DISCARD

The History of Music in Fifty Instruments

A FIREFLY BOOK

Published by Firefly Books Ltd. 2014

First printing

**Library and Archives Canada Cataloguing in
Publication**

Wilkinson, Philip, 1955–, author
The history of music in fifty instruments/Philip
Wilkinson. — First edition.
Includes bibliographical references and index.
ISBN 978-1-77085-428-4 (bound)
1. Musical instruments—History. I. Title.
ML460.W687 2014   784.19   C2014-
900697-7

Publisher Cataloging-in-Publication Data (U.S.)

Wilkinson, Philip, 1955–
The history of music in fifty instruments/Philip
Wilkinson.
[224] pages : ill., photos. (some color) ; cm.
Includes bibliographical references and index.
Summary: A popular history of fifty instruments
that have had an impact on history. Each entry
explores the origins and evolution of one instrument, and explains its role in the development of
music. Sidebars highlight the type of instrument
(woodwind, brass, strings, percussion, etc.) and
the period during which it was introduced.
ISBN-13: 978-1-77085-428-4
1. Musical instruments – History. I. Title.
784.19 dc23 ML460.W4544 2014

Published in the United States by
Firefly Books (U.S.) Inc.
P.O. Box 1338, Ellicott Station
Buffalo, New York 14205

Published in Canada by
Firefly Books Ltd.
50 Staples Avenue, Unit 1
Richmond Hill, Ontario L4B 0A7

Cover and interior design: Lindsey Johns

Printed in China

Conceived, designed and produced by
Quid Publishing
Level 4, Sheridan House
114 Western Road
Hove BN3 1DD
England

The History of Music in Fifty Instruments

written by Philip Wilkinson

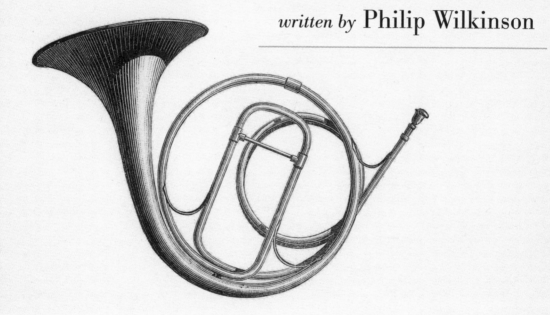

FIREFLY BOOKS

Contents

Introduction

From the serpent to the synthesizer, the piano to the piccolo, Western music has a huge range of instruments to draw on. Most of these instruments have a long history, and they have changed continuously — and as they have evolved, music has changed, too. This book tells the story of 50 of these instruments, showing how they have developed and how they have had an effect on Western music, from the Medieval period to today.

PLAYERS, INSTRUMENTS AND COMPOSERS

There has always been a complex relationship between musicians and instrument-makers. Craftsmen have been stimulated to make new and better instruments at the request of musicians. Players have honed techniques or found different approaches to playing as they have come across unfamiliar instruments. Composers have found in the latest instruments and the abilities of their players new expressive powers that have encouraged them to write in different and exciting ways.

The story of the violin is a good example. The great violin-makers of early 18th-century Cremona, Venice and other Italian cities made it possible for the talents of a generation of brilliant Italian violinist-composers (such as Corelli and Vivaldi) to blossom, and ultimately for the violin to dominate much of the music of the late Baroque period. Later violin-makers, inspired partly by the dazzling playing of the great virtuosos and partly by the demand for more volume as orchestras grew in size, evolved a modified design to produce a bigger sound. This in turn made possible the spectacular playing of 19th-century virtuosos like Paganini. The louder violin also helped 19th-century composers such as Brahms and Mendelssohn write their outstanding concertos for the instrument. Other instruments with a long history, from the clarinet to the piano, had a similar influence.

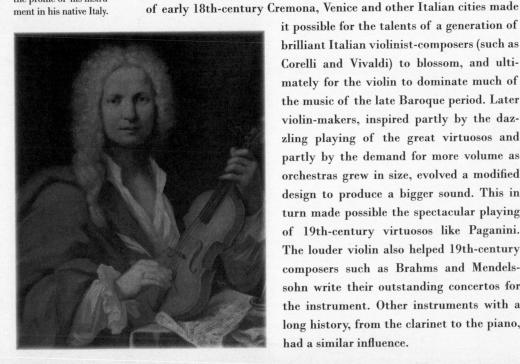

ANTONIO VIVALDI
The great composer Vivaldi wrote many violin concertos, helping to raise the profile of his instrument in his native Italy.

REASONS FOR CHANGE

Over the centuries, instruments have evolved in many ways and for many reasons. The changes can be linked to developing technology (as with the valves on brass instruments), to player convenience (as with the appearance of the end pin that helps cellists hold their instrument firmly in one place), to great inventors or craftsmen (as with the saxophone), or to the demands of composers (as with the special tuba that Wagner commissioned for his opera orchestra).

A major factor for change was simply musical or cultural fashion. When a prominent musician or patron took up an idea, it caught on widely and the fashion spread. The violin orchestras at the French court in the 17th and 18th centuries showed the huge potential of groups of stringed instruments playing in multi-part harmony. The advocacy of new piano designs by great pianist-composers such as Beethoven was highly influential. And 19th-century improvements to instruments like the harp made them increasingly popular.

THE INSTRUMENTS AND THEIR FAMILIES

This book concentrates on the classical orchestra, together with a few instruments, such as the piano and the guitar, that sometimes appear in or alongside the orchestra. Each instrument is given a key date, which may be the date of its invention, of a major development, or of the moment when it began to make a major musical impact.

THE VALVED TRUMPET
This instrument became common at the top of the orchestral brass section in the 19th century.

The type of the instrument is specified according to the system of classification devised in the early 20th century by German scholars Erich Mortiz von Hornbostel and Curt Sachs. Based on how instruments work, it divides the majority of instruments into types — idiophones, membranophones, cordophones and aerophones. Idiophones produce a sound when the whole body of the instrument vibrates — for example, gongs and chimes. Membranophones are instruments like drums that make a sound when a membrane vibrates. Cordophones, such as violins, guitars and pianos, produce their sound by means of vibrating strings. In aerophones, the movement of a column of air produces a sound, as is the case in oboes, flutes, horns and organs.

Another way of classifying instruments is by grouping them into the sections of the orchestra — strings, woodwind, brass and percussion — and this book gives these groupings too. Again, this system is based on the way in which the instruments work. Brass instruments, for example, are in that group not because of the material they are made of, but because they produce their sound as a result of the vibration of the player's lips.

INSTRUMENTS AND ERAS

All the groups of instruments have a long history, and this book tells their stories against a background of musical history stretching from the Middle Ages to the present. In the process, it uses the standard terms common in musical history to describe the key phases, from Medieval to Modern.

The Medieval period (roughly 500–1400 CE) was a vast era in which musical notation evolved and instruments were used to provide entertainment at festivities and to accompany dancing and singing. Vocal music, which featured a lot in church services, developed through many phases, but in particular from simple single-line chants to polyphony — complex music in which different vocal parts intermingled and produced the kinds of harmonies that influenced Western music for much of the rest of its history. Medieval instruments included ancestors of many of those played today. They ranged from plucked strings such as the lute and harp to bowed instruments like the lyra and fiddle, ancestors of the violin, and from wooden pipes resembling flutes to the sackbut, forebear of the trombone. The Medieval period also saw the development of the first keyboard instrument, the organ.

GHENT ALTARPIECE
One of the panels of the Ghent Altarpiece, painted in the 15th century by Jan van Eyck, shows musicians playing the organ and stringed instruments.

In the Renaissance period (in music, usually said to be 1400–1600), music shook off the conventions of medieval church music. The idea of tonality — according to which music is written in a specific key — became central and remained so until the 20th century. At the same time music tended to become more clearly expressive. As well as being a heyday of vocal music, it was also a boom time for instrumental music. Groups of musicians playing together in bands or consorts became common, and the instruments they played developed too. Valveless trumpets, wooden cornets and sackbuts dominated the brass; bowed stringed instruments, especially viols, were popular; and reed instruments such as shawms, the ancestors of modern woodwinds, were often heard. In addition, the harpsichord established itself at the heart of much instrumental music-making — it would keep this central role through the next period, the Baroque era.

The Baroque era (approximately 1600–1750) produced highly ornate music and established some of the major musical forms, such as the concerto, sonata and opera. This was the time of major composers such as Monteverdi, Bach, Handel and Vivaldi. The period saw the establishment of the strings (especially the violins) as the foundation of the orchestra, and the improvement of woodwind instruments such as the flute, oboe and bassoon, so that orchestras made up of strings plus woodwind became common. The harpsichord kept its place both as a solo instrument and within the orchestra, but in the later part of the period the piano was developed and began to inspire composers to produce increasingly expressive keyboard music.

By the time of the Classical period (around 1750–1820), composers such as Haydn, Mozart and Beethoven were writing symphonies, concertos and other works for an orchestra with strings, horns, oboes and bassoons. They often used additional wind instruments such as clarinets, trumpets and trombones. They began to incorporate further percussion instruments, adding the bass drum, triangle and cymbals to the orchestra, especially when they wanted to produce exotic musical effects. The Classical composers were also the first to exploit fully the expressive potential of the piano, which developed quickly during this period.

The piano was also a key instrument for the composers of the Romantic era (roughly 1820–1910). During this period, composers sought to extend the power and scope of the orchestra still further. They increasingly exploited brass instruments, which were now easier to play because of the introduction of valves in the first part of the period. They also added brand new instruments, many, such as the tuba, in the brass section. All these developments put a wide range of sounds at composers' disposal. From Berlioz to Wagner, they pioneered new ways of writing for these instruments, increased the size of the orchestra, and transformed music.

MOZART
From a very young age, Wolfgang Amadeus Mozart gave concerts with his father Leopold and sister Nannerl.

THE STORY CONTINUES

The Modern period (1910 onward) saw an explosion of musical ideas and a technological revolution. Classical composers continued to extend the range of sounds that could be produced with conventional instruments, but some used electronic instruments too, from early examples like the ondes Martenot, which has a distinctive sound, to the synthesizer, which, in theory at least, can make any sound at all. The variety of instruments and sounds available to composers has never been greater, and the number of musical styles in the 20th and 21st centuries is hugely varied too. The sheer number of performers, and the availability of their work through recordings and the internet, means that there has never been a better time to listen to the vast and diverse body of Western music, or to sample the variety of instruments that have transformed this music and brought it to life.

Lute

Location: Europe

Type: Cordophone (plucked)

Era: Medieval/Renaissance

+ WOODWIND
+ PERCUSSION
+ BRASS
+ *STRINGS*
+ OTHER

W ith its rounded body shaped like half a pear and its quiet but familiar tone, the lute is one of the most distinctive plucked-string instruments. Its fame is partly due to its long and widespread use. Over the centuries it has played solos, accompanied singers and taken its place in ensembles, exemplifying the great versatility of stringed instruments, which is one of the features of Western music throughout its long history.

FROM THE MIDDLE EAST TO EUROPE

The lute probably originated somewhere in the Middle East. Similar instruments were known to the ancient Egyptians and Mesopotamians, but the lute came to western Europe from the Arab world via Spain, which the Muslims conquered in the eighth century, and through Sicily, to which Muslim and Byzantine musicians brought the instrument. The word for lute in many European languages is derived from the Arabic word for the instrument, *al 'ud*, literally "the wood" or "the stick." During the Middle Ages, traveling musicians and others carried the lute around Europe and by the 13th and early 14th centuries, documents from France and England mention lutes and lute players, although no one knows exactly what their instruments were like.

AN ENDURING DESIGN
With its pear-shaped body and decorative sound hole, the lute looks, as well as sounds, distinctive.

By the beginning of the 15th century, the picture becomes clearer. Most lutes of this period probably had four "courses" (pairs of strings) and were played with a plectrum held between the fingers. Instrument-makers were beginning to add frets to the neck, to help players position the fingers of their left hand and hit the right pitch. The earliest surviving music for the lute dates from the 15th century, and as this century went on, players began to alter their technique, increasingly plucking the strings with their fingers rather than using the plectrum. At the same time, instrument-makers added a further course of strings to the lute. This was soon followed by another course, so that by the 16th century, the six-course, finger-plucked lute was the most common form of the instrument, although still larger lutes with up to 10 courses were available by the end of the century.

THE RENAISSANCE INSTRUMENT

The lute was hugely popular in the 16th century, at the height of the Renaissance era. The fashion for finger plucking made it possible to play more complex music and the extra courses gave the instrument much greater scope. Composers responded enthusiastically, and there was soon a huge repertoire of both solo lute pieces and songs with a lute accompaniment — players often accompanied their own singing. From royal courts to much more modest households, wherever music was being made on an intimate scale — the lute was not a powerful instrument — lutes and lutenists were to be found. The lute is as much a symbol of the musical Renaissance as the classical column is of Renaissance architecture.

The music that Renaissance composers wrote for the lute is some of the most beautiful ever produced in Europe. One of the first to exploit the polyphonic potential of the plucked lute was the great Italian composer, Francesco da Milano (1497–1543). Working at the papal court, Francesco produced several books of lute music (over 100 of his pieces survive). The fact that his works

COURSES

✦

Lute strings are usually described as being arranged in courses. This means that instead of single strings, the strings are arranged in pairs (or sometimes in larger groups) of identically tuned strings, which sound together when played. Having pairs of strings like this means that the instrument produces a stronger sound. In addition, some instruments had several single strings, known as diapasons. The courses were played by stopping (pressing them with a finger on the fingerboard), to vary their effective length and play different notes. The diapasons, on the other hand, were not designed to be played stopped, and were specifically tuned to the notes required in the particular piece being played.

THE LUTE PLAYER
Caravaggio's painting of c. 1596 shows a boy accompanying himself in a madrigal on the subject of love.

**Dowland to thee is dear,
whose heavenly touch
Upon the lute does ravish
human sense.**

*Richard Barnfield on the playing
of John Dowland*

were published commercially meant that his fame spread far beyond the Pope's court in Rome. John Dowland (1563–1626), one of the greatest English composers, produced several books of solo lute music, many songs to lute accompaniment, and music for ensemble consisting of viols and lute, including the famous *Lachrimae*, a collection centered on what the composer called "seaven [sic] passionate pavans" (sad tunes based on dances), which was dedicated to the wife of Dowland's employer, Queen Anne of Denmark. Dowland's fame as a player and composer helped sustain the love of his instrument in England during the 16th and 17th centuries.

NEW DIRECTIONS

During the 17th century the lute developed in different ways across Europe. In France and northern Europe, composers and instrument-makers experimented with various methods of tuning the strings, while in Italy the emphasis tended to be on extending the lute's bass range. A change in attitude to vocal writing in Italy led to the creation of new kinds of lute. Toward the end of the 16th century, Italian musicians began to write very dramatically for the voice, with expressive vocal solos being given major prominence. They accompanied such vocal lines with one or more instruments playing in harmony and reinforcing the bass line; this kind of accompanying bass group, which often included plucked strings, was called the *basso continuo.*

THE DUET
This painting of 1669 shows a musician accompanying a singer on the theorbo.

During the 1580s in Florence, Italian instrument-makers developed the theorbo, an extra-large lute with a long neck and up to seven or eight courses of double strings plus an additional seven or eight single "diapason" strings, which are plucked unstopped, like harp strings. The theorbo was widely used as a continuo instrument by early Baroque composers, such as Claudio Monteverdi (1567–1643), who flourished in the first decades of the 17th century. Its deep plucked sounds greatly enrich the orchestra in works such as Monteverdi's *Vespers* (1610), his operas, such as *Orfeo*

CLAUDIO MONTEVERDI
The great Italian composer
often used the theorbo to
enhance the sound of
his orchestra.

(1607) and *L'incoronazione di Poppea* (1643), and his accompanied madrigals. The continuo group used by Monteverdi and his contemporaries, which often comprises several instruments, can combine theorbo and chamber organ, or several theorbos plus harpsichord or organ, or sometimes a theorbo plus a bowed bass instrument. Although it originated in Italy, the theorbo spread to Central Europe and France too, especially among composers who were influenced by Italian music.

Another variation developed at around this time was the archlute, which, with its stopped courses and long diapason strings, combined the qualities of the ordinary lute and the theorbo. It was popular with players who wanted to exploit the instrument's qualities, not only in continuo playing and accompanying, but also in instrumental music that put the lute in the spotlight.

The lute and its cousins such as the theorbo and archlute fell out of widespread use by the end of the 18th century, but they are still played today in performances of music from the Renaissance and Baroque eras. They are often used to accompany voices alone or in passages where the voice is only lightly underscored with other instruments. In this kind of context they add beautiful color, complementing bowed strings or wind instruments and giving the early baroque orchestra a sound quite unlike that of later ensembles.

THE MANDOLIN

✦

With a body like a small lute, a fretted fingerboard like a guitar's, and strings tuned in a similar way to a violin, the mandolin is a hybrid instrument. It has four pairs of wire strings, with each pair tuned to the same note, so that the player can pluck a pair in quick succession to produce a fast tremolando — which has the effect of a sustained long note. The mandolin dates back at least to the 15th century, and was especially popular in Italy. The instrument can take various forms, including the Neapolitan mandolin, shaped like a lute, and the Portuguese mandolin, constructed and shaped more like a guitar, with a flat back. Various classical composers wrote for it. Vivaldi and Hummel produced mandolin concertos and Beethoven composed two sonatas for mandolin and piano. Mozart wrote a mandolin accompaniment for one of the arias in his opera *Don Giovanni* (1787), although this is sometimes played on the harp.

Organ

Location: Western Europe

Type: Aerophone/Keyboard

Era: Medieval

+ WOODWIND
+ PERCUSSION
+ BRASS
+ STRINGS
+ **OTHER**

RANKS OF PIPES
The organ, with its symmetrical arrangement of pipes above a central console, is a familiar fixture in churches across Europe and America.

During the 15th century in Europe the organ confirmed its place as the major instrument of the church. Capable of a wide range of tone qualities and ideal both as a solo instrument and for accompanying choral music, it was destined to have a major role in music, especially in the Renaissance, Baroque and late-Romantic eras. Because of its scope, tonal variety and considerable volume, writers and musicians began to refer to it as "the king of instruments."

ORGAN BASICS

The modern organ is a complex instrument, but all organs work in a similar way and have a small number of essential features. Organs function by producing air under pressure, storing this air, and releasing it through valves into groups of tuned pipes. To achieve this an organ requires, in addition to the pipes, a way of storing wind to supply the pipes, a mechanism to produce the wind and keep it under pressure, and at least one keyboard.

The sound of an organ is produced by the pipes. Each pipe has a single pitch, and groups of pipes are arranged in ranks, each rank forming a musical scale. Pipes also vary in timbre and volume, so organs have many ranks of pipes, each rank with different sound characteristics. The timbre varies according to how the pipes are made. For example, some pipes work like large recorders, by directing air along a flue or windway and against a sharp lip. In this kind of pipe, known as a flue pipe, the length of the pipe determines the pitch and the quality of its tone is affected by such things as the placing of the lip. Another kind of pipe has a reed and works in a similar way to a woodwind instrument. Again, the length determines the pitch.

Organists select which ranks of pipes to play by using controls called stops. These are linked to a mechanism, the stop action, which allows wind to flow to the relevant rank of pipes. Traditionally, the stops are operated by pulling out round knobs labeled with the name of the rank and its pitch; the stops control a mechanism

STOPS
Large organs have dozens of stops
that allow the player to control
which pipes are sounding.

that moves perforated wooden sliders that cut off, or open up, the wind supply to a rank of pipes. Some organs have electrical switches to control the stops.

Organs have a second mechanism, known as the key action, that connects the keyboards to the pipes, allowing wind under pressure to enter specific pipes. Most organs have at least two keyboards (known as manuals) plus a pedalboard. Organs vary in the way the key action works. For example, some make the connection using a series of metal rods. This kind of mechanism is called a tracker action. An alternative system, often used on very large organs, is the electropneumatic action; its use of electrical connections means that the manuals can be located at some distance from the pipes.

The wind to make the pipes sound was traditionally supplied by bellows that were pumped by hand. Nowadays, the bellows are nearly always electrically powered, so that the organist no longer has to rely on at least one other person to keep the instrument supplied with wind. The wind from the bellows is stored in a regulator, to keep it at the right pressure, and passes from here to windchests beneath each rank of pipes.

ORGAN STOPS

✦

Organs have many stops, some of which can be grouped together. Typical groupings include:

Foundation or diapason
Medium-bore flue pipes, open or stopped, that produce the organ's basic sound.

Chorus
Open metal pipes that can be added to the foundation stops to provide increased power.

Flutes
Wide-bore open flue pipes with a wide dynamic range. There are also stopped flutes with a smaller dynamic range and half-stopped flutes.

Strings
Narrow-bore flue pipes with a wide dynamic range, imitative of various stringed instruments, after which they are named.

Chorus reeds
Loud reed pipes, named after brass instruments.

Semichorus reeds
Softer reed pipes.

Imitative reeds
Reed pipes imitating such instruments as the oboe, clarinet, and bassoon.

Céleste
Two ranks of string pipes tuned to slightly different frequencies, producing a vibrato effect.

Mixtures
Stops that select ranks in combination, often giving a bright tone color.

ORGAN ORIGINS

The origins of the organ go back to the ancient world. In the third century BCE, Ctesibius, a Greek engineer working in Alexandria, was credited with the invention of the hydraulis, an organ that had a wind supply maintained by water pressure. The Romans played the hydraulis, but at some point in the Roman period, probably in the second century CE, they replaced its mechanism of pumps with an inflated leather bag; the use of bellows for an air supply came during one of the following centuries. When Rome fell, the tradition of organ-building and playing continued in the eastern empire, especially at its capital, Constantinople. In 757, the emperor Constantine V gave an organ to Frankish King Pepin the Short, and his gift marked the reappearance of the instrument in the West. From this period onward, the organ in the West was considered mainly as a church instrument.

PORTATIVE AND POSITIVE

Little information has come down to us about the earliest organs, but by the Medieval period, illustrations and documents show that the instrument had developed into forms that are recognizable as the ancestors of the modern organ. Several illuminated manuscripts show musicians playing the portative organ, a compact instrument that could be carried around. Instrument-makers of the Middle Ages also developed a larger instrument, the positive organ. Positive organs had more and larger pipes, a greater compass, and bellows that required a second person to operate. The larger manual could be played with both hands and so the positive organ was more suited to polyphonic music. The positive organ, although much bigger than the portative organ, could still be moved around. By the late Middle Ages, there were also still bigger instruments installed permanently in churches. These bigger organs

THE PORTATIVE ORGAN

◆

Popular in the Middle Ages, portative organs have one or two ranks of small pipes, a single short keyboard played with the right hand, and a bellows operated by the left. The musician could take a portative organ to any location and the instrument was used in religious and, especially, secular music. It would have played one melodic line and was used both to accompany singers and to add texture and harmony to instrumental ensembles. Many illustrations show it played by St. Cecelia, patron saint of music, or by a figure representing music itself, showing that the organ was seen as a symbol of the art.

FLUE PIPES
Sometimes organ pipes,
like these flue pipes, are
painted for decorative
effect. Some of these may
be dummy pipes, added to
make the arrangement
symmetrical.

had several manuals and many ranks of pipes. They are very similar to modern organs but with one major difference — they had no stops. Each key controlled a number of pipes that sounded simultaneously, en bloc, and these early church organs are usually known by the German term, *blockwerk* organs.

STOPS AND CASES

Although it is difficult to pin developments down to a precise date, the organ had reached a turning point by the 15th century. By this time it seems that it was increasingly common for organs in Europe to have multiple manuals, a pedalboard, and stop controls that enabled the player to play on selected ranks of pipes.

There were quite a lot of regional variations in the way the organ developed. Some of the most elaborate instruments were built in Germany, where most organs would have several manuals. In France and Italy, single-manual instruments were the norm, but organ-builders incorporated numerous stops so that their instruments gave plenty of scope for tonal variation.

When the full organ joins the tuneful choir, Th'immortal Pow'rs incline their ear.
Alexander Pope, "Ode for Musick on St Cecilia's Day"

Late-medieval organs often had elaborate wooden cases to hold and protect their increasingly complex mechanisms. The common arrangement, still seen on many instruments today, evolved, with the manuals and stops in the middle and the pipes ranked above and on either side. As well as protecting the mechanical parts of the organ from damage, the wooden case had its own acoustic properties, helping to blend the sound from the pipes.

The degree of control offered by stops gave the player much more scope to vary the tone colors produced by the instrument. During the Renaissance and Baroque periods, organ-builders developed this scope, creating stops that imitated all kinds of instruments — not just flutes or woodwinds, but instruments such as the viol — to create sounds of great richness. In addition, they added pipes that looked and sounded like brass instruments, giving trumpetlike sounds. As a result, the largest organs of the period were capable of a huge range of sounds. They could also play very loudly.

BAROQUE ORGAN
This 18th-century organ at the Monastery of Santa Cruz, Coimbra, Portugal, has a wide range of pipes, including some mounted *en chamade*, sticking out like trumpets.

ORGAN COMPOSERS OF THE BAROQUE

From the Middle Ages onward, the organ has been closely associated with church music, and, even today, most organs are installed in churches. From the Renaissance period, organists based in churches also composed music for their instrument. Among the first was the Dutchman Jan Pieterszoon Sweelinck (1562–1621), a master improviser, noted teacher, and pioneer of such forms as the fugue, which, with its separate voices, is well suited to the organ's polyphonic capabilities. Sweelinck, whose career spanned the Renaissance and Baroque eras, was the founder of a whole school of northern European organ music, which became especially strong in northern Germany. His music influenced the great Danish-German organist and composer Dieterich Buxtehude (1637–1707), writer of many organ works. The young J.S. Bach (1685–1750) famously walked 250 miles (400 km) from his home in Arnstadt to Lübeck, where Buxtehude lived and worked, to hear him play. Bach stayed in Lübeck for three months, learning much about the way Buxtehude played and composed; the young Bach subsequently produced a vast amount of music — chorale preludes, fugues, sonatas, toccatas and other pieces — for organ solo. Other influential Baroque organ composers included Girolamo Frescobaldi (1583–1643) from Ferrara, Italy, whose collection *Fiori musicali* (1635) remained influential for centuries in Italy and beyond, and a host of French composers who wrote music to accompany the celebration of the Mass.

As well as writing organ solos, Baroque composers used the instrument in their sacred choral music. Here, it reinforces the bass and adds harmonies — in other words, playing the continuo role. In a vast range of sacred music, such as the cantatas and masses of J.S. Bach and the oratorios of Handel, the organ features in this way.

There is nothing to it. You only have to hit the right notes at the right time and the instrument plays itself.

J.S. Bach (pictured left)

THE LATER ORGAN

The organ was used in church throughout the Classical and Romantic eras, but was less prominent in other kinds of music. Instrument-builders continued to develop the organ, however, partly as a result of a renewed interest in playing the works of J.S. Bach. Then, in the second half of the 19th century, the organ enjoyed something of a revival. Several Romantic composers included it in symphonic works — Liszt's Faust Symphony (1854–1857), Saint-Saëns' Symphony No. 3 (1886) and Mahler's Symphony No. 2 (1888–1894) all have prominent parts for the organ, as do several orchestral works by Richard Strauss and Scriabin. Among other Romantic composers who played the organ were Anton Bruckner, who was for a while organist at Linz Cathedral and incorporated organ parts in his sacred music, and César Franck (1822–1890), professor of organ at the Paris Conservatoire.

It was in France where the organ revival took hold especially strongly. Here, the organ-builder Aristide Cavaillé-Coll (1811–1899) hugely advanced organ design, introducing new stops, improved mechanisms and windchests, and higher wind pressures. He combined his innovations with high standards of craftsmanship. Composers such as Charles-Marie Widor wrote vast symphonies for solo organ, works on a grand scale that inspired other French composers to follow. This school of French organ players and composers stretched into the 20th century, when organist-composers such as Olivier Messiaen explored new and arresting sound worlds.

CÉSAR FRANCK
Franck was one of the great organists of the 19th century. He wrote numerous pieces for his instrument and was also a noted improviser.

c. 1555 | Guitar

Location: Andalusia, Spain

Type: Chordophone

Era: Renaissance

- ✦ WOODWIND
- ✦ PERCUSSION
- ✦ BRASS
- ✦ **STRINGS**
- ✦ OTHER

CLASSICAL GUITAR
The classical guitar is an instrument with a large following, especially in Hispanic countries.

Although it is associated especially closely with Spain, the classical guitar has a huge following worldwide. Its devotees range from beginners who want to try an instrument that is neither too costly nor too difficult to learn, to virtuoso players who can draw on a large repertoire from recent works back to music of the Renaissance period, when the guitar first began to find its identity.

GUITAR AND VIHEULA

The modern classical guitar is a plucked-string instrument with a figure-of-eight shaped body, a flat back and six strings, typically tuned in fourths with a major third between the second and third strings. But the term "guitar" has been used for hundreds of years to describe a variety of plucked-string instruments, some of which are quite different from the guitars of today. Because of their variety and the other instruments that share some of their features, tracing the early history of the guitar is very difficult.

During the Middle Ages the word "guitar" was sometimes used to describe a small instrument like a compact lute with a pear-shaped body and curving back. But in the later Middle Ages in Spain an instrument called the vihuela evolved, and this combined a more guitar-like waisted body with a flat back and a set of strings that were played by plucking. Vihuelas were popular in Spain in the 15th and 16th centuries. Their strings were arranged in courses, like those of the lute — in other words the instrument had six or seven pairs of gut strings, each pair tuned either to the same pitch or in octaves.

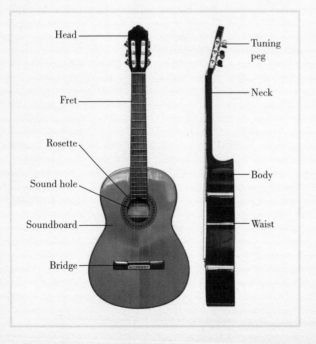

Head
Fret
Rosette
Sound hole
Soundboard
Bridge
Tuning peg
Neck
Body
Waist

Lean your body forward slightly to support the guitar against your chest, for the poetry of the music should resound in your heart.
Andrés Segovia

THE RENAISSANCE GUITAR

The 15th- and 16th-century vihuela seems to have been quite a large instrument — similar in size to the lute. But at the same time a smaller version was evolving, with a compact body of the same shape and four or five courses of strings, tuned in fourths with an interpolated third. Played by both plucking individual strings and by strumming to form chords, this instrument was the ancestor of the classical guitar. In 1555 the Spanish friar and musician Juan Bermudo published a treatise on musical instruments that distinguished between the guitar and the vihuela, and also described both four- and five-course guitars. This could be said to be the first milestone in the guitar's history, clearly pointing to its acceptance. This was confirmed by the appearance in the 1550s of several books of music for the guitar by the French lutenist, guitarist and composer Adrian Le Roy (1520–1598, pictured left) and by the publication in 1554 of Miguel Fuenllana's *Orphénica lyra*. Fuenllana's collection, published in Spain and dedicated to the Spanish king, Philip II, is described on its title page as for the vihuela. But as its music implies an instrument tuned like a modern guitar less the lowest string, it has been described as the first published music for the five-course guitar.

By the 16th century, the four-course guitar (as well as larger five- and six-course instruments) was quite widely played in Spain, where it probably first evolved, and in Italy, France and England. It was often used to accompany singers and also amassed a repertoire of solo music that included dances and other pieces. The guitar had arrived.

THE ELECTRIC GUITAR

◆

In a classical or other acoustic guitar, the sound is produced by the vibrating strings and amplified by the wooden guitar body. In an electric guitar, on the other hand, the string vibrates and its movement induces an electric current in a device called a pickup (basically a magnet wound with fine wire), from where the current is sent to an amplifier. Electric guitars, therefore, do not have to have a resonant, hollow body — most have solid bodies. Electric guitars have become increasingly common since they were invented in the 1930s. Jazz musicians working in big bands in the 1940s liked them because they could be heard alongside other loud instruments such as saxophones. Since then electric guitars have transformed pop and rock music and a few modern classical composers have used them too.

SINGLE STRINGS

During the Baroque era, the guitar began to evolve into an instrument closer to the modern guitar and to increase in popularity. This was in part due to the advocacy of notable players. In England, for example, the guitarist Francesco Corbetta (1615–1681) became court musician to King Charles II, giving his instrument a high profile that it had not had in the country before. As a result it began to supplant the lute.

To stand up on a stage alone with an acoustic guitar requires bravery bordering on heroism. Bordering on insanity.

Richard Thompson

A further reason for the increasing success of the guitar was a trend toward instruments with more courses and, therefore, more musical scope. In the Baroque era the five-course and, by the 18th century, the six-course guitar became the most popular. The 18th century also saw improvements in the strings themselves, including the use of overwound strings in the bass. These are strings that have a core of one material, such as gut, that is wound around with another material, such as silk thread, to make the string thicker. This led makers to abandon the idea of courses and fit six single strings. Whereas early guitars had often been thought of as treble instruments, these six-string guitars could supply their own bass, and more and more composers thought of them as self-contained solo instruments.

As a result of these improvements, the guitar repertoire increased in the 18th and early 19th centuries and in this period a number of guitarist-composers emerged, especially in Spain and Italy. One of the most famous was the Neapolitan Ferdinando Carulli (1770–1841), a renowned guitar virtuoso who toured Europe giving concerts and wrote more than 400 works — solos, chamber music and concertos — for his instrument.

The most famous Spanish guitar composer of the period was Fernando Sor (1778–1839). He traveled Europe, giving concerts, composing, and helping to gain the guitar a wider audience.

SOR'S MÉTHODE
Fernando Sor's influential book published in 1830 explains guitar technique and related musical topics.

ANTONIO DE TORRES

Although the guitars played by such masters as Sor and Carulli were very similar to the classical guitar of today, one further stage in the instrument's development improved it significantly. This was due to the work of the great Spanish instrument-maker Antonio de Torres Jurado (1817–1892), who worked in the second half of the 19th century. Torres adapted the shape of the guitar's body, enlarging it by

increasing the radius of the top and bottom curves and placing their centers farther apart. On his guitars, therefore, the bridge is positioned in the middle of a big resonating area, the strings are longer and the body rests comfortably on the player's knee. These changes give the instrument a strong, clear, balanced sound that projects very well.

Torres' instruments were taken up enthusiastically by the greatest player of the time, Francisco Tárrega (1852–1909), who was especially well known for making transcriptions of the works of past composers so that they could be played on the guitar. Tárrega stood at the beginning of a whole succession of guitar players, from Andrés Segovia to Julian Bream, who achieved international fame. Their playing inspired composers such as Joaquín Rodrigo (1901–1999), whose haunting *Concierto de Aranjuez* (1939) is one of the most widely performed concertos of the 20th century. The same composer's *Fantasía para un gentilhombre* (1955), written for Segovia, is almost as well known. Rodrigo, together with other 20th-century composers, produced guitar works that continue to enthrall listeners and ensure that the classical guitar retains its widespread appeal.

CONSTRUCTION

✦

The body of the classical guitar is made of wood — the soundboard of softwood (typically spruce) and the back and sides of hardwood such as maple or rosewood. The fingerboard is usually of ebony, with frets of nickel silver. The soundboard is hugely important in creating the instrument's distinctive timbre. Guitar soundboards are, at about $3/32$ inches (2.5 mm), thicker than those of the lute, and are braced with wooden bars on the underside. The placing of these bars and the thickness of the soundboard itself govern the way the instrument resonates — more than a lute at low frequencies but less so at higher frequencies — and contribute to the warmth of the instrument's sound.

Harpsichord

Location: Antwerp, Belgium

Type: Chordophone/Keyboard

Era: Renaissance/Baroque

+ WOODWIND
+ PERCUSSION
+ BRASS
+ STRINGS
+ **OTHER**

THE HEART OF BAROQUE
The harpsichord was central to music in the 17th and 18th centuries and is still widely played by specialists in Baroque music.

Some time between 1570 and 1580 a new instrument-maker set up his workshop in Antwerp. His name was Hans Ruckers and the harpsichords he made were soon prized for their rich tone and sustaining power, influencing other manufacturers and inspiring musicians all over Europe. From the drawing room to the opera house, music would never be quite the same again.

KEYBOARDS AND STRINGS

Keyboards were familiar to musicians from the organ, which had existed since ancient times. But in the late Middle Ages, inventors started to devise mechanisms that allowed stringed instruments to be played with a keyboard. The earliest of these were the clavichord, a kind of ancestor of the piano, in which the mechanism or action of the instrument strikes the strings, and the harpsichord, which has an action that plucks the strings.

> **Two harpsichords playing — and there's a robust heaven.**
>
> Norman MacCaig, "Down-to-earth heaven"

Adding a keyboard to a stringed instrument in this way gave a huge musical advantage. A harpist, or the player of a psaltery (a type of box zither played by finger-plucking or with a plectrum) can only pluck one or two strings at a time. With a keyboard, it is possible to play complex chords, or to play more than one line of music at once. The implications for music turned out to be game-changing, and the instrument that changed the game decisively was the harpsichord.

THE CLAVICEMBALUM

The harpsichord may have been invented around 1397 by an instrument-maker called Hermann Poll (c. 1368–1400) in the north Italian city of Padua. His instrument is referred to in a contemporary account as a "clavicembalum," and this name suggests that the instrument was based on a psaltery with the addition of keys ("clavi") that controlled a mechanism to pluck the strings. The name clavicembalum was also used in a document describing a German instrument in 1404. Harpsichords became more common through the 15th century, although in this period it is often impossible to tell whether music written for a keyboard instrument is for organ or harpsichord. By the 16th century, however, the harpsichord was well established, and collections of music were written that brought out the unique sound of its plucked strings.

THE PLUCKING ACTION

Instrument-makers developed various mechanisms to pluck the strings when the player pressed a key. The most enduring of these is based on a component called the jack. Each key has a jack, which consists of a length of wood (typically pear, service tree, or beech) with a slot cut in it at one end. In the slot is the tongue, a second piece of harder wood (holly is often used for this) pivoted on a pin and held upright by a spring made of hog bristle. At the upper end of the tongue is attached the part that actually plucks the string, the plectrum, usually made of quill. The jack rests on the end of the key, with the plectrum just below the string. When the player depresses a key, the jack moves upward, and the plectrum plucks the string. When the player releases the key, the jack drops back and the pivoted tongue moves, so that the plectrum passes the string without plucking it again. As the jack falls back a cloth damper rests on the string, cutting off the vibrations and the sound.

ZELL HARPSICHORD
The open lid reveals the strings of this 1737 harpsichord by the German maker Christian Zell (c.1683–1763).

HARPSICHORDS AROUND EUROPE

The harpsichord developed along slightly different lines across Europe. In Italy, the instrument usually had quite a lightweight build quality. Its brass strings were at relatively low tension and Italian harpsichords generally had only one manual, although by the 18th century, larger, two-manual instruments were being produced by some Italian makers.

From the late-16th century on, there was a major center of harpsichord-building in the Low Countries, thanks largely to the Ruckers family of Antwerp. The Ruckers workshop, which began at some time around 1570, was headed by

REGISTRATION

✦

On many harpsichords there are two sets of strings for each key, or in some cases even three sets of strings, with a separate jack for each string. Stops allow the musician to select which set of strings is played by mechanically moving the jacks away from their strings. This allows the player not only to control pitch but also to vary tone colors because the jacks are necessarily placed so that they pluck the sets of strings at different points along their length, affecting the tone. In addition, many harpsichords have more than one manual, enabling further tonal variations.

Hans Ruckers, who was assisted and followed by his sons Joannes and Andreas, and his grandson, another Andreas. They produced harpsichords of many sizes and shapes, but were particularly known for harpsichords with heavier cases and well-made spruce soundboards. Ruckers also preferred to use iron strings in the treble (although he retained brass strings in the bass because iron bass strings would have been inconveniently long). All this added up to instruments that had an impressive tone that sustained well. By around 1590–1600 the Flemish makers were also producing harpsichords with two manuals that sounded strings one fourth apart, enabling the player to transpose with ease — a useful ability when accompanying a singer, for example. As well as sounding beautiful, Flemish harpsichords are very attractive — their cases are commonly covered in painted decoration featuring flowers, fruit, birds and marbled effects.

> **Sounds like two skeletons copulating on a corrugated tin roof.**
>
> *Thomas Beecham, conductor*

The tone and build quality of Ruckers harpsichords soon became well known and influenced instrument-builders in other parts of Europe, such as England and France. Some makers even specialized in buying Ruckers harpsichords, taking them apart, and extending their compass, fitting larger soundboards and bigger cases.

In Germany there were thriving workshops in Hamburg and Saxony. These makers were also influenced by the Flemish and French workshops, but some of the German builders, especially in northern Germany, were interested in producing a wider variety of sounds. To achieve this, they fitted extra sets of strings; for example, a set

FLEMISH HARPSICHORD
Many early harpsichords, like this one dated 1618 from Antwerp, have beautifully decorated cases.

pitched two octaves above the main set of strings and sometimes also a further "choir" of strings pitched an octave below the main ones. The player selected different registers of strings using stops.

AN EXPANDING REPERTOIRE

A great deal of music was written for the harpsichord (and its siblings the virginals and spinet; see box) from the 16th century onward. The processes of instrument-manufacture and composition influenced one another in a virtuous circle, with better harpsichords stimulating composers and the increased availability of music encouraging the instrument-builders to produce more and better harpsichords. The 15th and 16th centuries saw a strong group of keyboard composers emerge from Italy, including such figures as Girolamo Frescobaldi (1583–1643), who wrote canzonas and toccatas; Claudio Merulo (1533–1604); and the great Venetian Andrea Gabrieli (c. 1533–1585) and his nephew Giovanni Gabrieli (c. 1554–1612). Germany was the home of the great 17th-century organist and composer Johann Jacob Froberger (1616–1667), whose toccatas and suites later had an influence on J.S. Bach.

One major center of keyboard music was Tudor and Stuart England, where composers William Byrd (c. 1540–1623), a great choral composer and music publisher, and John Bull (1562–1628), a noted keyboard player and organist at Antwerp Cathedral, were major writers of keyboard music. Their work, and that of others, was collected in a major manuscript album of keyboard music, the *Fitzwilliam Virginal Book*, which was compiled around 1609–1619 and contains some 300 pieces, mainly dances, fantasias and works in variation form. The first English collection of keyboard music to be printed and published was *Parthenia, or The Maydenhead of the First Musicke that ever was printed for the Virginalls* (1611), which includes 21 keyboard pieces by Byrd, Bull and another English master, Orlando Gibbons (1583–1625).

VIRGINAL AND SPINET
✦

The harpsichord has two sibling instruments, the virginal and the spinet, which work in a similar way. Both were designed primarily for domestic use and to save space they have their strings arranged at right angles to the keys, rather than parallel with the keys as in the harpsichord. The virginal has a boxlike shape, a single set of strings and one keyboard. The origin of its name is uncertain, but most illustrations of the instrument show it being played by young women. The spinet is usually trapezoid in shape, with the keyboard set in one of the long sides.

THE HEART OF BAROQUE MUSIC

By the 18th century, the harpsichord was at the heart of Baroque music, for continuo playing, as a solo instrument and, increasingly, as the soloist in stunning virtuosic concertos. Two German composers of the High Baroque contributed hugely to the repertoire and use of the harpsichord: J.S. Bach (1685–1750) and G.F. Handel (1685–1759). Bach was a skilled keyboard player and organist. He wrote outstanding music for unaccompanied harpsichord, including the Italian concerto (a solo piece in spite of its title) and numerous fugues and fantasias. His concertos for the instrument are also outstanding. G.F. Handel, also a noted keyboard player, wrote a series of suites for the instrument.

I shall always feel grateful to any who, by the exercise of infinite art supported by fine taste, contrive to render this instrument capable of expression.

François Couperin, Pièces de Clavecin, *Book I, Preface*

The most celebrated Italian composer for the instrument was Domenico Scarlatti (1685–1757), who wrote 555 solo sonatas for keyboard instruments, mostly for the harpsichord. For the last 25 years of his life Scarlatti lived in Madrid, where he was musical teacher to Princess Maria Barbara. Most of his sonatas were written for the princess to play, and show the influence of Spanish music, with the use of the Phrygian mode (often used in Spanish folk music), passages imitating such flamenco techniques as foot-stamping, and sections in which the harpsichord plays music reminiscent of the guitar.

A fourth composer, François Couperin (1668–1733), advanced the harpsichord in France. Between 1713 and 1730 he produced four books of harpsichord works, consisting of more than 230 short pieces arranged in groups or *ordres*. The *ordres* mix dance pieces with descriptive works that often have colorful and sometimes enigmatic titles, such as "Le Rossignol en Amour" ("The Nightingale in Love"). They range from the quirky to the vividly descriptive.

DOMENICO SCARLATTI
The great Italian master was probably the most prolific composer for the harpsichord.

HARPSICHORD REVIVAL

During the 18th century the piano, invented in 1711, gained popularity. Both composers and players appreciated its ability to play loud and soft notes and, as pianos became more common, the harpsichord increasingly fell out of fashion in the second half of the 18th century. After that time, new music and also the harpsichord works of such composers as Bach and Scarlatti were generally played on the piano. But the harpsichord did not die. In the 20th century, makers began to produce new harpsichords, generally building them with strong iron frames like grand pianos, and players explored the Baroque repertoire using them. These big "revival" harpsichords also attracted the interest of composers such as Francis Poulenc (1899–1963) and Bohuslav Martinů (1890–1959), who wrote concertos for them.

But many were unhappy with these loud, revival instruments, and sought to recreate the softer, more subtle sound of historical Baroque or Renaissance instruments. During the second half of the 20th century, scholars and instrument-makers studied the instruments of the 17th and 18th centuries and built copies using authentic materials and techniques. The research and attention to detail shown by these instrument-makers has enabled musicians to get closer to the sound world of composers from Byrd to Bach.

THE CONCERTO

✦

During the harpsichord's Baroque heyday, one of the most popular musical forms was the concerto for one or more solo instruments and orchestra. J.S. Bach wrote a series of harpsichord concertos that give the soloist scope to display great virtuosity. The Italian composer Vivaldi wrote hundreds of concertos, not only for his own instrument, the violin, but also for many other instruments, from trumpet to bassoon. These great Baroque works inspired later composers to develop the concerto genre, which became a showcase for composer-pianists such as Beethoven and Liszt to display their genius in both invention and performance. The way the concerto pits the soloist against an orchestra and explores their musical dialogue makes the form one of the most absorbing and entertaining of musical genres.

c. 1590

Serpent

**Aye, but not the Serpent
that seduced Eve.**
G.F. Handel

Location: Auxerre, France

Type: Aerophone

Era: Renaissance

+ WOODWIND
+ PERCUSSION
+ **BRASS**
+ STRINGS
+ OTHER

Fundamentally a bass member of the cornet family, the instruments that predate the modern brass section, the serpent began its life accompanying choral music in the 16th century. It found its way into the orchestra around 200 years later to add strength and depth to the bass line among the brass. Never a permanent member of the orchestra, it was superseded when other instruments, especially the tuba, entered the brass section in the 19th century. The serpent's distinctive soft voice, however, is still appreciated by many, especially period-instrument players.

THE SERPENT IS BORN

According to a long-standing tradition, the serpent was invented in 1590 by Edmé Guillaume, a canon from Auxerre. It is a hybrid instrument, made of wood and with holes, like the woodwind family, but it has a mouthpiece like a brass instrument rather than a reed. The player has to control the pitch using the lips and the serpent is therefore generally played by brass players. The instrument's wooden tube is covered in leather and the bore of its tube is similar to that of the cornet (the serpent is sometimes referred to as a bass cornet) but the bore is wider and the serpent lacks the cornet's thumb hole. The tube's sinuous shape, which gives the instrument its name, is designed so that the finger holes are easy to reach. At the top of the main tube is an elbow-shaped brass tube (the crook) that holds the mouthpiece, which is usually of brass or ivory.

The serpent's original role was supporting singers of plainchant and so for most of the 17th century the most likely place to come across the instrument was in a church in France. By the end of the century it was in use in England and a few decades later serpents featured in military marching bands in Germany.

BRASS IN DISGUISE
Although mostly made of wood, the serpent has a brass-style mouthpiece, so is classified as a brass instrument.

FROM BANDS TO ORCHESTRAS

Serpents were quite popular in wind bands in the 18th and 19th centuries — in military music, among the wind players who accompanied the singing in church, and in the Harmonie bands (brass, woodwind and percussion) that were popular in the Classical period. By this time it had also made the transition into symphonic music. Haydn included it in his oratorio *The Creation* (1798), Berlioz enforced the bass line with it in works such as his *Grande Messe des Morts* (1837) and *Symphonie Fantastique* (1830), and Mendelssohn included it in several works. A few opera composers liked the soft bass sound of the serpent and included it in their orchestras too. Wagner, for example, used it in his early opera *Rienzi* (1841), and it also appears in the work of some of the Italian opera composers, such as Gaspare Spontini (1774–1851) and Vincenzo Bellini (1801–1835).

HECTOR BERLIOZ
The French composer Berlioz, who was always an inventive orchestrator, included the serpent in some of his works.

More modern low brass instruments such as the ophicleide and tuba gradually replaced the serpent in the job of strengthening the bass line in the brass, so by the end of the 19th century the serpent had virtually died out. The instrument's fate was not helped by the fact that, left lying around uncared-for, the wooden tube tended to deteriorate. When someone picked up one of these neglected instruments, the sound was likely to be awful, and the verdict damning. The serpent became little more than a curiosity.

In the 20th century, however, there was a serpent revival. The researchers of the period-instrument movement encouraged players to try the serpent in historically informed performances of works by composers such as Berlioz, and instrument-makers started to build serpents again. In addition, ensembles made up entirely of serpents sometimes get together. Their performances, and those of single serpents in period-instrument groups, have led to a renewed appreciation of the instrument's sound and scope, and in 1987 a serpent concerto was written by British composer Simon Proctor (b. 1959). For its serious followers, the serpent is far more than a musical curiosity.

SERPENT VARIATIONS

✦

During the early decades of the 19th century, when the serpent saw quite frequent use in the orchestra, instrument-makers helped to expand its potential further by building models at different pitches. Some of these instruments soon acquired their own zoomorphic nicknames — from the anaconda (the big contra-bass serpent) to the worm (the soprano version of the instrument). Only the original tenor and bass instruments were used widely, but a whole family of serpents meant that small bands made up of the instruments were possible.

1597

Trombone

Location: Venice, Italy

Type: Aerophone

Era: Baroque

The trombone is unlike any other brass instrument in general use today because it has a slide — a simple way of increasing the effective length of its tubing, and therefore lowering the pitch. The trombone emerged in the 15th century and since then has changed relatively little in design. Throughout its long history it has played a variety of music, from the church music of Baroque Venice to modern jazz, as well as playing a key role in the brass section of the orchestra from the 19th century onward.

+ WOODWIND
+ PERCUSSION
+ *BRASS*
+ STRINGS
+ OTHER

SLIDES

Like the trumpet, the trombone is a brass instrument with a cylindrical bore. In other words, the tube has the

> In my opinion, the trombone is the true head of the family of wind instruments.
>
> *Hector Berlioz*

same diameter along all of its length until it flares into the bell at the end. Both instruments have a common ancestor in the signaling and ceremonial trumpets that were used in the ancient world and through the Middle Ages. The idea of the trombone's special feature, the slide, may also have come from the trumpet, because in the Middle Ages an instrument called the slide trumpet was devised. The slide trumpet was in two parts: the length of tubing connected to the mouthpiece, and the body of the instrument, connected to the bell. The player could slide these two sections in and out, altering the effective length of the instrument and so changing the pitch of any note played. As on any brass instrument, the musician produced the basic notes by means of the embouchure (the use of the facial muscles and lips to control the sound), but could lower the pitch of any note by sliding the body of the instrument away from the mouthpiece. According to how far you moved the slide trumpet's body, you could lower the pitch by one, two or three semitones; this enabled the player to produce complete chromatic scales.

The slide principle was ingenious, but the slide trumpet itself was unwieldy to play because it was the larger, heavier part of the instrument that the player had to move. It is not known how widely slide trumpets were used in the Middle Ages and Renaissance periods — no early slide trumpets

MODERN TROMBONE
The basic design of the trombone has changed little for hundreds of years.

have survived. Some authorities believe that their unwieldy nature made them unpopular. This was overcome in the trombone, in which the slide is relatively light. The slide is also double (so that the required movement to change the pitch by one semitone is relatively shorter) but also long (so that the slide can accommodate seven positions, meaning that the player can lower the pitch by up to six semitones).

TROMBONE CENTERS

The trombone appeared in around 1460, probably first in Burgundy, a state with strong links not only to France but also to the Hapsburg family who ruled the Holy Roman Empire. The instrument was soon being used alongside other winds in bands that played at ducal and royal courts. It also found a place in city bands that played on important civic occasions.

The city of Nuremberg, where several trumpet-makers were based, also became a center for trombone manufacture, and from there the instrument spread across the empire and beyond. Musicians were taken with its compass, its agility and its sound. Because Renaissance trombones had a narrow bore and a bell that flared only slightly, their sound was thinner than that of the modern instrument, but still impressive and capable either of blending with other winds or combining together in impressive trombone "choirs."

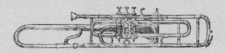

THE VALVE TROMBONE
✦

Early in the history of the trombone, there were lower-pitched instruments than the standard tenor trombone. These instruments had longer tubes. Their heavier slides and longer distances between the slide positions made them challenging to play, especially in fast passages. This problem was addressed in 1839, when Christian Friedrich Sattler (1778–1842) of Leipzig devised a trombone that took advantage of the valves that began to be used in brass instruments in the early 19th century. Sattler's trombone incorporated an additional length of tubing that could be brought into use by means of a valve, lowering the pitch of the instrument. This type of trombone could therefore play either tenor or bass parts. It found particular favor in Germany, where composers such as Wagner and Strauss wrote for it in their orchestral works.

FROM VENICE TO GERMANY

The 16th century saw the trombone well established in all kinds of music, both religious and secular. In 1526 the cathedral of Seville hired a dedicated wind band of shawms and trombones, and by the mid-16th century, trombones were quite common in church wind ensembles. Instrument-makers were also producing a whole family of trombones by this time. The availability of soprano, alto, tenor, bass and, sometimes, contrabass trombones extended the scope of the instrument and opened up more possibilities for trombone-only groups.

Some of the greatest music for trombone was written at the end of the 16th century, by the noted Venetian composer Giovanni Gabrieli (c. 1557–1612). Gabrieli was organist at San Marco and the Scuola Grande di San Rosso in Venice and wrote music for both. His music was revolutionary in that, unusually in this period, he often carefully specified both dynamics and instrumentation. Gabrieli also tailored his pieces to the architecture of the churches in which they were performed, expertly placing groups of singers or players in different parts of the building so that he could create dramatic spatial effects. This worked especially well in San Marco, where there were two choir lofts facing each other, so that the musicians in one could respond to the sounds coming from the other. Gabrieli used trombones in works such as his *Sonata pian' e forte* (1597), in which two groups, each containing trombones, cornetto and violin, answer one another. In another work, the *Canzon quarti toni*, Gabrieli has three different groups, while another of his Canzoni has no fewer than 17 separate trombone parts.

> **The trombones are too sacred for frequent use.**
>
> *Felix Mendelssohn-Bartholdy*

This music, in which the church of San Marco rang with the glorious sounds of differently pitched trombones, was hugely influential. A number of other Italian composers used the trombone, with or without voices, in religious music. But Gabrieli's biggest influence was probably in Germany, where composers such as Heinrich Schütz (1585–1672) combined trombones with voices to highly dramatic effect.

SAN MARCO
Some of the most dramatic music of the 16th and 17th centuries was first performed in the church of San Marco, Venice.

Schütz was born in Germany but traveled to Venice to be a pupil of Gabrieli. His books of *Symphoniae Sacrae* (1629 and 1647) contain some of the best examples of his dramatic blending of trombones and voices, one of the most celebrated being the solemn setting for bass voice and trombone choir of "Fili mi, Absolon," the Biblical King David's lament after the death of his rebellious son.

Composers such as Gabrieli and Schütz put the trombone on the map of serious music in the 16th and 17th centuries. The trombone also remained a regular feature in bands playing in royal and ducal courts and kept a strong presence in the Holy Roman Empire, where court composers used it in music for the imperial chapel. No doubt the strong tradition of instrument-making in Nuremberg helped keep the trombone popular in the German-speaking states too.

THE TROMBONE AND THE ORCHESTRA

With the rise of the orchestra in the late 17th and 18th centuries, trombones took a back seat. Orchestras were based on groups of stringed instruments (see p. 38), to which winds might be added in various combinations, and to begin with, trombones were not much used in symphonic or operatic music.

There were some notable exceptions to this. Trombones quite often took part in the orchestras used in oratorios, large-scale narrative choral

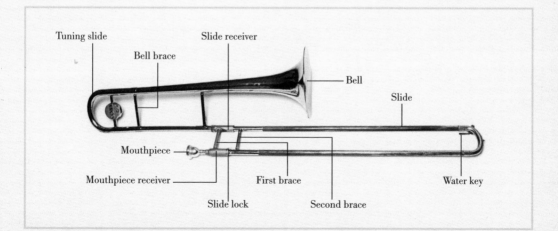

Tuning slide — Slide receiver — Bell brace — Bell — Slide — Mouthpiece — Mouthpiece receiver — First brace — Water key — Slide lock — Second brace

works often on religious subjects. At the end of the 17th and beginning of the 18th century, the Italian composer and conductor Arcangelo Corelli (1653–1713) included trombones in oratorios that he conducted.

One of these was by the young George Frideric Handel (1685–1759), who specified trombones in several oratorios — for example, *Israel in Egypt* and *Saul* (both first performed in 1739). Although Handel was born in Germany, these works were composed during his long residence in England. Even here, there was probably a strong Germanic influence, since the trombones may have been played by German musicians from the household of the country's Hanoverian rulers.

Handel's oratorios were popular, and they may have caught the attention of other composers, such as Gluck (1714–1787), who recognized the qualities of the trombone and brought it into the orchestra for several of his operas. After Gluck, trombones became quite popular in the opera orchestras in Paris. Mozart, too, used the trombone sparingly but tellingly, signaling the appearance of the Commendatorte in *Don Giovanni* (1787) with trombones and using the instruments powerfully to create the somber atmosphere of his final work, the Requiem (1791). In an 18th-century orchestra with a trombone section there were usually three instruments; an alto, a tenor and a bass.

THE TROMBONE IN JAZZ

✦

The profile of the trombone was increased hugely when jazz musicians adopted it. The instrument was present in jazz from the beginnings in New Orleans, where musicians such as Kid Ory exploited its ability to play glissandi, growls and smears, while others, including Miff Mole, played more melodically, with fewer of Ory's raucous effects. In the swing era of the 1930s and 1940s, some bands were actually led by trombonists and the instrument got more solos. Jack Teagarden is one example of such a prominent swing-era trombonist and bandleader. Other players, such as Bennie Green and J.J. Johnson, adapted to the very different rhythmic style of bebop. As jazz has continued to evolve, so trombone players have developed their style, exploring the range of sounds that their instrument can produce and keeping the trombone in the spotlight.

THE MATTHEWS BAND
This brass band of 1904 from Lockport, Louisiana, had a lineup that included both slide and valve trombones.

CHANGES IN THE 19TH CENTURY

The 19th century saw various adjustments to the design of the trombone family, in order to make the instruments more widely useful. In particular, military bands took up the instrument (sometimes as an alternative to the serpent, see p. 30) and instrument-makers came up with adaptations to make the instruments easier to play when marching or riding a horse. One such development was to give the bass trombone a double slide, to make the movements shorter. Another was to produce a modified tenor trombone with a wider bore to extend its lower register, or to keep the bore narrow but widen the bell, with a similar effect.

There were also national and regional variations in trombones. British and French tenor trombones tended to have a narrower bore, and therefore a brighter sound, than the wide-bore trombones of Germany and Austria. The wide-bore instrument is now used generally, because its power in loud passages is suitable for the large halls in which many orchestras play.

For much 19th- and 20th-century music, orchestras have a trombone section of three instruments: two tenor trombones, and a bass or tenor-bass trombone to play the lower part. Outside its orchestral work, the trombone rarely hits the spotlight. Concertos for the instrument are rare, but there are solo works by a number of Romantic and Modern-era composers, from Saint-Saëns and Darius Milhaud to Paul Hindemith and Frank Martin. However, thanks to a number of remarkable players, the trombone has been used widely in both jazz and in recent avant-garde music. Berio's fifth *Sequenza* (1966) is for trombone solo, and trombonist-composers such as Vinko Globokar and Christian Lindberg have added to the repertoire, extending its range of sounds and techniques in the process.

ON THE MARCH
Trombones commonly form part of military and marching bands, where they lie toward the lower end of the pitch range, above the tubas.

Violin

... the violin — that most human of instruments.

Louisa May Alcott, Jo's Boys

Location: Paris, France

Type: Chordophone (bowed)

Era: Baroque

+ WOODWIND
+ PERCUSSION
+ BRASS
+ *STRINGS*
+ OTHER

The violin, the most familiar stringed instrument of all, has four strings tuned in perfect fifths. It is the highest member of a family of instruments that also includes the viola, cello and double bass and has been at the heart of Western classical music since the Baroque period, when composers based their orchestras on the violin family and stringed instrument manufacture, especially in Italy, enjoyed a golden age. Since then it has been the most widely played of all stringed instruments, with a repertoire that is vast and rich in masterpieces.

ANCESTORS OF THE VIOLIN

The violin has a long and complex history, and evolved from the first bowed stringed instruments that were made and played in the ancient world and the early Middle Ages. The lyra, played in the Byzantine empire from about the ninth century, was a pear-shaped instrument with three, four or five strings, played by bowing with the right hand and stopping the strings with the left; the player rested the instrument on the knee. Contemporary with the lyra was an Arabic instrument, the rebab, which usually had a round, drumlike body, a long neck, and one, two or three strings.

Arriving in Europe via early-medieval trade routes, the lyra and rebab led to the evolution of the first European bowed instruments. The lyra evolved into the fiddle, which could have up to five strings on an oval body with two crescent-shaped slits. The rebab became in Europe the rebec, which had a pear-shaped body. Both of these instruments were played held against the chest, shoulder or neck. They were very popular and widely used, especially by minstrels who sang as they played.

CLASSICAL MAINSTAY
Since its emergence in the Renaissance period, the violin has become the mainstay of the classical orchestra, central to much chamber music, and a popular solo instrument.

There is nothing more to be said or to be done tonight, so hand me over my violin and let us try to forget for half an hour the miserable weather and the still more miserable ways of our fellowmen.

Arthur Conan Doyle, The Five Orange Pips

PARNASSUS
In this painting of
c. 1510 by Raphael,
the god Apollo plays
the lyra, holding it on
the shoulder in a similar,
but not identical,
fashion to a violinist.

TWO TYPES OF "VIOLA"

By the end of the Middle Ages these two kinds of instruments were
becoming more sophisticated and developing into two different groups
or families, both known by the Italian name viola (which bears the
meaning "small stringed instrument" rather than the modern English
viola, which is larger than the violin), but with an addition to indicate
the way in which they were held while playing. One type, called viola
da gamba (leg), was played held between the knees; the
other, the viola da braccio (arm), was held at the
player's neck or shoulder, like the medieval fiddle.
Both types of instruments were made in different
sizes and pitches.

**APOLLO THE
LYRE PLAYER**
A Roman copy of
an earlier sculpture
shows Apollo with
his lyre, traditionally
the ancestor of the
stringed instruments.

These two kinds of stringed instruments look
superficially similar but have several key differences. The viola da gamba family have flat backs,
sloped shoulders, c-holes (or occasionally f-holes)
in the body, and frets. They have six strings,
which are played holding the bow with an underhand grip. The bridge is flat, making it easy to
play more than one string at the same time.
Violas da gamba come in a range of pitches,
from small instruments the size of a modern
violin to bass instruments as tall as a man. The
viola da braccia family have rounded backs,
squarer shoulders, f-holes and no frets. They have

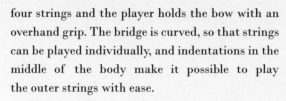

four strings and the player holds the bow with an overhand grip. The bridge is curved, so that strings can be played individually, and indentations in the middle of the body make it possible to play the outer strings with ease.

These two families of bowed stringed instruments had evolved by the 15th century. They had different sounds and tended to be favored by different kinds of musicians. The violas da gamba, with their soft but sonorous tone and suitability for chordal playing, appealed to keen amateurs who liked to play in groups for their own entertainment, and by professionals who wanted to exploit their potential in contrapuntal music. The violas da braccia, on the other hand, with their brighter, sometimes more strident, tone, appealed to professional musicians accompanying dancing, and to folk musicians. Perhaps surprisingly, given these humble origins, it was the viola da braccia family that eventually took center stage and evolved into the modern violin.

ENTER THE VIOLIN

Italy was a hive of musical activity in the 16th century, and the northern part of the country, especially the cities of Venice, Milan, Brescia and Cremona, was a center of stringed-instrument manufacture. This was where the violin evolved between about 1520 and 1550. Andrea Amati (1505–1577) of Cremona made the oldest surviving violins, and he is often credited with inventing the instrument. Italian players took up the violin quickly, exploring its range of expression and powerful sound. The 17th century and the first half of the 18th century was a golden age of violin-making in Italy, where the violin quickly became the dominant stringed instrument played at the shoulder. These great craftsmen made their violins in a range of sizes and pitches — they did not think of them as the high-pitched instruments that we call violins today — so that whole ensembles of violins could be formed.

THE KING'S VIOLINS

The fame of the violin soon spread beyond Italy and, unlike the older viola da braccia of the 15th century, began to find favor not just among popular entertainers but in much more prestigious surroundings. Decisively, in 1626, the French king, Louis XIII, gave his royal approval to a violin band, Les Vingt-quatre Violons du Roi (The King's 24 Violins), that provided a range of music at court. They played at important royal occasions, sometimes as a strings-only ensemble, sometimes in combination with the royal wind band, the Grand Écurie, and so were a high-status ensemble — members had to have a good character and reputation, and were rewarded with tax exemption. Their number eventually included some of the most notable composers and performers of the period, including the greatest French composer of his generation, the founder of French Baroque music, Jean-Baptiste Lully (1632–1687).

The Violons du Roi was a balanced ensemble consisting of six *premier violons* (similar to modern violins) at the top, six *basses de violon* (similar to cellos but tuned a step lower) in the bass, and, between these two extremes, four each of three intermediate viola-like instruments called *hautes-contre*, *tailles* and *quintes*. This gave composers five separate subgroups for which to write parts, and five-part string writing became a speciality of French Baroque composers. The implications, however, went further than France. The Violons du Roi, with their five-part playing of music such as symphonies and suites, have been seen as the forebears of the modern, string-dominated orchestra.

This French ensemble was not the only early orchestra. It was an important part of a wider trend of composers writing for mixed groups of instruments, and was also influenced by the rise

... they esteemed a violin to be an instrument only belonging to a common fiddler ...

Anthony Wood, Antiquities *(1674)*

FIRST AND SECOND VIOLINS

✦

Modern symphony orchestras have two violin sections, the first and second violins, which play separate parts. Each section usually plays in unison (although a composer may divide the strings into more parts). Their musical functions vary, but traditionally, the firsts carry the melody and the seconds play supportive harmony. Their positions in the orchestral layout also vary. There was a long tradition of placing the two sections on opposite sides of the platform, although for many decades in the 20th century there was a fashion for placing the two together, on the left-hand side of the platform as the audience looks at it. Today, many conductors are reverting to the "two sided" approach, and some try to adopt a historically informed position, placing the sections where they were most likely to have sat when the work was originally played. The principal first violin is known as the concertmaster (or orchestra's leader) and he or she leads the tuning, makes decisions about the section's bowing and other technical matters, and plays any violin solos that occur in orchestral pieces.

of opera. Violins (as opposed to the softer-toned violas da gamba) were especially suitable for opera orchestras, which needed to project across large theaters. Another factor in the increasing popularity of orchestras was the fashion for rulers and aristocrats to maintain private orchestras for their own entertainment and prestige. In each case, the violin was increasingly at the heart of the ensemble and at the heart of Western classical music. Meanwhile, composers and players developed the potential of the violin as a chamber and solo instrument, discovering new, expressive ways in which to play it, such as playing on two strings at once or plucking the strings. Composers of solo violin music, such as the Bohemian Heinrich Biber (1644–1704) in his sonatas, developed these techniques.

VIOLIN-MAKERS

Where Andrea Amati began, others followed, from Andrea's son Nicolo to other great Cremonese makers such as Stradivari and Guarneri, whose instruments were loved by generations of musicians and are still played today. Stradivari made around one thousand instruments, more than half of which survive, and his instruments are revered for their brilliant sound. Violins by Guarneri are in the same league, and some players even prefer their rich, sustaining tone to that of the Stradivarius.

In addition, the craft of violin-making spread to Austria, where Jacob Stainer (c. 1617–1683) was one of the best makers. Both J.S. Bach and Mozart's father Leopold were admirers and owners of Stainer violins. Other countries, especially England and France, developed strong traditions of violin production.

CONCERTOS AND SINFONIAS

The violin dominated the Baroque music of the 18th century. Many of the great composers were violinists themselves, and used their instrument (together with its stringed siblings, the viola and cello) enthusiastically in their music, whether writing accompaniments to choral works or operas, orchestral works, or small chamber pieces to be played in a domestic setting. Bach was a master in all these

contexts, interweaving vocal solos in his cantatas with a violin part, and writing his extraordinary Sonatas and Partitas for unaccompanied violin (c. 1720), works that explore the instrument's range of tone and technique in a way that sounds extraordinarily modern. He also wrote several concertos in which the violin soloist (and, in one memorable work, two violin soloists) are able to shine.

Still more enthusiastic were the composers of the violin's home country, Italy, where the superlative quality of the local violins must have inspired composers and players alike. Arcangelo Corelli (1653–1713) led the way, with a series of *concerti grossi* (Grand Concertos, 1714), in which a small group of string players is contrasted with the orchestra as a whole in a way that combines memorable melody, sparkling ornament and lush layers of sound. But most prolific of all the Baroque violin composers was probably the Venetian Antonio Vivaldi (1678–1741). Concertos for every instrument poured from his pen, but his violin concertos are especially memorable — works for one, two,

three or even four soloists, often in sets of four or more concertos. The most famous are the set that include *I Quattro Stagioni* (*The Four Seasons*, 1723), but the high level of invention they achieve is matched in sets such as *L'Estro Armonico* (1711), *La Stravaganza* (1716) and *La Cetra* (1727).

BAROQUE VIOLINS
Violins from the 17th and 18th centuries are sometimes ornately decorated, with shorter necks and generally lower, thicker bridges than modern violins.

ARCANGELO CORELLI
A fine violinist as well as a composer, Corelli had a number of talented pupils and helped make Rome a center of good violin playing.

THE EVOLVING VIOLIN

The violin has kept its key position in classical music from the Baroque era to the present, but not without big changes. The key transformation came about in the late 18th and early 19th centuries. A major change was the way the bow developed, mainly as a result of the work of Parisian bow-maker François Tourte (1747–1835). Tourte changed the curvature of the bow. Baroque bows had a straight or convex stick; Tourte's bows were concave, curving toward the hair in the center. With a Tourte bow it was possible to press harder throughout the whole length of the bow, making strong, sustained playing easier — this was ideal for playing long, singing lines at high volume, something that the composers of the Classical period liked and used in concertos and other works.

The violin itself changed in this period. Strings were longer, heavier and held at greater tension, and makers fitted thicker sound posts and bass bars to their instruments to cope with the extra

STRINGS

✦

The traditional material for violin strings is gut. Sheep's gut was the most popular material, and although this material is often referred to as "catgut," no cats were ever harmed in the production of violin strings. In the second half of the 17th century the practice began of winding the "G" string with a thread of silver wire to give it a more powerful sound. In the 19th century it was common to have "E" and "A" strings of plain gut, a twisted gut "D" string, and a "G" string wound with silver or copper wire. Steel "E" strings became popular in the late 19th century, and various metallic windings were adopted for the other strings — metal strings were preferred because they lasted longer and stretched less. In the 20th century synthetic fibers were used for strings, but the historic performance movement ushered in a return to gut strings among players who wanted to get closer to the sound of the early violin.

VIOLIN BOWS
From top to bottom, the heads of a transitional Tourte bow, a long 18th-century bow, and a 17th-century bow, showing the move away from the convex stick.

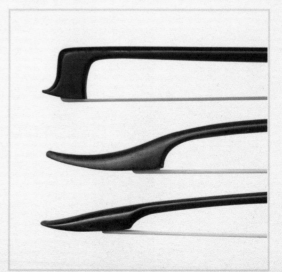

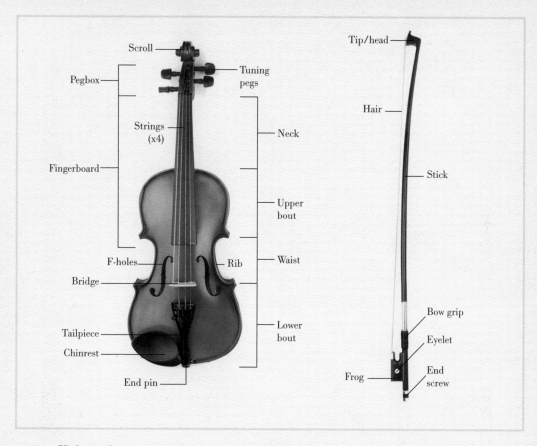

Scroll

Pegbox

Tuning pegs

Strings (x4)

Neck

Fingerboard

Upper bout

F-holes

Rib

Waist

Bridge

Tailpiece

Lower bout

Chinrest

End pin

Tip/head

Hair

Stick

Bow grip

Eyelet

Frog

End screw

tension. Violin necks were made longer to accommodate the longer strings and the joint between the neck and body was strengthened. The material used for the strings also changed. These modifications were applied not only to newly made violins, but to older ones too. The result was instruments with a more powerful sound, ideal for the expressive, often loud, music of the Romantic era, and for the virtuoso playing of such famous violinists as Niccolò Paganini.

In the hands of Romantic composers such as Brahms, Mendelssohn and Tchaikovsky, the violin concerto became a highly expressive, emotionally charged form, and performances of these concertos have remained popular ever since. The tradition continued into the 20th century, with many major composers writing concertos that explored the potential of the violin while keeping much of the Romantic emotional power — the concertos of Shostakovich and Prokofiev are good examples. The violin remains as prominent as ever in the orchestra, where there are usually two violin sections playing different parts and adding to the rich string sound.

VIOLIN PARTS
The parts of a modern violin and its bow, showing how the stick of the bow curves toward the hair in the center.

Is it not strange that sheep's guts should hale souls out of men's bodies.
William Shakespeare, Much Ado About Nothing

Oboe

Location: Paris, France

Type: Aerophone (double reed)

Era: Baroque

The clear sound of the oboe, near to the top of the woodwind section, can command a range of musical moods from plangent to jaunty. From its 17th-century beginnings it has been used in various ways, doubling the violins in early orchestras, playing en masse in Baroque wind bands, or taking orchestral solos and underpinning the human voice in choral music. Its facility for long, singing lines is much loved by musicians and listeners alike.

ANCIENT DOUBLE REEDS

The idea of a double-reed instrument, in which the vibrations of a pair of reeds make the air inside the instrument vibrate in turn, has been around since ancient times. The ancient Greeks played the aulos, an instrument consisting of a pair of pipes, each with a double reed — the musician played both pipes at once, keeping the two double reeds together in the mouth. The aulos was a high-status instrument, and was used to lead the chorus at the theater, to accompany religious sacrifices, and to provide music during processions and banquets. The aulos is often included in ancient Greek vase paintings, and is especially associated with Greek civilization. However, it probably went back to long before the Greeks. It is mentioned in the Bible, where it is noted that its music could either raise the spirits or accompany sadness and lamentation. The Romans had a similar instrument, which they called the tibia.

AULOS PLAYER
A youth plays the aulos in the painting on an ancient Greek red-figure cup of the fifth century BCE.

> I used to compose like the devil in those days, chiefly for the hautboy, which was my favorite instrument.
>
> George Frideric Handel, *remembering works he composed as a boy*

THE SHAWM

At some point in the Middle Ages the work of the aulos was taken over by the shawm. Shawms may have come to Europe from the Middle East, perhaps during the Crusades. By the Renaissance period they were very familiar in many parts of Europe. The shawm is a double-reed instrument with a one-piece wooden body, swelling to a bell at the lower end and with a cap or "pirouette" at the top end, in which the reed is placed. A variation on the design, used in Germany and called the Rauschpfeife, had a wind-cap over the reed. Shawms, like many medieval and Renaissance wind instruments, were made in a series of sizes and pitches from treble to great bass. The larger members of the family may have been devised slightly later than the higher shawms, but by the 16th century, shawm bands were popular, playing entertaining music but not generally taking part in the more serious compositions played in church. Shawms did find their way into the French royal court, however — playing dances in groups that sometimes also contained cornet, trombone and dulcian (the precursor of the bassoon, see p. 52).

LULLY'S OBOES

The composer Jean-Baptiste Lully (1632–1687) reformed the wind band at the royal court in the 17th century, replacing the old shawms with a new instrument: the oboe. The oboe began life in the mid-17th century, during the period of change in woodwind instruments that was going on in France. As with other instruments, such as the flute, these developments may well have been spearheaded by the Hotteterre family, noted makers of wind instruments, though this is not known for sure. Members of the Philidor family, also musicians at the French royal court, may have been involved too.

UNUSUAL OBOES

✦

During the 18th century variations on the oboe evolved and these instruments found special favor with J.S. Bach (1685–1750). The one he used especially widely was the oboe d'amore. This oboe is slightly longer than the standard oboe and pitched a minor third lower. Bach found its slightly veiled sound ideal to accompany singers in his cantatas. When Bach lived and worked in Leipzig, there was a skilled maker of woodwind instruments called Eichentopf, and several of his oboes d'amore have survived. They allow modern listeners to get a good idea of the soft sound Bach wanted when he wrote for the instrument. Occasionally Bach wrote a part for a different variation on the oboe, the oboe da caccia ("hunting oboe," see p. 104).

The instrument's name betrays its origins — "oboe" comes from the French words "*haut*" (high) and "*bois*" (wood), and in 17th- and 18th-century England the French name *hautbois* was often used, sometimes Anglicized to "hoboy."

The oboes made in 17th-century Paris and adopted by Lully had no wind-cap or pirouette, so the double reed could vibrate freely in the mouth of the player, whose lips were in continuous contact with the reed. The instrument had an attractive tone, although the timbre varied at different points in its compass. It was prized because it could play loudly, taking on the same kind of outdoor music played by the shawm, but also had a beautiful tone when played softly — especially when in the hands of a skilled player who took full advantage of the lip control allowed by the lack of pirouette. Musicians rapidly got used to "overblowing" — a woodwind technique in which the player increases the flow of air in the instrument to alter the vibrations and produce higher pitches.

The oboe soon found a place in all kinds of music, from chamber and orchestral pieces to a new genre, opera, in which the oboe could accompany an aria, weaving ornamental arabesques around the singer's words. Players found it was an ideal instrument with which to play long, cantabile lines, because the small gap between the reeds did not require a large amount of air, so that the player could produce long streams of notes on a single breath.

French composers were quick to exploit such qualities of the oboe, but the instrument spread around Europe too. J.S. Bach wrote beautifully for it, using it in his cantatas and Passion settings to accompany some of his most touching arias. Some Baroque composers also exploited it as the solo instrument in concertos. Albinoni wrote notable concertos for it, while Handel composed chamber sonatas with

... it is to the oboe that they [Gluck and Beethoven] both owe the deep feelings aroused by some of the most beautiful passages in their music.

Hector Berlioz, Treatise on Orchestration *(1843–1855)*

oboe. A large number of oboists were among the musicians in the extra-large wind band assembled to perform one of Handel's most famous works, the *Music for the Royal Fireworks* (1749), a piece in which Handel brought his sophistication and melodic invention to the kind of outdoor wind music that had been played by shawms before the Baroque oboe evolved. Handel's work was written for performance in London, where a strong tradition of oboe playing had developed in the previous century. Many of the works of the British composer Henry Purcell (1659–1695) make luminous use of the oboe.

The musicians of the Baroque period also experimented with oboes at different pitches. A baritone oboe, for example, sounding an octave below the standard treble instrument, was developed and used in some music; it was later largely replaced by the heckelphone (see p. 198). The English horn or cor anglais (see p. 104) is the tenor member of the oboe family. But although the English horn appears in many orchestral pieces it is the standard treble oboe that has found the most lasting place in the orchestra.

TWO SYSTEMS

✦

There are various differences in oboe design involving variations in the way in which certain notes are produced. One such variation is between the thumb-plate and conservatoire type instruments. There is a long tradition in Britain of using the "thumb-plate" system oboe. In this type of instrument, B-flat and C are produced by lifting the left thumb from a plate. In the much more common conservatoire system oboe, these notes are made by lowering the right-hand first finger.

OBOE PLAYER
An oboist features in this late 17th-century Gobelins tapestry on the theme of the Dance of the Nymphs.

MECHANICAL REFINEMENTS

The composers of the Baroque era used the oboe so widely that the instrument had no problem winning a place in the orchestra during the Classical and Romantic periods that followed: most of the composers recognized the instrument's expressive powers and by the time of Haydn, Mozart and Beethoven, orchestral woodwind sections regularly included a pair of oboes alongside pairs of flutes and clarinets. Examples of these composers harnessing the oboe's expressive potential include the way in which Haydn makes it imitate a hen in his Symphony No. 83 (1785), while Beethoven uses it to recreate the song of the quail in his Symphony No. 6 (The Pastoral, 1808). As with the flute, there was also a long-standing link between the oboe and pastoral scenes — in his *Symphonie Fantastique* (1830), Berlioz uses an off-stage oboe to evoke the piping of shepherds. Both Baroque and Classical instrument-makers added keys to the oboe — usually two, one for low C and one for E-flat. By the time the Classical era was coming to an end, makers were adding further keys — up to eight — to eliminate cross-fingerings, making the oboe easier to play and opening it up to more complex music.

German manufacturers led the way with further mechanical improvements, such as adding more keys until there was a key-operated tone hole for each semitone. The French makers took the technical lead with innovations such as the speaker key (which enabled the player to produce higher pitches without overblowing) and various enhanced key and lever mechanisms.

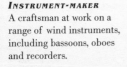

INSTRUMENT-MAKER
A craftsman at work on a range of wind instruments, including bassoons, oboes and recorders.

At the same time, two overall tendencies in the sound produced by these instruments emerged. German instruments tended to keep the Classical oboe's dark tone, which blended well with the orchestra, while French instruments tended to sound brighter, making them sing out above the rest of the orchestral texture.

By the 1860s, French manufacturers were perfecting what became the standard modern instrument. This has a very narrow bore and speaker key. Adopted by the Paris Conservatoire, it became known as the conservatoire oboe and was used throughout much of Europe by the 20th century. Such instruments were ideal to play the long lines that featured in oboe solos in Romantic-era works such as

1.

2.

3.

4.

5.

A VARIETY OF OBOES
This selection of 18th- and 19th-century oboes includes examples in a variety of woods and one musette, a higher-pitched oboe-like instrument.

1. German oboe, c. 1744, with boxwood tube, brass keys and ivory ferrules

2. Dutch oboe, 1716–1727, with ebony tube, silver keys and carved ivory ferrules

3. French oboe, late 18th century, with ivory tube, black horn ferrules and silver keys

4. French musette, c. 1850, with cocus tube and nickel keys and ferrules

5. English oboe, c. 1870, with boxwood tube, nickel silver keys and ivory ferrules

Tchaikovsky's ballet *Swan Lake* (1876) or the long, keening passages in the second movement of Elgar's Symphony No. 2 (1911). But there was a long gap in the concerto repertoire in the early Romantic period — there were few concertos written for the instrument in between Mozart's time and the flowering of solo music that took place in the 20th century. Concertos by Richard Strauss, Vaughan Williams and Eugene Goosens (brother of the great oboist Leon Goosens), plus sonatas by Hindemith and Poulenc and solo pieces by Britten, greatly extended the solo repertoire. So did the work of virtuoso players, notably Leon Goosens (1897–1988), who did much to win his instrument a larger following, and more recently the great Swiss oboist Heinz Holliger (b. 1939). Holliger commissioned numerous solo pieces for his instrument — many of them experimental or avant-garde works that exploited the range of unusual sounds that the oboe can produce. The creative explorations of players like Holliger, and of composers such as Luciano Berio and Harrison Birtwistle, ensure that the expressive qualities of this instrument have been explored and extended through the 20th century and into the 21st.

Bassoon

Location: Paris, France

Type: Aerophone (double reed)

Era: Baroque

Sometimes seen as the comedian of the orchestra, the bassoon is in fact a highly versatile low-pitched woodwind instrument. Its voice, which ranges from gruff to plaintive, has inspired composers to produce interesting and engaging music since the instrument evolved in the 17th century, probably as a refinement of an earlier wind instrument, the dulcian. Since then it has found a regular place in the classical orchestra, as well as occasional solo spots.

THE DULCIAN

The predecessor of the bassoon is the dulcian (also known as the curtal), a double-reed instrument with two parallel bores joined at the bottom (like an elongated letter U). Both bores were usually made in the same piece of wood, with a cap at the bottom containing the connecting curve. The construction of the dulcian, with its two parallel bores, effectively "folded" the instrument in two, so that a long tube could be housed in a relatively short instrument. The advantage of this, apart from keeping the instrument compact, was that the tone holes were well within reach of the player's fingers. Dulcians were made in various lengths and pitches, from soprano to great bass, but by the mid-16th century the bass dulcian especially was widely used in wind bands. It was powerful enough to hold its own among the shawms (ancestors of the oboe) and sackbuts (early trombones) used in outdoor groups and in ensembles that played in church.

BASSOON
The tube of this low-pitched woodwind instrument is longer than it looks because it is "folded" at the bottom.

It is a bass instrument without proper bass strength, oddly weak in sound, bleating burlesque.

Thomas Mann, Doctor Faustus *(1947)*

THE JOINTED BASSOON

Making the conical bore was very difficult to do with precision, especially as the dulcian was made out of one piece of wood. In the middle of the 17th century, instrument-makers came up with a new way of making the bass woodwind instrument that to some extent overcame this problem. Instead of forming it out of a single piece of timber, craftworkers produced it in four sections, known as joints, which the player pushed together to assemble the instrument. By making the instrument in four sections, manufacturers found it much easier to match the bore, which had always been a challenge when making an instrument by boring two parallel holes in a single piece of wood.

This new instrument became known as the bassoon. Some historians believe it evolved naturally from the dulcian, others that it was a completely separate invention. Like the dulcian, it was produced in different sizes and pitches, but (apart from the rare tenoroon) only the bassoon and its still lower-pitched sibling the contrabassoon (see p. 94) have found a permanent place in Western classical music.

The instrument-maker usually credited with producing the first bassoons is the eminent French craftsman Martin Hotteterre (d. 1712), although other French makers may also have been involved in the bassoon's evolution. But whoever had the original idea for it, the bassoon with four joints, three keys, and a double reed held in a curving metal crook seems to have taken hold in France by about 1660. Twenty years later, the instrument was also being made in Germany.

The bassoon arrived on the musical scene just as Baroque music was about to reach its peak. It found ready recognition as a continuo instrument,

THE ORCHESTRA
WITH WOODWINDS

✦

The development of the oboe and bassoon in the mid-17th century encouraged some composers to make woodwinds a regular feature of their orchestra. For example, the French composer Jean-Baptiste Lully (1632–1687) used for his operas a body of strings together with oboes, bassoons, flutes and sometimes trumpets and timpani. Although his "oboes" were not modern instruments and his "flutes" were recorders rather than transverse flutes, Lully was still an important figure in expanding and enriching the orchestra.

OPERA ORCHESTRA
A bassoonist sits at the front of this opera orchestra of 1870, painted by Edgar Degas.

providing a bass line under singers in operas, but composers soon realized that the bassoon could do a lot more than this. Several Baroque composers wrote concertos for bassoon, the most prolific being Antonio Vivaldi (1678–1741), who produced some 39, of which 37 survive. Vivaldi's bassoon concertos are demanding works. No one knows for sure why the composer wrote so many of them, but there must have been at least one highly accomplished musician available in Vivaldi's native Venice to play them. Talented bassoonists must have been available in Central Europe too, as Bohemian composer Jan Dismas Zelenka (1679–1745) exploited the instrument's potential in chamber music by giving the bassoon an important role in his charming trio sonatas.

The bassoon was also increasingly included in the orchestra as the Baroque period went on, balancing the flute and oboe at the other end of the woodwind section. Many composers of the Baroque and Classical eras saw it as a generic bass instrument, using it, the cello and the double bass to give the bass plenty of weight in orchestral pieces. Haydn often used the bassoon in this way. Often, when the composer had not written a bassoon part, the bassoon players doubled the cello or double bass parts.

Mozart more often gave the bassoon its own part, recognizing its distinctive voice, and Beethoven exploited the voice of the bassoon still more. His later symphonies, violin concerto and other works include solos for the instrument. Among Classical era composers, Mozart, Hummel, Danzi and Rosetti all wrote bassoon concertos — the Mozart and Hummel works are enjoyable and quite often performed. Both Haydn and Mozart wrote *sinfonie concertante*, in effect concertos for several solo instruments, one of which was the bassoon.

IMPROVING THE BASSOON

In the early 19th century, once musicians had begun to explore the bassoon's potential, manufacturers and players started to develop ways of improving both the instrument and standards of playing. One of the chief improvers of the bassoon was the German player and instrument-maker Carl Almenräder (1786–1846). He worked with an expert in acoustics, Gottfried Weber (1779–1839), and the pair carried out experiments at Germany's Schott instrument factory. By rearranging the bassoon's keys and adding more keys, they were able to produce an instrument that not only had a greater compass but was also easier to play and provided improved intonation. By the 1820s Almenräder's 15-key and 18-key bassoons were impressing players.

One of the people Almenräder came across at the Schott factory was a young instrument-maker called Johann Adam Heckel (1812–1877).

The bassoon is one of my favorite instruments. It has a medieval aroma.

Frank Zappa

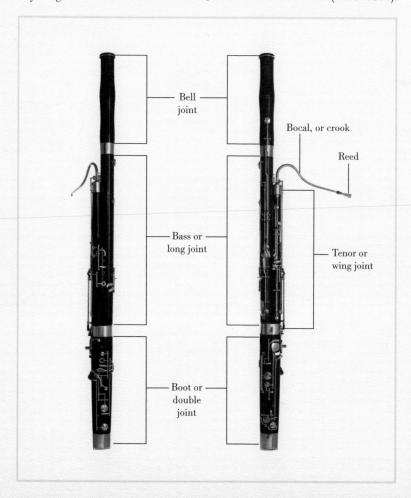

Bell joint

Bocal, or crook

Reed

Bass or long joint

Tenor or wing joint

Boot or double joint

THE PARTS OF A BASSOON
A bassoon is made up of four sections or joints. The bottom joint, the boot joint, is like a U-bend that connects the long joint and wing joint. The wing joint joins the boot at the bottom and the bocal, or crook, at the top.

In 1831 the pair left Schott and set up their own firm, continuing to experiment with improvements and to publish the results of their work, just as Almenräder had done when working with Weber. When Almenräder died in 1846, Heckel and his son Wilhelm continued the firm, and carried on improving their products. By the 1870s, Heckel instruments had achieved most of Almenräder's goals: the conical bore was precisely made with an even taper, many keys helped eliminate difficult fingerings, and relocated note holes also made the instrument easier to play. "Heckel system" bassoons remained popular throughout much of Europe.

The Wedding-Guest here beat his breast,
For he heard the loud bassoon.

S.T. Coleridge, The Rime of the Ancient Mariner

The main exception was France, where a rival system, the Buffet system, developed. Buffet bassoons also evolved gradually, generally by adding keys to the existing bassoon. Playing them involved different fingerings from those used on Heckel bassoons and the Buffet instruments tended to be easier to play in the higher register, but produced a reedier, more edgy tone, which not all musicians liked. The Buffet system was widely used in France and was also popular in Italy and England, but it gradually fell out of favor. Heckel system bassoons are now by far the most common.

During the 19th century the bassoon kept its place in the orchestral woodwind section. A lot of its work was to do with reinforcing the bass — the increasing popularity of French horn solos in orchestral pieces edged the bassoon out of the orchestral limelight. But the instrument still had occasional solo passages that exploited its range from deep bass to a surprisingly high, yearning upper register. Tchaikovsky wrote beautiful passages for the instrument in his last three symphonies and Giuseppe Verdi gave it the spotlight in his powerful Requiem (1874).

The bassoon's range was also exploited in a few concertos and solo pieces. Several Romantic composers, including Weber, produced concertos for the instrument and Glinka wrote a striking trio for bassoon, clarinet and piano. Many of these composers exploited the two contrasting images of the bassoon. The instrument's deep, sometimes gruff voice, when used in fast passages and unusual rhythm, could cast the bassoon as the orchestra's comedian. On the other hand, like all reed instruments, the bassoon also has a lyrical side and can present singing lines and lamenting slow movements very effectively. Successful concertos make good use of this contrast with their fast outer movements and gentle, lyrical slow movements.

Quiet and low, the bassoon is often out of the limelight. But late 19th-century composers made good use of the instrument, as shown by Debussy in his orchestral *Nocturnes* (1899). For many people, the modern era in music could be said to be heralded by Stravinsky's revolutionary ballet music for *The Rite of Spring*, premiered in 1913. This work is begun by the bassoon, which opens the piece with a haunting, high passage in which it hardly sounds like a bassoon at all. Perhaps picking up on the instrument's eloquence in this pivotal music, 20th-century composers have used it widely. A good example is Shostakovich, in his Symphony No. 9 (1945). He gives the bassoon melancholy music in the slow third movement, then rapidly moves to faster, light-hearted material at the start of the fourth movement, one mood following the other almost instantly in a showcase of the instrument's great expressive range.

THE TENOROON

✦

Just as Renaissance woodwind instruments like the dulcian were made in families of different pitches, so some makers produced a range of bassoons from a small soprano instrument to the large standard bassoon and contrabassoon familiar in today's symphony orchestras. The higher bassoons are very rare today, but one that is occasionally used is the tenoroon, which is pitched a fourth or fifth above the standard bassoon. Its sound is somewhat similar to the English horn (cor anglais) and there was once a theory that the English horn part in Rossini's *William Tell* overture (1829) was intended for the tenoroon, though this is now thought unlikely. Few works have been written specifically for the tenoroon, apart from pieces by little-known Baroque composers and the occasional military march that has a part for the instrument.

IGOR STRAVINSKY
When Stravinsky (pictured left) began his landmark work *The Rite of Spring* with a high solo on the bassoon, he presented the instrument in a light that was quite unfamiliar to most listeners.

Double Bass

Location: Bologna, Italy

Type: Chordophone (bowed)

Era: Baroque

- ✦ WOODWIND
- ✦ PERCUSSION
- ✦ BRASS
- ✦ **STRINGS**
- ✦ OTHER

DOUBLE BASS
The lowest of the orchestral stringed instruments is distinguished not only by its size but also by its shoulders, which slope more than those of the higher strings.

Seen and heard in every modern symphony orchestra and widely used in jazz, the double bass is the lowest member of the string family. In classical music, however, this large and familiar instrument has a low profile — it has few solo opportunities and its low notes, though they can be impressive, are often heard in the background, beneath the brighter violins and the louder cellos. This role of underpinning, however, is vital, and the double bass has a long and interesting history.

A HYBRID INSTRUMENT

Although the double bass is part of the violin family, it is different from the other members in several ways. Its body is deeper in proportion to its height than those of the other strings; the instrument's "shoulders" have a gradual slope, in contrast to the more rounded shoulders of the violin; and the instrument is tuned in fourths rather than in fifths. Some of these differences make the bass more like the early string family known as the viols. Viols have sloping shoulders and are usually tuned in fourths (with a fifth in the middle). So one of the ancestors of the bass was probably the lowest member of the viol family (often known as the violone), which was certainly in existence by the beginning of the 16th century. This kind of bass or contrabass viol was impressive for its size as well as its sound.

However, in other ways the double bass is much more like a violin. It has f-holes rather than the viol's c-holes; its internal construction is more violin-like; it has four strings rather than the six common in the viol family (in some eras three-stringed basses were common); and its neck lacks frets, in contrast to the fretted viol. So the double bass has dual origins, taking some features from the viols, some from the violins, and the exact way in which it evolved is not clear.

The double bass is as we know the foundation of the orchestra.

François-Joseph Fétis (Belgian musicologist)

THE VIOL AND ITS MUSIC

✦

Although the viol has never had a regular place in the symphony orchestra, it survives because so much beautiful music was written for it in its Renaissance heyday, and during the Baroque era. Many of the great English composers of the Tudor and Stuart period wrote for viols — the English viol tradition stretches from Elizabethans William Byrd (c. 1540–1623) and John Dowland (1563–1626) to the less well known but almost equally fine Stuart masters William Lawes (1602–1645) and John Jenkins (1592–1678).

Most of this music was written for small groups, or consorts, of viols of different pitches, from the small viola da braccia held at the shoulder to the larger viola da gamba held between the legs, and, at the bottom of the group, the violone. There was also a strong French school of viol composition that stretched well into the Baroque period, with such exponents as Monsieur de Sainte-Colombe (1640–1700; his first name is unknown), Marin Marais (1656–1728) and viol virtuoso Antoine Forqueray (1699–1782). The French masters excelled at solo music for the instrument. Viol consort music from various parts of Europe, especially from England and France, has been revived by period instrument groups and is still widely played and recorded.

ORCHESTRAL BEGINNINGS

Although it was evolving in the 16th and 17th centuries, the double bass did not find its way into the orchestra quickly. It was not an original member of the famous Vingt-quatre Violons du Roi, the notable string ensemble that played at the French court that is often described as the first orchestra (see p. 41). But by the end of the 17th century, the double bass had been admitted to the orchestra, and by this time it was starting to appear in opera orchestras as well. The low string section of the orchestra was very fluid in this period. Orchestras had various combinations of cellos, double basses and violones. Sometimes all three were present at the same time, doing a combined job of providing the low parts of the string harmony, with the cellos usually handling any passages that required more agile playing.

REHEARSAL
Various low stringed
instruments are visible
in Marco Ricci's painting
Rehearsal of an Opera,
c. 1709.

STRINGS AND TUNING MECHANISMS

One problem with large stringed instruments playing at low pitches was
with the strings themselves. The strings on all early violins, cellos and
double basses were made of gut. On the double bass these gut strings
had to be very thick and heavy, and such strings made it difficult to
play fast passages. In the 17th century, probably first in Italy, strings
wound with thin copper wire were introduced. These were easier to play
quickly, and greatly increased the expressive power of the double bass.
There is a strong case for saying that the addition of wire-wound strings
enabled the double bass to fulfill its true expressive potential.

**He came to seek his beloved wife,
alias his double bass ...**

Mary Novello on Dragonetti

But there was a problem with the new strings. They
had to be kept at a high tension, and this made tuning
difficult using the traditional wooden pegs found on
stringed instruments. Berlin instrument-maker Carl
Ludwig Bachmann (1743–1809) came up with a solution
to this problem in 1778. Bachmann was one of those instrument-makers who was also a musician: he was employed as both violin-maker and
chamber musician at the Prussian court. His invention was a new
tuning mechanism using screw pegs — thumb screws turned small cog
wheels that allowed the strings to be tightened with great precision.
This made the double bass a much more practical instrument.

A SLOWLY EXPANDING ROLE

Even with Bachmann's invention, however, the double bass did not achieve the same prominence in the orchestra as its higher-pitched siblings. The reason for this was the way in which orchestral harmony had developed. By the 18th century, the trend toward four-part string harmony was clear. In chamber music, this was represented by the string quartet (see p. 125), a medium developed by Haydn and seized upon by nearly every major Classical era composer and many later ones too; these writers found the quartet's composition of two violins, viola and cello ideal. The orchestra developed a similar four-part pattern of string sections, with first and second violins, violas, and cellos.

When the double bass arrived in the orchestra its main job was playing the same music as the cellos, but an octave lower, to reinforce the bottom of the string sound. In the Classical period, therefore, playing double bass was most of the time like playing a low cello, sometimes dropping out when the cello part was too agile or difficult for the larger instrument. For the most part, double basses in the 18th century had three strings.

Haydn occasionally extended the role of the double bass in his symphonies: there are memorable solo passages in numbers 6, 7 and 8 (*Le matin*, *Le midi* and *Le soir*, 1761). There are very few double bass concertos, and they were rare in the Classical period. Carl Ditters von Dittersdorf (1739–1799), who played in a string quartet alongside Mozart and Haydn, wrote one, as did Johann Baptist Vanhal (1739–1813), who was the fourth member of the same quartet. Many double bass players regret that the group's two other members did not leave behind a concerto or two for their instrument.

In chamber music, the double bass occasionally had interesting work to do. Mozart included it in several chamber pieces. A few of Mozart's divertimenti feature double bass in combination with two violins, viola and two horns, and his popular Serenade for 13 Wind Instruments is famously misnamed — the part labeled "basso" is in fact for double bass.

If the double bass had little chance to shine in the Classical era, there was one musician who was determined to make the instrument stand out. His name was Domenico Dragonetti (1763–1846), and from humble beginnings in his native Venice he rose to be principal double bass in the chapel of San Marco before leaving to

GIOVANNI BOTTESINI
Italian composer and double bass player Giovanni Bottesini (1821–1889) was one of the most talented players of his time, famous for composing elaborate works for his instrument based on tunes from popular operas.

JAZZ BASS

✦

From large jazz orchestras to trios,
the bass has been a major presence
in jazz since the 1890s. It is nearly
always played pizzicato, sometimes
using the "slap" technique in which
the string is pulled and bounces off
the fingerboard, which helps to
amplify the instrument's sound.
The bass began in jazz playing a
"walking bass" line to underpin the
harmony in New Orleans bands of
the 1890s. By the 1930s it was a
key part of the rhythm section in all
kinds of jazz groups, ranging in
style from bebop to cool. Although
some groups from the 1940s on
favored the amplified sound of the
electric bass guitar, the double bass
is widely loved for its unique sound
and is still played in many jazz
rhythm sections.

pursue a brilliant career in London. Becoming
famous as the Paganini of the double bass, he was
known for his large, strong hands and his agile
playing, and he showed off his skills in many of his
own compositions. These included several double
bass concertos, numerous pieces for double bass
and piano, and a number of solo works.

THE ROMANTIC BASS

In the Romantic era orchestras tended to get larger,
as composers demanded more volume, more variety of timbre, and more expressive power in their
large-scale works. One result of this trend was
bigger string sections with a complement of double
basses. Another was the gradual adoption of
instruments with four strings. Although many
players liked the three-string bass, which had a relatively powerful sound, its lower register was
restricted. Composers wanted more lower notes,
and the four-string bass could provide them, but its
sound was weaker. Adding more basses to the string
section — something that was happening anyway
as the Romantic orchestra got bigger — helped
address this weakness. At the same time instruments such as the bass clarinet and contrabassoon
were entering the orchestra in the 19th century,
and their arrival helped to strengthen the bass line.
The mellower sound of the four-string bass,
together with this extra emphasis on the lower
parts of the harmony, helped to give the Romantic
orchestra its richer, darker sound.

The burnished sound of Romantic symphonies
such as those by Brahms and Tchaikovsky, the
richness of Wagner's orchestration, the powerful
bass in symphonies by Mahler and Sibelius —
all these were helped along by the expanding
double bass sections of orchestras in the Romantic
period. A few composers also highlighted the bass
by giving it solos in orchestral works. Saint-Saëns
exploits it for comic effect in his portrait of the
elephant in his *Carnival of the Animals* (1886).

Mahler puts the instrument in the spotlight in his Symphony No. 1 (1888). Stravinsky includes a solo in his ballet *Pulcinella* (1920), a score based on 18th-century music but rewritten with a 20th-century voice. In each case, the sonority of the double bass contrasts effectively with the other instruments. As the 20th century went on, classical composers, in part influenced by the use of the bass in jazz, in part by the adventurous playing of avant-garde improvisers, and in part by the work of notable players, have explored the range of the instrument still further. All of these interests come together in the work of bassists like the British virtuoso Barry Guy (b. 1947). Guy has improvised, played in ensembles and composed. He has opened up new possibilities for the bass with a range of adventurous techniques — plucking and bowing beneath the bridge, hitting the strings with percussion mallets, and incorporating objects with the strings. The scope of the double bass has never been greater.

BARRY GUY
The British master double bass player is seen here during a Moscow performance with the Aurora Trio.

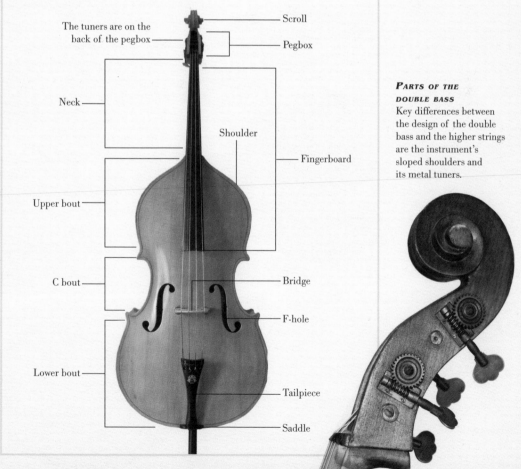

The tuners are on the back of the pegbox

Scroll

Pegbox

Neck

Shoulder

Fingerboard

Upper bout

C bout

Bridge

F-hole

Lower bout

Tailpiece

Saddle

PARTS OF THE DOUBLE BASS
Key differences between the design of the double bass and the higher strings are the instrument's sloped shoulders and its metal tuners.

Cymbals

> The cymbal must not be attached to the drum.
>
> *P.I. Tchaikovsky, score of Symphony No. 6*

Location: Germany

Type: Idiophone

Era: Baroque

+ WOODWIND
+ **PERCUSSION**
+ BRASS
+ STRINGS
+ OTHER

The arresting clash of the cymbals entered orchestral music in 1680, when German composer Nicolaus Adam Strungk (1640–1700) included them in his opera *Esther*. Cymbals had been around for centuries, but Strungk gave them prominence in Western classical music, and, ever since, in combination with drums, they have been attracting listeners' attention, signaling climaxes, contributing to an atmosphere of exoticism, or startling audiences with a sudden clash.

A SPECIALIZED INSTRUMENT

Cymbals have a long history and have been played in many parts of Asia, including India, Tibet, China and Japan, for centuries. They were also used in western Asia and Egypt, and probably came to Greece from these areas of the world. Several pairs of cymbals have survived from ancient Greece — they are typically about 3.5 inches (9 cm) in diameter with a deep central dome and curved rim. Similar cymbals, as well as much larger ones, were played by the Romans — cymbals up to 16 inches (41 cm) across were found among the ruins of Pompeii. In both Greece and Rome, cymbals were played during the worship of Dionysus (also known as Bacchus), god of wine and revelry, and Cybele, a mother goddess. Worship of both of these deities was accompanied by orgiastic rites, in which the excitement was heightened by the frenzied clashing of cymbals.

From the Romans the cymbals passed to medieval Europe. Medieval illustrations show cymbals between 6 and 10 inches (15–25 cm) across with quite large domes. Players of dance and military music often held them horizontally. Some illuminated manuscripts show small cymbals played by angels, so they may have been used in religious music too. But they seem only to have been played occasionally and were not much used in mainstream art music.

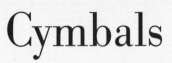

PAIR OF CYMBALS
Modern cymbals are generally played in pairs and held using leather straps.

ANCIENT CYMBAL
The typical cymbal of ancient Greece (see right) was made of bronze and had a higher, larger dome than modern cymbals.

RECLINING BACCHANTE
This 18th-century painting by French artist Jean-Simon Berthélemy shows a devotee of the Greek god Bacchus playing the cymbals.

FROM EXOTIC TO MAINSTREAM

When Adam Strungk employed large cymbals in his opera *Esther*, he alerted European composers to a striking new sound. Slowly, the cymbals were taken up, initially when composers wanted to evoke the musical style of Turkey. This they did in the so-called "janissary music" fashionable in the 18th century, which made use of a battery of tinkling percussion including the cymbals, triangle, tambourine and bell tree. Mozart's opera *Die Entführung aus dem Serail* (1782) is a famous example. When Gluck wanted to evoke the music of the Scythians in his opera *Iphigénie en Tauride* (1779), he also resorted to the cymbals. By the time the next generation of composers was established, the cymbals were taking a more regular place among the percussion in the orchestra, and Beethoven gave them prominence in the final movement of his great Symphony No. 9 (1824). Here, along with other "Turkish" instruments, they accompany a marchlike passage, and perhaps for the first time do so without involving any explicitly "exotic" meaning.

HOW THEY WORK

✦

When a player clashes together a pair of cymbals, the rim area of each cymbal begins to vibrate. The thin metal of the cymbals allows the vibrations to continue and develop, and the instrument produces a range of vibrations, some very deep, some much higher. When an instrument produces a sound, this is not one note, but a series, consisting of the fundamental note and many above it; the overtones. This note and the overtones are together known as the partials. In the case of the cymbal, the instrument produces many inharmonic partials, and the effect of these is to create a sound of mingled pitches, so the cymbal is an instrument that is said to be of no definite pitch.

The stage was set for the Romantic composers to make still greater use of the dramatic clash of the cymbals. Hector Berlioz (1803–1869), always eager to expand the range of sounds produced by the orchestra, led the way. In his Requiem (1837), he makes a deafening impact with large numbers of drums, three pairs of cymbals and a tam-tam. In his Te Deum (1849), he asks for four or five pairs of cymbals, and in *The Trojans* (1856–1858) and *Romeo and Juliet* (1839), he calls for the small ancient cymbals, played edge to edge to produce a tinkling sound, rather than clashed together; the composer had these cymbals specially made, probably as copies of cymbals found at the ancient Roman site of Pompeii. Berlioz was critical of composers who used cymbals in a dull or predictable fashion. He particularly objected to a fashion among some composers for emphasizing accented beats with a stroke of the bass drum and a clash of the cymbals (often both played by the same musician), which he described as an effect fit only for dance music for monkeys.

JOYFUL NOISE
Salvation Army bands included cymbals in their percussion sections, as satirized in this image from the humorous magazine *Puck*.

ESTABLISHED IN THE ORCHESTRA

By the end of the 19th century the cymbals were well established in the orchestra and they were brightening the color of the percussion section in works by composers from Bizet to Tchaikovsky. Mostly these composers used standard cymbals, which are round, with a central raised dome containing a hole for a leather strap or metal stand. They are carefully manufactured to produce the best tone. Percussionists have the choice of a wide range in different gauges of metal and diameters, commonly between 8 inches (20 cm) and 24 inches (60 cm). The thickness of the cymbal affects the sound, with heavy gauges producing more of a "clang" and lighter gauges a higher "zing." Musicians choose a gauge that suits the piece. The other type of cymbal sometimes used in

CROTALES
Also known as antique cymbals, crotales (see right) are small tuned cymbals. They are hit with hard beaters.

classical music is the small cymbal or crotale, based on the instruments from the ancient world that Berlioz had copied. These are made of thicker metal and may have a dome that is large in size relative to the rim. They produce a high note, often bell-like in tone.

The most familiar cymbal sound is the clash, produced by bringing the cymbals together in a glancing motion, then either raising them so that the sound rings on or damping them against the player's body. A cymbal may also be played suspended, either in the player's hand or on a stand, and hit with beaters. A pair of different cymbals on stands can be used to make contrasting sounds.

Many composers expected percussionists to do more than simply clash their cymbals together. Berlioz was one of the first to require the player to hit a single cymbal with a drumstick. In the late 19th and 20th centuries, composers became more adventurous in their use of the cymbals. Wagner, for example, required the percussionist to produce rolls, both by hitting the cymbal with sticks and by producing a two-plate roll, in which the edges of the cymbals are rubbed against one another, an effect also used in Bartók's Violin Concerto No. 2 (1938). Other composers ask for various beaters, from hard to soft, to vary the sound, and some employ metal rods or wire brushes. Schoenberg, in his *Five Pieces for Orchestra* (1909), requires the player to produce a tremolo by playing a cymbal with a cello bow, while William Walton, in *Façade* (1923), even has the player strike a suspended cymbal with a triangle, to imitate the sound of a cowbell. A bell-like sound can also be achieved with the small cymbal or crotale, a favorite with French composers such as Debussy. Debussy's languorously beautiful *Prélude à l'après-midi d'un faune* (1894) uses them at the end, an example of the cymbals recreating the mood of exoticism for which they were first valued by composers back in the 18th century.

CYMBALS IN THE DRUM KIT

✦

The cymbal has been prominent in the rhythm and percussion sections in popular music, dance music and jazz since the early 20th century, and the typical drum kit has several cymbals. The hi-hat was popularized in the jazz and dance music of the 1920s. It consists of a pair of cymbals, horizontally mounted on a stand and connected to a pedal that moves the upper cymbal down to hit the lower one with a clicking sound. Drum kits also have a "top" or "ride" cymbal, a suspended symbol used for rapid repeated notes, and a "crash" cymbal, a smaller suspended cymbal. Some players also use a sizzle cymbal, which has loose rivets sets around the rim to make a rattling but less sustained sound.

Cello

Location: Italy

Type: Chordophone (bowed)

Era: Baroque

+ WOODWIND
+ PERCUSSION
+ BRASS
+ **STRINGS**
+ OTHER

MAINSTAY
The cello is a key member of the string section of every orchestra, and has one of the largest repertoires of any instrument.

The second-largest member of the string family, the violoncello — usually called by its shortened name of cello — is one of the most versatile of all instruments, familiar in its roles in the string section of the orchestra, in many different chamber-music groups and as a solo instrument. Its wide dynamic range, generous compass and appealing tone make it one of the most ubiquitous and popular instruments, with a repertoire second only to that of the violin in quantity and quality.

THE BASS VIOLIN

Bowed stringed instruments have a long history stretching back to the early Middle Ages, but the crucial period for the evolution of the modern strings was the late 15th and early 16th centuries. This was when the two basic families of stringed instruments — the viols, with their fretted necks, flat blacks and sloping "shoulders," and the violins, with their unfretted necks, curving backs and generally more hunched, rounded shoulders — were diverging. At the lower end of the viol family was the viola da gamba (viol for the leg), which the player held between the knees. Toward the lower end of the violin family were various forms of bass violin, some held between the knees, some held at the shoulder. These bass instruments were known by a confusing variety of names, including bass violin in England and *basse de violon* in France. They were sometimes also called "violones," which means simply "large violas."

One of these Renaissance stringed instruments was mentioned in 1556 as a "*violoncello da spalla*," the first printed reference to an instrument with this name. "*Violoncello*" means a violone that is on the small side or, as some writers put it, a smallish large viola; "*spalla*" means "shoulder." Holding even a smallish violone at the shoulder was not easy, so instrument-makers also

If only I had been told that one could write a cello concerto like that!

Johannes Brahms, on the Dvořák Cello Concerto

made a similar, slightly larger, violone that the player could hold
between the legs, like a viola da gamba. This violin-shaped low-pitched
instrument, typically with four strings tuned in fifths, was the ancestor
of the modern cello. Players held it supported between the calves. Later
cellos were fitted with a spike or endpin, so that the instrument could be
rested on the floor.

To begin with, the cello was played mostly in
consorts or bands made up of several different
members of the violin family — the violin itself,
plus larger instruments of various pitches. In the
early 17th century, most of the solo music
for strings was written for the violin.
The cello had more of an accompanying or continuo role (see p. 12), although
it is likely that many cello players
adapted music written for the solo
violin and played it on their lower-
pitched instruments.

LIRA DA GAMBA
This low stringed instrument
had up to 16 strings and was
held between the legs like a
viola da gamba. It was popular
in the 17th century.

THE ARPEGGIONE

✦

Held and bowed like a cello
but with frets and guitar-like
tuning, the six-stringed arpeggione
was invented in the 1820s by
Viennese guitar-maker Johann
Georg Stauffer (1778–1853).
Schubert wrote a sonata for
arpeggione and piano, which is the
only work now widely known from
the period when the instrument
was in fashion. Schubert's
arpeggione sonata is usually
played today transposed for the
cello or viola.

THE FIRST SOLO WORKS

A crucial change in the cello's fortunes came about in the late 17th century. In around 1660 in Italy, instrument-makers began to produce strings that were wound with wire, instead of being made of gut alone, for the cello and double bass. These wire-wound strings gave the instrument a better bass sound and also made it possible for the cello to be shorter. Soon after this change in the way the strings were made, composers began to think of the cello as a solo instrument. The first composer to spotlight the cello was the Italian Giovanni Antonii (1660–1697), who in 1687 published a set of 12 pieces known as ricercare for solo cello. These ricercare vary in content — some are like studies that give the player practice in producing various rhythmic patterns; others have more lyrical passages. Two other Italian composers, Domenico Gabrielli (c. 1651–1690) and Domenico Galli, were writing ricercare and sonatas for the cello at around the same time as Antonii: Gabrielli's first solo pieces are dated 1689. These groups of pieces show the cello finally emerging as a solo instrument in its own right. There were probably other similar pieces that have not survived, since much music in the 17th century was not published and our knowledge of it depends on the chance preservation of unique manuscripts. As they played them, cellists honed their skills, and the stage was set for still more adventurous and interesting music for the instrument in the 18th century.

I fell in love with the instrument because it seemed like a voice — my voice.

Mstislav Rostropovich

IMPROVED TECHNIQUES

By the beginning of the 18th century, the cello's length was becoming standardized at about 30 inches (75 cm) in the workshops of the great Italian instrument-makers, especially Antonio Stradivari (1644–1737). The size and proportions of Stradivari's cello remained standard, and today's cellos are still roughly the same size and shape.

At around the same time as Stradivari was defining the size and shape of the instrument, cello playing methods were evolving. For example, cellists were developing the left-hand fingering techniques (in particular the use of the thumb) that are still used today, as well as changing the way they used the bow. During the 17th century, players held the bow in a variety of ways — some images show them holding it with an underhand grip similar to that used by a viol player; other pictures show the musician holding the bow overhand, but gripping it farther from the heel than a modern player, restricting the bow's movement. Altering the grip, and also using bows that were more curved, gave players more control, enabling them to play more loudly and more expressively.

PABLO CASALS
The great Catalan cellist was famous for his performances and recordings of Bach's solo cello suites, which he practiced for 13 years before playing in public.

These improvements in technique, combined with the work of the great stringed instrument-makers of Italy, encouraged composers to write more, and more demandingly, for the cello. Among the Baroque composers, Giuseppe Jacchini, Antonio Vivaldi and Leonardo Leo all wrote cello concertos; a number of composers, again including Vivaldi, wrote chamber music in which the cello was the main instrument. But the jewels in the crown of Baroque cello music are the six suites for unaccompanied cello by J.S. Bach. Bach's Cello Suites were written around 1720 and it is not known who, if anyone, performed them in the composer's lifetime. They brilliantly combine tuneful, dance-like music with polyphony — music in several parts, as if more than one instrument was playing at once. This is an extraordinary achievement on an instrument best suited to playing one continuous melodic line and the suites remain among the greatest masterpieces of cello music. They are endlessly performed and recorded.

CELLISTS AND COMPOSERS

Toward the end of the 18th century, Classical composers such as Haydn and Mozart exploited the cello in various ways. Mozart was inspired by a Parisian cellist, Jean-Pierre Duport (1741–1818), who was a famed virtuoso, able to reach very high notes. He played in the last of Mozart's string quartets (1790), which give a starring role to the cello, and also performed Beethoven's early sonatas for cello and piano. Duport's brother, Jean-Louis, was also a well-known player; he published a book on cello technique in 1806 that became something of a bible for players. In the same period both Haydn and C.P.E. Bach (1714–1788) added to the cello repertoire with concertos and other works.

What cellists needed, though, was a composer who played their instrument, understood its capabilities from the inside, and could act as its advocate. They found him in the Italian Luigi Boccherini (1743–1805). Boccherini was a brilliant player, highly skilled in playing in the upper register, who extended the scope of his instrument by developing various techniques such as tremolo and playing *sul ponticello* — bowing

STRING FAMILY
This engraving shows the cello in the context of its string siblings, the violin and double bass.

very close to the bridge to bring out the higher harmonics and give a distinctive, ethereal sound. Boccherini's command of the cello's higher register encouraged him to see the cello as not just a bass instrument but also a melody instrument. All these ways of increasing the cello's scope are explored in his numerous cello sonatas, 12 cello concertos, several cello duets, and various other works he wrote for the instrument. Most notable are a large number of string quintets featuring two violins, viola and two cellos (an unusual combination; quintets usually have two violas rather than two cellos). Boccherini makes full use of the cellos, often treating one as a solo instrument so that the pieces function as miniature cello concertos. Highly successful, Boccherini worked for the Spanish royal family, the king of Prussia and Lucien Bonaparte (brother of Napoleon). His work vastly increased the profile of the cello in Europe.

EXPANDING HORIZONS

Players like Boccherini undoubtedly helped composers of the subsequent generations appreciate the cello. The Romantic era produced a lot of music for this most expressive of instruments. Schumann, Saint-Saëns and Elgar all produced concertos. Dvořák's concerto (1895), for many the greatest of them all, made the aging Brahms wish he had tried to write a concerto for the cello. Instead he composed a Double Concerto for violin and cello (1887), which is one of the most popular featuring the instrument. Few followed Boccherini's path with quintets with two cellos, although Schubert produced one such quintet that is among his greatest works. The cello's potential in chamber music, however, was realized through a vast number of sonatas for cello and piano — Mendelssohn, Chopin, Brahms and Grieg all produced examples, and in the 20th century many composers followed suit, including Rachmaninov, Debussy and Prokofiev.

When the cello enters in the Dvořák concerto it is like a great orator.

Mstislav Rostropovich

A notable trend in the 20th century was the phenomenon of the "cello choir" or group of cellos playing together. A pioneer of this kind of ensemble was the Brazilian composer Heitor Villa-Lobos (1887–1959). Villa-Lobos wrote a series of pieces under the collective title *Bachianas Brasileiras*, for various combinations of instruments. The most famous of these are *Bachianas Brasileiras* No. 1 for cello ensemble (1930) and No. 5 for cellos and soprano (1938–1945). Arvo Pärt and Pierre Boulez are among the others who have written for groups of cellos, and the most famous players of such works are the cello choir of the Berlin Philharmonic Orchestra, a group known as the "12 cellists." At the other end of the scale are 20th-century works for unaccompanied cello by Britten, Hindemith, Dutilleux, Ligeti and Xenakis among others. Many of these works have been inspired by notable players, especially the celebrated Russian cellist Mstislav Rostropovich, the greatest of many great players and advocates of the instrument in the modern era.

VOICE AND CELLOS
Accompanied by an ensemble of cellos, soprano Lucy Shelton performs *Bachianas Brasileiras* No. 5 by Villa-Lobos.

Clarinet

Location: Nuremberg, Germany

Type: Aerophone (single reed)

Era: Baroque

+ **WOODWIND**
+ PERCUSSION
+ BRASS
+ STRINGS
+ OTHER

CHALUMEAU
A low-pitched precursor of the clarinet, the chalumeau had a brief vogue and was admired for its mellifluous tone.

Chalumeau replica

I n around the year 1700 a woodwind instrument appeared with a distinctive, mellifluous tone that would earn it a major role in all kinds of music, from orchestral to jazz. The instrument was the clarinet, and it was probably invented by the instrument-maker Johann Christoph Denner (1655–1707) of Nuremberg, or his son Jakob. Since the Denners' time, a huge extended family of clarinets has evolved. They are much-loved instruments, prized by listeners and composers alike for their appealing, liquid tone, which has often been compared in its eloquence to the human voice.

THE CHALUMEAU

Denner created the first clarinets by modifying an existing instrument, the chalumeau. The chalumeau is a single-reed instrument, in which the reed beats against the mouthpiece. It has an attractive sound but a limited range, so Denner increased its effective compass by adding a speaker key. The two instruments were otherwise very similar and for a while existed side by side, the chalumeau being used for its rich lower notes, while the clarinet was prized for its ability to produce a higher register, accessed with the aid of a special key called the register or speaker key. To this day, musicians refer to the lower notes of the clarinet as the instrument's "chalumeau register," while the higher notes are often called the "clarinet register."

HOW IT WORKS

By blowing into the instrument the player provides the power source or energy, the flow of air. But this is a steady stream of air, and in order to make a sound, the air inside the clarinet has to vibrate. What makes this happen is the reed, which vibrates in response to the player's breath. When the air inside the tube vibrates, it creates energy, some of which is lost as friction on the sides of the tube, some of which emerges from the instrument's bell as sound. It is also possible to alter the way in which the air in the tube vibrates with the aid of the register or speaker key; this makes the instrument sound at a different pitch — an interval of a 12th higher than normal.

THE FAMILY GROWS

During the 18th century, instrument-makers developed the clarinet, adding more keys to make it easier to play and introducing larger tone holes, which improved the sound of the instrument's lower register. They also produced clarinets in a variety of different pitches — clarinets in C and B-flat were the most common — to enable musicians to play a wider range of music while avoiding difficulties with complicated fingering. By the end of the century makers were also producing instruments in which the mouthpiece and barrel were separate, to make tuning easier.

By this time the clarinet had quite a substantial repertoire. Vivaldi began adding clarinet parts to his music in the early 18th century and the first solo concertos for the instrument appeared in the 1740s from the pen of Johann Melchior Molter of Karlsruhe, Germany. During the next few decades clarinets were in use in the prestigious court orchestra in Mannheim, a body of players much admired by Wolfgang Amadeus Mozart (1756–1791), the first great composer to take full advantage of the clarinet's range of tone and expression. One of Mozart's friends, Anton Stadler (1753–1812), was a noted player of the basset horn and clarinet. He was praised for the beauty of his tone — which was said to be similar to the human voice — and the great delicacy of his playing. Between 1786 and 1791 Mozart wrote three masterpieces, a trio, a Clarinet Quintet and a Clarinet Concerto, for Stadler. The concerto and quintet made full use of the whole range of the instrument, from the lowest notes of the chalumeau register to the very top, for the first time. In their full exploitation of the instrument, Mozart's pieces show that the clarinet had arrived.

The ability to play the clarinet is the ability to overcome the imperfections of the instrument.

Jack Brymer, clarinetist

> ## BASSET HORN AND BASSET CLARINET
> ◆
> The basset horn, developed in the late 18th century, is a clarinet in F, a fourth below the standard B-flat clarinet, and has extra keys to extend the bass range. Its body is usually bent, so that some models look rather like alto saxophones or the instrument's larger cousin, the bass clarinet. There were local, differently pitched variations, including basset horns in G and D. Some Classical pieces, most famously Mozart's Clarinet Concerto, were written for an instrument called the basset clarinet, a similar but different instrument with a lower range than the standard clarinet. Today, some players play the concerto on the standard clarinet, others on the basset clarinet.

JOHANN MELCHIOR MOLTER
The German composer wrote the first concertos for clarinet, as well as concertos for other instruments including the trumpet.

SERENADER
This charming painting by Carl Heyden shows a man serenading a kitchen maid with his clarinet.

HYACINTHE KLOSÉ
As well as developing the successful Boehm system clarinet, this talented player and teacher (pictured right) had many successful pupils during his time at the Paris Conservatoire.

MÜLLER AND BOEHM

From Mozart's time onward, the clarinet was assured of its place in music, and the Classical orchestra of the late 18th century, as used by Haydn, Mozart and Beethoven, commonly included a pair of clarinets. But the clarinet was far from perfect, and its popularity encouraged makers to improve it still further. One problem was that the pads generally used to cover the key-operated holes were made of felt. Felt did not provide a good seal, and so air leaked out of the holes when they were closed, affecting the sound quality. To minimize this problem, makers kept the number of pads and keys to a minimum, but this in turn restricted the instrument's usefulness.

Ivan Müller (1786–1854), a clarinetist and inventor born in Russia, saw a way around this problem. He developed a new kind of pad made of leather, which provided a much better seal. Müller's clarinet of 1812 had 13 keys and seven finger holes. It enabled users to play in any key with relative ease and caught on widely, as did another Müller invention, a metal screw ligature to hold the reed in position.

Müller is a good example of a player who also developed instrument technology. Another player, Hyacinthe Klosé (1808–1880), a French clarinetist and professor at the Paris Conservatoire, had a similar impact. Klosé admired the improvements to the keywork of the flute developed by Bavarian musician and composer Theobald Boehm (1794–1881). One of the key inventions of Boehm was the ring key. When the player's finger covers one of the instrument's holes, it also pushes down a ring that surrounds the hole. This ring is connected to an axle, which moves a padded key to cover a hole in another part of the instrument.

Klosé, working with instrument-maker Louis-Auguste Buffet (1816–1884), adapted the Boehm mechanism

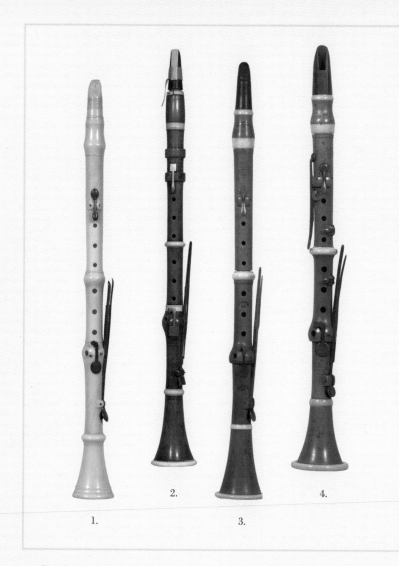

This selection of American and European clarinets dates from the first half of the 19th century. Boxwood was the most popular material for the body of the instrument, with ivory for the ferrules, and brass or silver for the keys. One example has a body made completely of ivory.

1. Ivory, silver keys, clarinet in D, c. 1800

2. Boxwood, clarinet in A made of boxwood with brass keys, U.S., c. 1800

3. Boxwood, brass keys, ivory ferrules, clarinet in C, 1830–1850, U.S., Graves & Co.

4. Boxwood, brass keys, ivory ferrules, 1837–1847, England, but with later French mouthpiece

1.

2.

3.

4.

to the clarinet; instruments made in this way are therefore known as Boehm system clarinets, even though Boehm himself did not design them. The ability to close two holes with a single movement of the finger in this way eliminates troublesome fingerings and the need to slide from key to key, a difficult technique that players of the Müller clarinet had to master. But the Boehm system did not catch on quickly because it required players to learn a completely different system of fingering. Eventually, however, the Boehm system clarinet, which was launched in 1843, became standard. Modern clarinets are very similar, although slight variations in the size of the bore and holes gives them some differences in tone.

JAZZ CLARINET

✦

Well established in classical music, the clarinet has played a major role in many types of popular music too: there were clarinets in the ragtime bands of the U.S., and when jazz evolved in New Orleans the clarinet had a prominent place. Players such as Leon Roppolo gave it a starring role in the 1920s hot jazz of Chicago, while in the same decade instrumentalists such as Johnny Dodds put it center stage in the blues. In the Swing era of the 1930s and 1940s, the clarinet was particularly prominent, especially in the hands of Benny Goodman (1909–1986, pictured above), the "King of Swing." The sheer virtuosity of Goodman's playing electrified audiences and impressed musicians working in other fields too. Artie Shaw was another swing player who had a huge following. The long and illustrious careers of Woody Herman and Buddy DeFranco took jazz clarinet through the second half of the 20th century and in DeFranco's case into the 21st, but in the era of modern jazz the saxophone was much more dominant. Even so, the expressive clarinet still plays a part in many jazz combos.

THE ROMANTIC CLARINET

The expressive qualities of the clarinet appealed greatly to the Romantic composers of the 19th century. Most included it — usually in its B-flat form — in their orchestral works, where its vocal qualities sometimes earned it a solo passage. Occasionally, composers gave the other forms of the instrument a special prominence — Berlioz, for example, capitalized on the arresting, high-pitched sound of the E-flat clarinet in his *Symphonie Fantastique* (1830), as did Richard Strauss in his tone poem *Till Eulenspiegel* (1895).

Weber composed two concertos for the instrument in 1811 and his contemporary Louis Spohr, one of the most famous composers of the time, wrote four. But the Romantic composer who produced the most enduring clarinet works was Johannes Brahms (1833–1897). Like Mozart before him, Brahms had a respected clarinetist friend, Richard Mühlfeld (1856–1907). Mühlfeld's playing of the Weber and Spohr concertos greatly impressed Brahms, who went on to compose a great quintet for the instrumentalist, as well as a trio and some clarinet sonatas. Many other Romantic composers, from Mendelssohn to Rimsky-Korsakov, wrote pieces with a solo part for the clarinet, but it is the pieces by Brahms that, along with Mozart's clarinet works, remain among the most popular for the instrument. All these composers seized on the range of moods and emotions that the clarinet can express, from the mournful or yearning to the upbeat or jocular.

I would not have thought that a clarinet could imitate the human voice so deceptively as you imitate it.

Johann Friedrich Schink on the playing of Anton Stadler

THE CLARINET TODAY

Today, clarinets in A and in B-flat are the most common, while some composers ask for the higher-pitched sound of the E-flat clarinet or the rich, mellow tones of the bass clarinet (see p. 174). The clarinets in A and B-flat are very similar and can be used with the same interchangeable mouthpiece. Players use both instruments, resorting to the A clarinet to play difficult sections of music in sharp keys.

Throughout the 20th century their followers have continued to find inspiration from the instrument's expressive variety. Some have gained from listening to jazz clarinet. George Gershwin's *Rhapsody in Blue* (1924) is a famous piece of jazz-classical fusion that begins with a trill and an arresting rising glissando on the clarinet — one of the most extraordinary openings in all music. Passages like this showed musicians the huge expressive range of the clarinet, and composers such as Ravel, the third movement of whose Piano Concerto (1931) features a raucous high clarinet wail, were eager to learn the lesson. The clarinet's resources seem inexhaustible.

KEYWORK
The keywork of a modern clarinet.

GEORGE GERSHWIN
Gershwin produced music for both Broadway and the classical orchestra. His *Rhapsody in Blue*, which begins with this long glissando on the clarinet, is the archetypal "crossover" piece, with versions for both jazz band and classical orchestra.

Piano

Location: Florence, Italy

Type: Chordophone/Keyboard

Era: Baroque

✦ WOODWIND
✦ PERCUSSION
✦ BRASS
✦ STRINGS
✦ **OTHER**

UPRIGHT PIANO
The affordable upright became popular in the late 19th century, when millions of homes had a piano.

Although the piano is not a standard member of the orchestra, it is one of the most widely played classical instruments of all. Millions of musicians learn to play the piano, and the instrument has a vast repertoire, embracing all kinds of solo pieces, chamber music, and concertos. It is also used widely to accompany singers and many composers use it as a tool when writing music. For this range of roles, the piano has been at the heart of classical music for well over 200 years.

THE KEYBOARD "WITH SOFT AND LOUD"

By the early 18th century the harpsichord had established itself as the keyboard instrument of choice for those who wanted to play solos, concertos and continuo parts. Its generous compass and sparkling timbre beguiled listeners and it was more convenient in a domestic or concert-room setting than the organ. But there was one problem with the harpsichord — there was no way of controlling the volume. This problem was to some extent solved by the clavichord, a small keyboard instrument in which the strings were struck by tangents. But the clavichord was a quiet instrument, suitably only for playing in a very small room.

In around 1709, the Florentine inventor and instrument-maker Bartolomeo Cristofori (1655–1731) came up with a keyboard instrument that was louder than the clavichord and enabled the player to vary the volume: the first piano. Cristofori called his invention a *gravicembalo col piano e forte*, in other words a "harpsichord with soft and loud." It replaced the quills of the harpsichord, which plucked the strings, with tiny hammers that struck them. This meant that the player could control the volume by varying the force with which the keys were struck.

In order to achieve this, Cristofori had to devise quite a complex mechanism. It was not too difficult to build the keys and pivoted hammers so that when the player pressed the key down, the hammer moved

upward to hit the string. But Cristofori also needed to find a way of making the hammer drop away from the string as soon it had made contact, so that the string was left free to vibrate and sound. He did this with a mechanism called an escapement. He also created a system of levers that made the hammer travel much faster than the key. In addition, he provided a damper for each string, which fell onto the string when the player released the key, stopping the vibration and cutting off the sound. This combination of components — including key, hammer, escapement and damper — forms the heart of the piano's mechanism, which is known as its "action." In addition, the piano, like a harpsichord or a harp, has a soundboard. This resonates when the string vibrates, creating a much louder sound than the string alone.

Cristofori's piano had quite light, hard hammers, and strings that were thinner than those on the modern piano (although thicker than harpsichord strings). These features gave his piano a lighter, quieter, more harpsichord-like tone than later pianos. Over the piano's 300-year history, makers found different ways of designing it to give the tone more body, but the essential idea, of an action striking a series of strings, remains at the heart of the instrument.

THE PIANO TRAVELS

A few years after Cristofori began to make pianos, news of his invention started to travel, first of all to Germany. The great organ-builder Gottfried Silbermann (1683–1753) had already made clavichords and was clearly interested in other kinds of keyboard instruments; in around 1725–1726 he made several pianos that were very similar to Cristofori's prototypes. He showed his pianos to one of the greatest keyboard players of the day, J.S. Bach (1685–1750), but the great composer was unimpressed: he thought the treble was weak and the touch not light enough.

CLAVICHORD
With its very quiet tone, the clavichord (see left) was ideal for music-making in a domestic setting.

PIANO NAMES

✦

Early pianos have several different names, and the terminology, which mixes German, Italian and English, can be confusing.

Fortepiano:
Italian ("loud-soft"), an early form of the now standard pianoforte. Today this term is usually used for early, wooden-framed pianos.

Hammerflugel:
German, this name indicates an instrument with hammers in a case that is wing-shaped, like a grand piano.

Hammerklavier:
German, literally a keyboard with hammers; a term traditionally applied to a square piano and used by Beethoven in the title of one of his most famous sonatas, No. 29 in B-flat.

Klavier:
German, keyboard.

Some 20 years later, Bach tried some more Silbermann pianos when he visited the court of Frederick the Great at Potsdam. He found these instruments much better, but by this time Bach was nearing the end of his life, so he wrote no music for the improved piano. Bach's countless keyboard works were written for either the organ or the harpsichord.

THE "SQUARE" PIANO

However, Bach's youngest son, Johann Christian Bach (1735–1782), was a piano enthusiast. In 1762 he traveled to London, where he was to settle, and here he found an emigré piano-builder, Johannes Zumpe of Nuremberg, who had learned his craft from Silbermann. Zumpe's instruments were very successful, in part because he had developed a new kind of piano that took up less space and was ideal for people to play at home. Whereas Cristofori and the early builders had made pianos in the form of the standard harpsichord (similar also in shape to the modern grand piano), Zumpe developed a compact instrument in a rectangular case, similar in shape to the clavichord. This type of instrument became known as the square piano, and had come out in around 1760, just in time for J.C. Bach's arrival in London.

J.C. Bach liked these instruments, probably because they had a sweet tone and a light action that allowed the musician to play fast passages with relative ease. The square piano caught on with amateur players too — they liked the instrument's compact size, which was easier to fit into a drawing room than the larger pianos in the Cristofori tradition. Square pianos were also light, which meant that owners could

J.C. BACH
The youngest member of the Bach family liked the pianos available in London when he settled there, and composed numerous sonatas for these instruments.

SQUARE PIANO
Pianos like this small instrument made in 1767 by Zumpe impressed players such as J.C. Bach.

move them around with ease — some accounts mention that Zumpe's delivery man had no trouble carrying the small instruments on his back.

The popularity of the new instrument encouraged composers, and soon many were writing all kinds of works, from short dance-like pieces to more extended sonatas and even concertos, for the piano. Several of the younger members of the Bach family, especially J.C. Bach and his elder brother Carl Philipp Emanuel Bach (1714–1788), were prolific composers of keyboard works, although it is not always clear from their scores whether these works were intended for the harpsichord or the piano.

Bach is the foundation of piano playing, Liszt the summit. The two make Beethoven possible.
Ferruccio Busoni

TWO TRADITIONS

Zumpe could sell as many square pianos as he could make and he was soon joined by other manufacturers, such as Scotsman John Broadwood (1732–1812). As a young man Broadwood walked the 400 miles (650 km) from his home in East Lothian to London, where he got a job with harpsichord-maker Burkat Shudi (1702–1773), for whom Zumpe had also worked for a while. Shudi was already making pianos and, when Shudi died, Broadwood took over the business. The Broadwood company became one of the world's best-known piano manufacturers.

As well as exporting pianos widely, including many to the U.S., Broadwood improved the Zumpe piano. Square pianos became the most popular keyboard instruments for use in the home. Those produced by Broadwood, and other quality makers such as Clementi, were well-crafted, serious instruments, with a loyal

PEDALS

♦

In the 18th century, piano-makers devised several ways of altering the sound of the instrument. On today's pianos these devices are controlled by pedals (all pianos have at least two; many have three). But on early pianos there were other controls, such as handstops or levers moved by the pianist's knee.

The first of these controls to be added to the piano was the *una corda* pedal (the left-hand one on a modern piano), which on a grand piano moves the whole action to one side so that only one bass string or two treble strings per note are struck by the hammers, producing a quieter, less brilliant sound. (On an upright piano the effect is achieved differently, by reducing the distance traveled by the hammers and therefore also their speed.)

The second pedal (the right-hand one) is the sustaining or damper pedal, which removes the dampers from all the strings so that any note played sustains (continues to sound) even after the player removes their finger from the key. A second effect is that other adjacent strings, because they are undamped, are free to vibrate "sympathetically" with those actually played, producing a fuller, richer tone.

Some pianos have a third pedal in the middle, called the *sostenuto* pedal. This acts on the dampers of keys that the player has already depressed, so that the specific notes just played can be sustained, while other notes played subsequently are not affected.

following. Although Broadwood and other early makers did well with the square piano, many musicians, especially those playing in a large room or hall, preferred the louder harpsichord-shaped grand pianos, which were also built in large numbers.

Broadwood and his followers, generally known as the English school of piano-manufacture, gained a reputation for quality instruments with a particular character. Their pianos were rich in tone and color, but with a rather heavy, slow-speaking action that made the rapid playing of repeating notes difficult because of the time it took for the keys to return to rest before they could be played again. Pianos by Broadwood and his colleagues attracted players who liked expressive melodies and colorful sound, but were prepared to sacrifice speed. Two noted composers of the Classical era, the Austrian Johann Nepomuk Hummel (1778–1837) and the Italian but English-based Muzio Clementi (1752–1832), favored English pianos. Although neither of these composers is widely played today, they were very famous in their time for both their playing and their compositions. They carried the fame of the English piano far and wide.

At the same time there was an alternative style of piano-building, coming from Vienna. Viennese pianos had a lighter action, lent themselves more to fast playing, and had a slightly thinner tone that was brilliant, light and clear. This approach was pioneered by Johann Andreas Stein (1728–1792) of Augsburg and refined by Anton Walter (1752–1826). The piano-makers of Vienna excelled at producing instruments along these lines, and so pianos in the Stein-Walter mold are

THE PIANO SONATA

✦

The development of the piano, with its expressive power and wonderful range of color, led composers to write vast amounts of piano music. Many of these pieces were piano sonatas, a genre developed by Classical-era composers such as the Italian Muzio Clementi (who wrote more than 100), Haydn, Mozart, Beethoven and Schubert. Typically, the piano sonata is a three-movement work in which the first movement follows "sonata form." Put very simply, this means that the movement begins with an exposition, in which two musical themes are introduced, followed by a development, in which the themes are elaborated or varied, followed by a recapitulation, in which the themes return. The sonata's other two movements are commonly a lyrical slow movement and a faster finale. Piano sonatas are among the greatest works of the Classical composers and Beethoven especially was the master of the sonata, bringing to it the most arresting and inventive music and incorporating into it all kinds of musical techniques and forms, from fugues to themes-with-variations.

described as Viennese in style. Such instruments were the favorites of Haydn and Mozart. Their many sonatas and piano concertos are among the first great piano pieces to find a permanent place in the repertoire, works that explore the expressive potential of the piano, as well as stretching the abilities of the player. They were written for the Viennese piano, but sound well on the modern concert grand too.

Beethoven was a virtuoso pianist who transformed piano music in his five concertos and 32 piano sonatas. His piano works are endlessly inventive, and his sonatas (see box) especially are revolutionary, every one a masterpiece. To begin with he favored the brilliance of Viennese pianos by makers such as Walter and Streicher, but he also had a piano made by the French manufacturer Sébastien Érard (1752– 831), which was built more along the lines of the English pianos. To play his groundbreaking sonatas and other piano works, Beethoven needed the best of both Viennese and English traditions.

The pianoforte is the most important of all musical instruments: its invention was to music what the invention of printing was to poetry.

George Bernard Shaw

YOUNG BEETHOVEN
In this steel engraving of 1882, Mozart listens to the young Beethoven at the piano.

THE 19TH-CENTURY PIANO

In around 1808 Érard came up with a new kind of action, the "double escapement action," in which after striking the string the hammer does not fall back to its rest position straight away, but takes up a halfway position, meaning that the player can repeat the note quickly. Other makers adopted this feature and it remained an important part of the piano action.

... this instrument works wonders.

Alfred Brendel, A Pianist's A–Z

The next challenge for manufacturers was that musicians wanted pianos with more power. The way to achieve this was to increase the tension of the strings. With a wooden frame, however, the scope for higher tension was limited, so the logical next step was to create a stronger metal frame. The first one-piece metal frame was patented in 1825 by American manufacturer Alpheus Babcock. Babcock's frame was for a square piano, but by 1843 Babcock's colleague Jonas Chickering had produced a cast-iron frame for a grand piano.

A metal frame has another advantage as well as power and volume. Because a heavy frame of iron is less susceptible to variations in temperature or humidity, it offers more stable tuning. Metal-framed grand pianos were soon in production in the U.S. and they quickly impressed pianists. Franz Liszt (1811–1886) praised one of Chickering's pianos, and with the advocacy of one of the piano worlds's greatest celebrities, news of their quality traveled fast. The metal-framed grand piano became the standard, and pianos today are very similar to those produced in the 19th century.

One of the first manufacturers to produce metal-framed pianos was Henry Steinway (1797–1871), who had started his firm in New York in 1853. Steinway became the world's most prestigious maker of grand pianos, and the Steinway brand still exists. Most of the world's foremost concert halls have Steinway pianos. Steinway is also the piano of choice for the majority of the world's concert pianists, although a few prefer other makers such as the Austrian company Bösendorfer, or the Italian maker Fazioli.

While grand pianos were the choice for serious musicians, many amateur players at home opted for square pianos until

STEINWAY GRAND
Steinway grand pianos, such as this Model D, are the choice of most of the world's concert pianists.

the arrival of the vertically strung upright piano in around 1830. Uprights, marketed originally as "cottage" or "parlor" pianos, caught on because they saved space in small rooms. By the late 19th century millions of homes had an upright piano, and these pianos were at the center of home music-making, whether played as solo instruments, or accompanying singers or other instruments.

THE ULTIMATE INSTRUMENT

The development of the modern grand piano in the 19th century helped confirm the piano as the preeminent classical instrument. Many of the most important Romantic composers wrote extensively for it. Frédéric Chopin (1810–1849) was the composer most devoted to the piano — nearly all his music was written for the instrument and his mostly short pieces — such as nocturnes, waltzes, mazurkas and polonaises — make up a unique, melodic, endlessly absorbing and typically Romantic body of work. Liszt, the greatest pianist of his time and the first musical superstar, composed a vast body of piano music, exploring new forms, using the piano to tell stories and displaying his superhuman virtuosity. His sonata, piano concertos, Hungarian Rhapsodies and collections of shorter pieces such as the *Années de Pèlerinage* (published between 1855 and 1883) are among his masterpieces for the instrument. Of the other great 19th-century Romantics, Schumann, Brahms and Mendelssohn were all devoted to the piano.

Composers of the 20th century have continued to explore the piano's potential. There are too many, with outputs too diverse, to list, but highlights include the great Russians (Rachmaninov, Prokofiev), inventive Central Europeans (Bartók, Janáček), and the atmospheric and boundary-pushing French masters (Ravel, Debussy, Messiaen). Today, in spite of the rise of electronic keyboards, the rich tonal range of the piano continues to delight and absorb composers, players and audiences alike.

SINGING LESSON
Square pianos, like the one in this painting by Walter Firle, remained in use in the home during the 19th century.

Trumpet

Location: London, England

Type: Aerophone

Era: Baroque

+ WOODWIND
+ PERCUSSION
+ **BRASS**
+ STRINGS
+ OTHER

Known for its bright, high tone, the trumpet is a regular member at the top of the brass section in modern symphony orchestras. It has a long history, and associations with both military command and human destiny, summed up by the phrase "the last trump." But the instrument has not always played a prominent part in classical music. Some of its most striking music was written in the 18th century, when composers such as Bach and Handel saw its great potential.

SIGNALER
A German herald sounds a signal using a trumpet in this 17th-century woodcut.

IN WAR AND PEACE

Trumpets have existed for thousands of years. The Oxus civilization of Central Asia had metal trumpets in the third millennium BCE, and trumpets were found in the tomb of Tutankhamun (dating to around 1323 BCE) when it was opened in the 1920s. Similar instruments have been in use ever since in many parts of the world, from ancient China to medieval Europe.

The most common use of these early trumpets seems to have been for signaling, and by the Middle Ages trumpets were the signaling instruments of choice for the cavalry, for whom the trumpet's portability and loud, clear sound must have been key assets. Because clear and reliable signals were essential on the battlefield, trumpeters were both highly valued and carefully protected.

TRUMPET
After a long period of use for signaling, the trumpet became popular in orchestral music in the Baroque era.

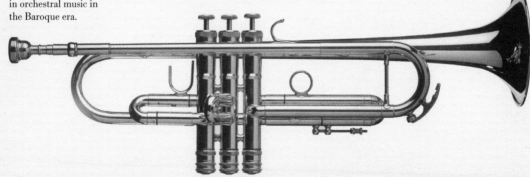

Perhaps because of their importance in warfare, and especially to prestigious mounted warriors, trumpets gained special status and became associated with pageantry and high ceremony. Fanfares on the trumpet accompanied all kinds of ceremonies, from the entry of a dignitary at a banquet to the climactic moment at a coronation or investiture. The fanfare is still a key element in music for the trumpet, both in actual ceremonies and in concert music where the composer wants to reflect pageantry, ceremony or history.

As a result of the importance of trumpets in both war and peace, trumpet-playing became a valued art. Guilds of trumpet-players were set up in many places to foster the art of trumpet-playing, to make membership exclusive and to regulate the use of trumpets by law. These guilds often had royal or imperial sanction. Holy Roman Emperor Ferdinand II gave his stamp of approval to the Imperial Trumpeters' and Kettledrummers' Guild in Germany 1623 and each emperor followed suit until 1767.

THE NATURAL TRUMPET

The trumpet that entered the modern orchestra was still a "natural" instrument — a length of tubing with a basically cylindrical bore, flaring to a bell and bent twice to create a rounded oblong shape. As it consisted of a single length of tubing without valves, it could play in only one key; to change keys the player had to change instruments or insert crooks — extra lengths of tubing that altered the instrument's pitch. Then, as now, the trumpeter played different notes by changing the tension of the muscles in the lips, cheeks and jaw. Doing this enables the player to produce the notes of a specific natural harmonic series, but a few of these notes are inherently out of tune. The player therefore has to "lip" or bend these notes. The higher up the trumpet's register the player goes, the more of these difficult notes there are, which made the natural

ON HORSEBACK
The Baroque frescoes of St Katherine's church, Wolfegg, Germany, dating from 1735, include a depiction of trumpeters and drummers on horseback.

trumpet particularly challenging to play. Modern reproduction baroque trumpets have vent holes that make the production of these notes much more straightforward. These holes also affect the tone of the instrument, but, even so, modern players striving for a historically informed style of performance still prefer the natural trumpet.

By the 17th century, the trumpet was being used widely in serious music, and players were developing the technique to master the instrument's difficulties in increasingly demanding parts. The more able players often specialized in the trumpet's difficult higher register (often referred to as the clarino register), which is exploited in such works as Monteverdi's celebrated opera *Orfeo* (1607). Trumpet-playing blossomed in Europe during the first half of the 18th century and composers began to explore the instrument's potential, using it both as a soloist in concertos and as a brilliant accompanist in choral works. This happened quite early in Italy, where composers such as Alessandro Scarlatti were writing brilliant trumpet parts in operas and choral pieces.

VARIATIONS ON THE TRUMPET

✦

Among the variations on the usual trumpets in B-flat and F, a bass trumpet was introduced in the 19th century with a similar compass to the trombone but a more trumpetlike tone. Wagner intended to use such an instrument in his Ring cycle, but had a modified version made so that higher notes were also more practical. The result was an instrument with a compass of three octaves, sounding an octave below the B-flat trumpet. It is usually played by a trombonist.

It is equally suitable for martial ideas, for cries of fury and vengeance, and for songs of triumph.

Hector Berlioz, Treatise on Orchestration, *on the trumpet*

THE TRUMPET'S FIRST HEYDAY

George Frideric Handel (1685–1759) traveled to Italy between 1706 and 1710, heard some of these pieces, and developed a particular liking for the trumpet. In 1711 he wrote his first opera for performance in London, *Rinaldo*. This was one of the biggest operatic spectacles of the age, with special effects that ranged from dragons spitting real fire to live birds released on stage. The spectacle was underpinned by the orchestra, which included four trumpets. Handel's subsequent works usually made do with two trumpets, or even a single one, but the parts were often stunning. One of the most famous accompanies the tenor aria "The Trumpet Shall Sound" in *Messiah* (1741–1742), but there are many others, including several of the composer's Coronation Anthems. Many of these parts, which can demand heroic stamina and breath, succeeded thanks to the talents of the composer's favorite trumpeter, Valentine Snow (1685–1759), the most respected trumpeter in England at the time.

Rinaldo

SPECTACLE AND SOUND
Handel's opera *Rinaldo*, for which the orchestra includes a group of four trumpets, was visually spectacular, as this 18th-century costume shows.

Similarly, J.S. Bach (1685–1750) explored the potential of the trumpet, writing high clarino parts in his Brandenburg Concerto No. 2, composed in about 1721. Two years later, when he moved to Leipzig, Bach began to work with the trumpeter Gottfried Reiche (1667–1734), penning demanding trumpet parts in his cantatas and other works. When Reiche died in 1734, another talented musician, Ulrich Heinrich Ruhe, took over, and Bach carried on creating challenging trumpet parts — his music for the instrument contains many high notes, requires the player to work hard playing the natural trumpet's difficult (normally out-of-tune) notes, and goes on for many bars without pausing. The use of the high end of the instrument's register was especially typical of the trumpet writing of the 18th century, and the demanding trumpet parts in the music of Bach, Handel and other Baroque composers gave the instrument a high profile; for many musicians, this was the trumpet's golden age.

GOTTFRIED REICHE
The talents of virtuoso brass player Gottfried Reiche inspired Bach to write some of his most elaborate trumpet parts.

SLIDE TRUMPET
Adding a slide to the
trumpet was one way of
enabling the pitch to be
changed with ease. This
example was produced by
the manufacturer Besson.

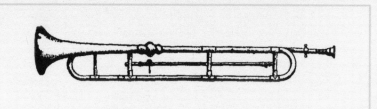

THE CHANGING TRUMPET

In the Classical period the role of the trumpet changed. There was less emphasis on the high notes and trumpets were used in a more restricted way, to fill in orchestral harmonies, add color, and sometimes to provide music of a martial quality. In roles like these, a pair of trumpets became a regular feature of the orchestras that played the music of Haydn, Mozart and Beethoven. By this time players were using a number of crooks (typically four or five) to play in a range of different keys. Some players used curved trumpets that enabled them to alter the pitch by placing the hand in or on the bell, a technique similar to that used by French horn players.

An alternative to changing crooks was the slide trumpet. In this version of the instrument the tube to which the mouthpiece was attached could slide in and out of the "yard" (the tube forming the instrument's body), altering its working length and thus changing the pitch. This worked in a similar way to a trombone slide, except that, because the mouthpiece was held steady at the player's mouth, the whole body of the trumpet had to be slid in and out. It is not known for sure how widely slide trumpets were used.

VALVES

A major breakthrough came with the invention of valves in the early 19th century. Valves enabled the musician to bring an extra length of tubing into play instantly, with a rapid movement of a finger. They appeared from the late 18th century onward and were taken up increasingly after the invention of the Stölzel valve in 1814 (see p. 119). By 1820 valve trumpets were a common sight in orchestras. Valves greatly improved the flexibility of the instrument, not only allowing quick key changes, but also enabling players to play faster more easily. The valve trumpet became the standard in orchestral brass sections throughout the Romantic period and into the Modern era. Composers such as Berlioz, in his opera *Les francs-juges* (1826), and Rossini, in his *William Tell* (1829), included parts for the valve trumpet, and other composers followed suit.

Later Romantic composers such as Wagner and Mahler wrote parts that stretched the instrument's higher register and, instead of the then-common trumpet in F, players began to favor the trumpet in B-flat, which remains common today. At the same time, manufacturers began to extend the potential of the trumpet the other way by introducing a bass trumpet that was exploited by some late-Romantic composers.

In classical music the trumpet is still mainly an orchestral instrument. There are relatively few concertos after the Baroque period, although Classical composers Haydn and Hummel wrote one each and a few 20th-century composers including Harrison Birtwistle, Mark-Anthony Turnage and Arvo Pärt have written concertos. Neither is the trumpet much used in chamber music, although notable exceptions include a striking septet by Saint-Saëns (written in 1881 for a Parisian chamber group called "La Trompette") and a sonata by Hindemith (1939). Modern players have also highlighted the trumpet by playing arrangements of music written for other instruments. Otherwise, composers have used trumpets for their unique sound in works as diverse as Copland's *Fanfare for the Common Man* (1942), Mahler's Symphony No. 5 (1901–1905), which opens with a trumpet solo, and Janáček's *Sinfonietta* (1926), which uses an orchestra with 25 brass players and begins with rousing fanfares on trumpets and tubas. It is interesting that, even in 20th-century pieces, the association of the trumpet with ceremonial music and fanfares is still very close. The trumpet and its music are enriched by this long heritage.

HISTORICAL AND MODERN INSTRUMENTS

✦

To play works like Janáček's *Sinfonietta* or Copland's *Fanfare for the Common Man*, trumpeters use a modern instrument with valves. However, when playing Baroque or Renaissance music, musicians taking a historically informed approach often use modern reproduction Baroque trumpets, which resemble 17th- or 18th-century instruments, but with the addition of vent holes to help the player hit the difficult notes. Increasingly, for still greater historical accuracy, early-music groups use natural trumpets without holes, which give a tone more akin to brass instruments of the Baroque era.

LOUIS ARMSTRONG
One of the greatest and most popular of all jazz musicians, Armstrong was known for his expressive playing of both the trumpet and the cornet.

1714

Contrabassoon

Location: Northausen, Germany

Type: Aerophone (double reed)

Era: Baroque

+ **WOODWIND**
+ PERCUSSION
+ BRASS
+ STRINGS
+ OTHER

From about 1650 the bassoon was the lowest member of the woodwind family, but at some point, probably toward the end of the 17th or the beginning of the 18th century, an instrument an octave lower was devised. This is the contrabassoon, sometimes called the double bassoon, a very large woodwind instrument that composers could call on when they wanted to extend the wind sound to the lowest possible depths. Impressive as its sound was, it was not widely taken up until the orchestra began to expand in the Romantic period, since when its impressive bass rumble has been a familiar presence among the woodwinds.

EARLY CONTRABASSOONS

The earliest surviving contrabassoon was made by Andreas Eichentopf (1670–1721) of Northausen in 1714. About 9 feet (2.7 m) high, it is made in a similar way to the bassoons of the time, with four joints (sections) and three keys. Eichentopf was a well-respected maker of wind instruments, and his contrabassoon is of high quality. So too were those of London craftsmen who followed in his footsteps, such as Thomas Stanesby, who was making similar instruments in the 1720s.

The contrabassoon was an impressive instrument, but it was very large and therefore also costly. It was not widely adopted in orchestral music in the Baroque era, although Telemann used it in one of his cantatas and J.S. Bach asks for a *bassono grosso* (a low contrabassoon) in his *St. John Passion* (1724). It was said that a contrabassoon was produced for Handel's famous *Music for the Royal Fireworks* (1749), but that the instrument was not used in the actual performance. Perhaps it was not loud enough to compete with the massed ranks of oboes, horns, trumpets and other instruments that were gathered together for the first performance of that imposing and noisy piece.

LOWEST WOODWIND
A total tube length of over 18 feet (5.5 m) enables the contrabassoon to produce the lowest notes of the orchestral woodwind section.

LOW NOTES IN THE ORCHESTRA

Bach's appreciation of the expressive quality of the instrument's low notes was emulated by the next generation of composers in the Classical period. When Haydn needed an especially solemn timbre in his choral setting of *Christ's Seven Last Words on the Cross* (1796), he called on the contrabassoon. When he went on to write his famous oratorios *The Creation* (1798) and *The Seasons* (1801) he once again exploited the instrument's dark tones. Mozart wanted a similar color in one of his most serious and heartfelt scores, the *Masonic Funeral Music* (1785). Mozart himself was a freemason, and wrote the music for the funerals of two aristocratic freemasons, Duke Georg August of Mecklenburg-Strelitz and Count Franz Esterházy von Galántha. This dark and solemn score was the only one in which he wrote a part for the instrument. Beethoven also reserved the contrabassoon for very specific occasions — it appears in some of his symphonies (adding weight to the double basses in the Symphony No. 5, 1808, for example), and in his only opera, *Fidelio* (1805). From around 1800, musicians playing these works had the benefit of a redesigned contrabassoon consisting of eight sections (known as joints) devised by the craftsman Simon Josef Truska of Prague and widely used in Central Europe during the first half of the 19th century.

THE SARRUSOPHONE

✦

Sarrusophones are double-reed instruments with a wide conical bore of metal construction, made in various pitches. They were patented in 1856 by Pierre-Louis Gautrot and named after bandleader Pierre-Auguste Sarrus, who is said to have come up with idea for the instrument. Sarrusophones became popular in 19th-century France, initially in outdoor band music, where they replaced the less powerful oboes and bassoons. The bass and contrabass models proved particularly popular among French classical composers, and Massenet, Ravel and Dukas included them in a number of their works. Parts for the contrabass sarrusophone are nowadays widely played on the contrabassoon.

FIDELIO
Set mainly in a prison, the opera *Fidelio* draws on a dark orchestral palette, in which the contrabassoon plays a notable part.

> **[The contrabassoon] seems to have been regarded as troublesome until the time of Wilhelm Heckel's reconstruction.**
>
> *James A. MacGillivray, in Anthony Baines, ed.,*
> Musical Instruments Through the Ages

Soon after Beethoven died in 1827, instrument-makers were experimenting with different ways of making and playing this unwieldy instrument. Their aims varied, but they were particularly interested in increasing the contrabassoon's volume, so that it could be used effectively with other winds in military music. Their attempts at a redesign included the compact *Tritonicon* of the 1850s, produced in *Königgrätz* by Červený, which had a narrow bore, and the wider-bore *Harmonie-Bass*, which was made of metal. Perhaps the most bizarre of all was the *Clavitur-contrafaggot*, which had a large bell and a keyboard. This ingenious but rather odd and ungainly instrument did not catch on.

Even the more conventional contrabassoon remained a rare instrument for much of the 19th century. In an anecdote recalled in the *Oxford Companion to Music*, it was said that there was only a single contrabassoon player in London in the Victorian period, and as he did not have enough work as a musician, he supplemented his income by running a brothel. On the few occasions when a contrabassoon was imported and placed on sale in London, this player bought the instrument and hid it, so that no competitors could reduce his workload still further.

HECKEL AND THE CONTRABASSOON

More influential than the mid-19th-century inventors and adapters of the contrabassoon were the Heckel family, who made woodwind instruments in Wiesbaden, Germany, and contributed widely to instrument design. Adam and Wilhelm Heckel (1812–1877 and 1856–1909) began producing innovative contrabassoons in 1877, with an instrument that impressed musicians with its ability to play demanding, fast passages without losing tone quality. One composer who was especially impressed with the sound of the Heckel contrabassoon was Wagner, who wrote for it in his opera *Parsifal* (1882).

The Heckels continued to improve the instrument, coming up in 1901 with the contrabassoon that was very widely adopted. The Heckel instrument — now made by other makers as well as Heckel themselves — is still the standard. It has a conical tube, some 18 feet (5.5 m) in length, arranged in five parallel parts linked by U-bends. The whole instrument stands on a short spike so that it can be rested on the floor. The holes are much farther apart than on other wind instruments (six times farther apart than on an oboe, for example), and a mechanism of keys enables the player to control them.

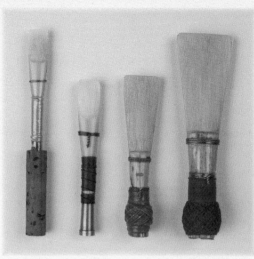

The Heckel contrabassoon impressed composers. Many included it in the woodwind sections of their larger-scale works. The composers who employed the instrument in the orchestra especially liked its low notes, which are dark and sometimes organ-like in sound. The middle notes, which can be played loud very effectively, are where the instrument excels at reinforcing the orchestral bass.

Composers sometimes gave the contrabassoon lyrical passages in which its rich, soft tone can be appreciated — the short solo in Mahler's Symphony No. 9 is an example. One of the most memorable passages for the instrument is in Richard Strauss's opera *Salome* (1905), where it has a solo as John the Baptist is taken to his subterranean prison, harking back to Beethoven's use of the contrabassoon in the opera *Fidelio*. The solo repertoire for the instrument is very limited, but a handful of composers, from Ruth Gipps to conductor Michael Tilson Thomas, have written contrabassoon concertos, and a few players have written chamber music and solo pieces for their own instrument, giving it a life outside the orchestra.

REEDS
The principal double-reed instruments have reeds of varying shapes and sizes. A comparison of the four (left to right: oboe, English horn, bassoon, contrabassoon) shows the wider reeds of the bassoon and contrabassoon.

HECKEL CONTRABASSOON
This contrabassoon, with its body in five sections, is an example of an instrument made in the German tradition by Wilhelm Heckel.

1719

Flute

> The flute is not an instrument
> that has a good moral effect
> — it is too exciting.
>
> *Aristotle*, Politics

Location: Paris, France

Type: Aerophone (edge-blown)

Era: Baroque

In the early 18th century one of the greatest instrumentalists at the French court was Jacques-Martin Hotteterre (1674–1763). As well as playing the flute and other instruments, Hotteterre may have been responsible for improving the design of the flute to make it more attractive to composers and musicians. But his greatest achievement was to write Europe's first manual for flute players, *L'Art de préluder sur la flûte traversière*, which he published in 1719. Hotteterre's book put the flute on the map, and the instrument enjoyed its first heyday during the following decades.

+ **WOODWIND**
+ PERCUSSION
+ BRASS
+ STRINGS
+ OTHER

ANCIENT BEGINNINGS

The idea of making music using a hollow pipe is a very ancient one. Archaeologists working on the earliest human remains have found instruments made from hollowed-out animal bones with finger holes bored into them so that the user could play different notes. One such bone pipe comes from a cave in Slovenia, occupied by Neanderthals some 45,000 years ago.

Most of these ancient pipes were open at both ends and were probably designed to be blown down, like a modern recorder. The modern flute, on the other hand, is closed at the head end and has a hole, known as the embouchure hole, that the player blows across and into, to make the air inside the flute vibrate. This is why the modern flute is sometimes called the transverse flute, to distinguish the sideways-held instrument from pipes and recorders that are held vertically and have a mouthpiece into which the player blows.

The earliest transverse flutes may have been made in China, where this form of instrument was called the *chi*. It dates back at least to the ninth century BCE, and a surviving *chi*, dating to 433 BCE, was found in the tomb of Marquis Yi of Zeng in Hubei Province. This flute, which is made of bamboo, is closed at both ends and has five finger holes. Later Chinese paintings show musicians playing similar instruments.

MODERN FLUTE
Most modern flutes have a metal body as well as metal keys. Wooden flutes are often used in historically informed performances of music from the Baroque and Classical eras.

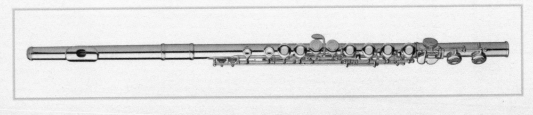

The Romans had side-blown instruments that are illustrated in some of
their works of art, but it is uncertain exactly what these were — they
may have been reed instruments of some kind. The flute probably came
to western Europe some time in the Middle Ages and continued in use
through the Tudor period and beyond — Henry VIII had many flutes
in his collection. These medieval and Renaissance flutes were usually
made of wood, and had six finger holes
in addition to the embouchure hole.
They were especially widely used in military music, especially the higher-pitched
examples, which were known as fifes (see
p. 108). In other kinds of music they had
to compete with the recorder; also
widely popular, this instrument was
used to play similar music, and was
available in a variety of pitches.

THE FLUTE COMES OF AGE

At the beginning of the 18th century
the flute's fortunes improved hugely.
This was in the first place due to developments in France, and especially the
work of Jacques-Martin Hotteterre. By
writing a manual for flute players,
Hotteterre increased the profile of the

MEDIEVAL FLAUTISTS
Flute players are shown
on this illustration from
the manuscript of the
Cantigas de Santa Maria,
produced in the Iberian
Peninsula in the 13th
century.

instrument, helped people to learn it and to play it better, and inspired
other composers to write music for it. This activity fostered interest in
the instrument and encouraged makers to improve it. One of these
makers might well have been Hotteterre himself — he is often credited
with inventing the features that distinguish the Baroque flute from its
Renaissance forebears. The Baroque flute was an instrument made in
three sections (known as joints), with a link between the head and main
body that could be adjusted by pulling in or out, for tuning. By making
the flute with a conical bore (rather than the cylindrical bore of the
Renaissance flute), the way the air vibrated inside changed, and the
maker was able to place the finger holes closer together, making the

BAROQUE FLUTE
Made of wood, baroque
flutes like this one, a copy
of a Parisian instrument of
c. 1740, often have ivory or
metal ferrules where the
sections join together.

instrument easier to play. It is not known for sure who came up with these design changes — they probably evolved over time, with different makers adding their input.

By the middle of the 18th century the Baroque flute was established and was becoming popular. Players were taking the instrument up and it was finding a regular place in orchestras playing music by such composers and J.S. Bach and Handel. Bach included a beautiful, lyrical part for the flute in his 5th Brandenburg Concerto (c. 1721) and Handel used flutes in his set of concertos op. 3 (1734). Vivaldi wrote some 18 flute concertos, including a famous one called *Il Gardellino* (*The Goldfinch*, c. 1728) in which the solo instrument imitates birdsong. It is not known for sure whether Vivaldi wrote his concertos for the transverse flute or the recorder.

No one did more for the flute, however, than the composer and flute player Johann Joachim Quantz (1697–1773), who became composer and flute teacher to Frederick II of Prussia in 1740. Frederick was an enthusiastic and skilled flautist himself, and kept an orchestra at court whose members included the great composer C.P.E. Bach, who was also a notable keyboard player. Unlike most monarchs, who were content to listen to their court musicians, Frederick wanted to play along with them. So Quantz was kept busy writing music for the king to play — around 300 flute concertos and 200 sonatas for the instrument flowed from his pen.

ROYAL MUSICIAN
Adolphe Menzel's painting
of 1852 depicts Frederick
the Great playing the
flute while C.P.E. Bach
accompanies him at
the keyboard.

> ... the people were playing on flutes
> and rejoicing with great joy, so that
> the earth shook at their noise.
>
> *I Kings, 1:40*

Quantz's other claim to fame was the book that he wrote about his instrument. *Versuch einer Anweisung die Flöte traversiere zu spielen* (usually known in English as *On Playing the Flute*) appeared in 1752. It helped not only Frederick but also other players master the instrument and, although Quantz's concertos are hardly ever played today, his book is remembered and consulted by musicians and scholars who want insight into the way the flute was played in the 18th century, its first golden age.

New developments

The flute survived into the Classical era as an orchestral instrument, although never again were so many solo pieces written for it as there were in the time of Quantz — Mozart composed only two concertos for the flute and was rumored to dislike the instrument. Instead, it became the voice of delicate solo passages in orchestral works, such as passages imitating birdsong in Beethoven's Symphony No. 6, the Pastoral. This delicacy, in many ways an appealing quality, was also one of the problems with the flute, and the instrument found it difficult to compete with the increasing volume produced by 19th-century orchestras.

The renowned 19th-century instrument-maker Theobald Boehm (1794–1881) tackled these problems, changing the design of the flute so that it was capable of producing a bigger sound while also retaining good intonation. By providing it with ring keys, giving it larger holes closed by pads, and carefully

THE RECORDER

✦

A flute that the player blows into, rather than across, the recorder developed in the Middle Ages, was very popular in the Renaissance period, and co-existed with the transverse flute in the Baroque era. Recorders have a beak-shaped mouthpiece into which the player blows, connected to a tube, usually turned from a single piece of wood, with a conical bore, a number of finger-holes and a thumb-hole. They were made in several lengths and pitches and in the Medieval and Renaissance periods often played together in consorts consisting of four types — descant (also called soprano), treble (also called alto), tenor and bass. To extend the range at either end of the group a small sopranino and larger great bass recorder could be added. By the Baroque period, the most common recorder was the treble or alto, for which many composers, including Alessandro Scarlatti, Vivaldi and Telemann, wrote concertos or chamber music. Many Baroque works may have been played on either the recorder or the transverse flute.

THEOBALD BOEHM
Using rod-axles to transfer the movement of the player's fingers to distant tone holes, Boehm revolutionized flute design.

positioning the holes so that the instrument was capable of good intonation, Boehm produced a flute that was capable of a powerful sound. He introduced other refinements too, such as a better embouchure hole, and made adjustments to the diameter and bore of the instrument's tube to reach the best balance between volume and response at the upper end of the instrument's register.

By 1847 Boehm had produced his definitive design. Not all players liked the new flutes, because they found their tone rather strident and not flutelike. But eventually they caught on, especially the more mellow wooden models, and Boehm's design became the basis of most modern flutes. Today's flutes follow Boehm's design quite closely, although modern makers often vary the hole sizes to give the most even response across the instrument's entire range. Boehm's work on the flute also influenced instrument-makers who were improving the design of the clarinet (see p. 74).

19TH-CENTURY FLUTES
This selection of 19th-century flutes shows one old-system example and four later Boehm system instruments. Both metal and wooden flutes were made by Boehm, and individual players differed in their preferences.

1. German flute in C, old system, 1828–1839

2. German Boehm flute in C, 1854–1861

3. German Boehm flute in C, c. 1860

4. American flute in E-flat, 19th century

5. German Boehm flute in C, 1847

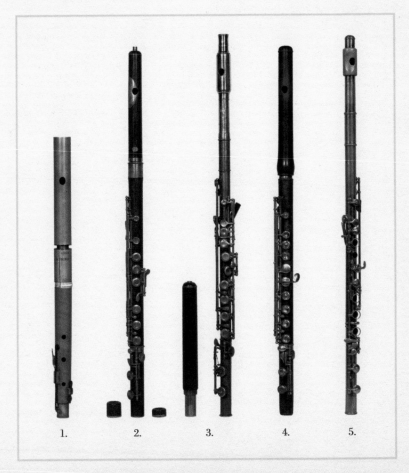

1.   2.   3.   4.   5.

THE FLUTE IN FRANCE

Although Boehm was a German inventor, his flute received international acclaim and was exhibited at the Great Exhibition in London's Crystal Palace in 1851. It caught on most quickly in France, where the flautist and teacher Louis Dorus (1812–1896) took it up enthusiastically. Dorus played both at the Paris Opéra and at the Société des Concerts, and was a professor at the Paris Conservatoire. He passed on his enthusiasm for the instrument to his pupils, including Paul Taffanel (1844–1908), who became one of the most renowned flute players and teachers of the century. An influential school of flute-playing stemmed from Dorus and Taffanel, in which consistent sound across the instrument's range was combined with playing of great sensitivity, bringing out all the varied colors of which the flute is capable.

By the end of the 19th century, France was well known as the home of the best flautists, who could bring out the full potential of the instrument. By the 1890s, this mastery of the flute was at the service of French composers who were taking music in new directions. Foremost among these was Claude Debussy (1862–1918), and his most famous orchestral work, *Prélude à l'après-midi d'un faune* (1892–1894), uses an orchestra with three flutes that are given a prominent part. The very beginning of the piece, in which a solo flute plays the main theme, is one of the most famous in all music. It evokes a faun, playing his panpipes, and the way the theme unfolds suggests sensual abandon and summer afternoons. For many musicians, this piece signals the beginning of modern music in the way it seems to dissolve tonality and conventional harmony. Debussy also wrote the haunting piece *Syrinx* (1912) for unaccompanied flute. His compatriots Maurice Ravel and Jacques Ibert also used the flute a lot in their works. The questing way in which these French composers explored the potential of the flute was continued in the 20th century as composers such as Luciano Berio and Pierre Boulez pushed the instrument into newer, still more adventurous directions.

CONSTRUCTION

✦

Early flutes, and the reproduction early instruments used in historically informed performances, are made of wood. Since the 19th century, in spite of the fact that the flute is classed as a woodwind instrument, many flutes have been made of metal — often brass or nickel-silver that is silver-plated to give a shiny finish that will not corrode. More costly instruments are made of silver. Specialists in historical performance generally play wooden flutes, which get closest to the sound of the instruments of the 18th and 19th centuries. Flautists in a "modern" symphony orchestra playing standard repertoire are more likely to use metal flutes. Players and instrument-makers do not think the choice of metal affects the tone of the instrument very much — the skill of the player has much more influence over how the instrument sounds.

English Horn

Location: Silesia

Type: Aerophone (double reed)

Era: Baroque

The tenor member of the oboe family is known in the U.S. as the English horn and in England as the cor anglais. It evolved in Central Europe during the 1720s, but only got a firm footing in the orchestra in the 19th century, when French composers were the first to take it up enthusiastically. Though it is rare as a concerto or chamber instrument, the English horn is a regular member of the symphony orchestra, where it often has beautiful, melodic solos to play.

FOREBEARS

Like its higher-register cousin the oboe, the English horn is a double-reed instrument descended from the earlier family of reeds known as the shawms. Shawms were made in a variety of pitches, and groups of shawms often played together in wind bands. When the oboe evolved, a number of other oboe-like instruments at lower pitches were also developed, the most enduring being the English horn.

However, the English horn did not evolve quickly, and in the 17th and 18th centuries several types of lower-pitched oboe were available for musicians to use. One was known in the English-speaking world as the tenor oboe, but was also often identified by its French name, the *taille de hautbois*, or *taille* for short. This was a straight instrument, longer than the standard oboe. From the end of the 17th century onward it was often made with a swelling, onion-shaped bell. It was used in both religious and secular music, including some of the theater works by Henry Purcell (1659–1695), and was used throughout much of the 18th century, dropping out of fashion in the last two decades. At around the same time, some groups, especially wind bands, favored the vox humana, a similar tenor oboe but lacking the rounded bell of the *taille*.

An alternative to these was the oboe da caccia. This instrument's name, meaning "hunting oboe" in Italian, gives a clue to its hybrid nature. It was an

AN EXPRESSIVE VOICE
Although it is not the most widely used of the woodwinds, the English horn has an expressive tone that has been beautifully exploited by composers from the 18th century onward.

HENRY PURCELL
This great English composer sometimes wrote for the tenor oboe, forbear of the English horn.

odd-looking instrument with a double reed, a curving body and a conical metal bell rather like that of a hunting horn. This bell gives the instrument a different sound, a sonic combination of oboe and horn that is very distinctive. Anthony Baines, historian of wind instruments, described the effect as one of distant horns across forest glades. He adds that a German encyclopedia describes how such "hunting oboes" were "taken out on hunting parties and played in the mornings and evenings before the quarters of the Chief Master of the Hunt."

The oboe da caccia was not only used out of doors. It was especially favored by J.S. Bach in his later years — he wrote parts for it in some of his cantatas, his Christmas Oratorio and his settings of the Passion. But the instrument had only a short vogue (roughly 1720 to 1760) and because it fell so completely out of fashion it was thought for many years that no oboes da caccia survived from Bach's time. However, in the 1970s the Swedish museum curator and scholar Cary Karp discovered two of the instruments (one in Stockholm and one in Copenhagen). Now modern instrument-makers make copies of them so that Bach's oboe da caccia parts can be played on the correct instrument.

THE CURVED HORN

The English horn is closely related to both the *taille* and the oboe da caccia. Like these instruments it is pitched in F, a fifth below the conventional oboe. Like the oboe da caccia, it was originally made in a curved shape, but with a bulbous bell rather than the flaring, hornlike bell of the oboe da caccia. The curved shape was probably popular with musicians because it meant the player did not need to stretch the hands as far to reach the lower tone holes as they would if the instrument were straight.

Craft workers made the curved body of the early English horn out of wood. They first bored out the center then cut the tube in numerous places along its length, sawing almost all the way through and removing tiny wedges of wood. The tube could then be bent gently and the instrument-maker secured the bend in position by gluing and adding a thin wooden rib to the inner part of the curve. Once this was done the tube was covered in leather.

This curved form of the instrument developed in the 18th century, probably around 1720 in Silesia, alongside the oboe da caccia. It started to become popular in the mid-18th century and remained widely played through much of the 19th century. There was also an angled version, made in two straight sections jointed together. Both forms of the

OBOE DA CACCIA
With its hornlike metal bell, the oboe da caccia is an odd-looking instrument, but it has a distinctive mellow tone.

instrument became known as the English horn, or the equivalent in the various European languages, but it is not known exactly how this name came about.

By the 1740s and 1750s, parts for the English horn began to appear quite often in theatrical and orchestral music. Italian opera composer Niccolò Jommelli included one in the score of his opera *Ezio* in the 1740s; Haydn, Mozart and Gluck were using the instrument in the second half of the 18th century. Before the end of the century a number of concertos — mostly by minor Central European composers — were written for the instrument.

A MYSTERIOUS NAME

✦

A mystery surrounds the naming of the instrument. It was once thought that the name used in England, cor anglais, came from the phrase *cor anglé*, angled horn. Another explanation notes the visual similarity between the instrument and the hornlike instruments played by angels in religious paintings. The German phrase for these instruments was *engellisches Horn* ("angelic horn"), and in the 18th century the adjective *engellisch* was close to *Englisch*, "English" — hence the term "English horn." Whatever the reason, the German term *Englisches Horn* was in use by 1723, when it is written in the score of a cantata by Tobias Volckmar (1678–1756), music director at a church in Hirschberg in Silesia, the apparent home of the English horn.

IN THE SPOTLIGHT

The English horn became much more prominent in the 19th century. This was due to two developments: firstly, some changes to the instrument itself, and secondly, the way in which the English horn was taken up by several prominent composers, especially in France.

The modifications to the instrument began in around 1820, when various makers began to construct versions with a straight tube, shaped more like the oboe, but retaining the distinctive bulbous bell of the English horn. A number of makers in France began to produce straight versions of the instrument, creating a more resonant, louder, sound but losing some of the romantic hornlike quality of the earlier instrument. Using straight tubing also made it easier to add more keys.

These new straight instruments found favor with English horn players at the Paris Opera — indeed, the horn was created together with the oboe. They were popular because of their resonant sound and perhaps because their tone was more similar to that of the standard oboe, so that the woodwind section blended well together.

This new attention to the design of the English horn undoubtedly made composers more interested in the instrument. But the straight instrument did not oust the earlier curved version, which many preferred because of its gentle and distinctive voice. Though not as piercing as its sibling the oboe, which can sound through and above a large body of orchestral instruments, the English horn was still admired and given solo work.

The composer who exploited it above all others was Hector Berlioz (1803–1869), one of the greatest of all orchestrators, who was alert to the characteristic sounds of all the instruments and knew how to use them to best advantage. Berlioz gives the English horn several prominent solos, drawing on its lamenting, almost vocal, quality, and its suitability for painting pastoral scenes, evoking the piping of shepherds. This effect is beautifully realized in the slow movement of his *Symphonie Fantastique* (1830), which starts on the instrument and includes moving solo passages. The English horn also has memorable solos in *Harold in Italy* (1834) and the *Roman Carnival* overture (1844). He also uses it effectively in his vast choral work *The Damnation of Faust* (1846), where it accompanies Marguerite's beautiful aria, "D'amour l'ardente flamme," in which she declares her love for the tragic hero.

The instrument itself had no special connection with England.

Anthony Baines, Woodwind Instruments and Their History *(1967)*

It is likely that these solos, along with those in the works of other composers such as Rossini and Bellini, were first played on the old-style, curved English horn. This design lasted well into the 19th century in France and for virtually the whole century in Italy; these were the two countries where the English horn was especially popular. But here, as in the rest of Europe, the straighter instrument eventually prevailed. As it spread composers continued to write solos for it, many of them slow, atmospheric ones.

Among the great English horn solos from the end of century is the one in Dvořák's Symphony No. 9 ("From the New World," 1893), one of the most famous melodies in all symphonic music. Solo passages in César Franck's Symphony in D minor (1889) and Debussy's orchestral *Nocturnes* (1899) are no less touchingly beautiful.

No doubt inspired by such pieces, 20th-century composers continued the tradition. Rachmaninov (*Symphonic Dances* and *The Bells*), Ravel (Piano Concerto), Shostakovich (Symphonies No. 8, 10, and 11) and Vaughan Williams (Symphony No. 5) all made use of the English horn. Perhaps the most outstanding is Sibelius's *The Swan of Tuonela* (1895), in which the English horn portrays the gliding path of the swan as it swims around Tuonela, the isle of the dead in Finnish mythology.

Piccolo

Location: Paris, France

Type: Aerophone (edge-blown)

Era: Baroque

Resembling the flute but half its length and pitched an octave higher, the piccolo is the highest member of the woodwind family and also the highest-register flute. A regular member of the modern symphony orchestra, it came to prominence in the 18th century, especially when French composer Jean-Philippe Rameau (1683–1764) began to include it in his opera orchestra. The piccolo is usually played by a flautist, and its scope ranges from a piercing shriek to lyrical soft tones.

+ **WOODWIND**

+ PERCUSSION

+ BRASS

+ STRINGS

+ OTHER

A MILITARY ROLE

As the highest-pitched member of the flute family, the piccolo traces its origins back to the earliest transverse flutes in ancient China. Simple cylindrical-bore wooden flutes were common in the Middle Ages, and short, high-register ones, known as fifes, were widely played in military music, generally accompanied by a drum. These short, six-hole instruments were used both to play marching tunes and for signaling in infantry regiments (cavalry troops used trumpets, which could be held in one hand while riding). They were particularly associated with Switzerland, and some people called them "Swiss flutes," although they were played all over Europe.

... it is mere prejudice to think that [the piccolo] should only be played loud.

Hector Berlioz

YANKEE DOODLE
In this print by Archibald M. Willard, the figure on the right is playing a fife.

COMPACT PIPE
Shorter than the flute, the piccolo's tone holes are very close together. They are controlled by keywork similar to that of the flute.

ORCHESTRAL BEGINNINGS

The transverse flute began to enter the orchestra at the end of the 17th century and the beginning of the 18th century, a time when instrument-makers were improving it by adding keys. The same improvements began to be made to the flute's high-register cousin, and the military fife began to evolve into the orchestral piccolo. To begin with, though, the instrument was still made of wood like the fife, with a cylindrical bore.

The German flautist, composer and writer Johann Joachim Quantz (1697–1773) published his major treatise *On Playing the Flute* in 1752. In it, he mentions the keyless fife, describing it as an octave higher than the standard flute. Another writer and composer, Frenchman Michel Corrette (1709–1759), describes it as sounding similar to the flute but with a sharper, louder and more brilliant tone. He also mentions that Parisian craft workers were making small flutes that create a "charming" effect in concertos by such composers as Albinoni, Quantz and Corette himself. Clearly, the high flute was starting to make its mark in the world of "serious" music.

A number of surviving early 18th-century pieces have parts for a high-register flute, but it is not always clear from the scores that have survived whether the instrument originally used was a piccolo or a high recorder. This is because composers often named the part "flautino" (small flute), which could mean either. Vivaldi wrote several concertos for "flautino," and the compass of these works suggests that they were almost certainly played on the piccolo. Among the other Baroque first composers to add high flute parts to their works were Handel (in his opera *Rinaldo*, 1711) and J.S. Bach (who included a flute in the orchestra for his Cantata No. 103 in 1725).

JOHANN JOACHIM QUANTZ
The flautist, writer and composer Quantz, portrayed here in a statue in Scheden, Germany, was among the first composers to write music for the piccolo.

RAMEAU AND THE PICCOLO

But the composer who did most for the piccolo was the French composer Jean-Philippe Rameau, who rose to fame quite late in life when he began composing operas in the 1730s. Rameau's operas were a new departure in Baroque music, with their striking harmonies, rich orchestration, and winning combination of singing and dancing. Part of the richness of his orchestral sound came from the piccolo, which Rameau included in many of his operatic works from about 1735. He used it in a number of his dances, in vivid storm scenes, and also in lyrical passages. Largely as a result of Rameau's work, there was a permanent piccolo player in the orchestra of the Paris Opera in the mid-18th century.

Rameau's operas were both popular and, because of their new harmonies, controversial when they were first performed; their fame increased the profile of the piccolo as well. Other Baroque composers followed suit, notably French master Jean-Féry Rebel, who included a piccolo part in his extraordinary ballet *Les élémens* (1737), which describes the creation of the world.

PICCOLO EFFECTS

In both the Baroque era and the Classical period that followed it, the piccolo was used by composers only occasionally. Mozart, for example, wrote for it in his *Posthorn Serenade* (1779), in which it plays a solo over strings in the trio section of the second minuet — a beautiful addition to the orchestral color of this already colorful work. The instrument also has a key role in his opera *The Magic Flute* (1791), in which it represents the reed pipes played by the bird-catcher Papageno. For sensitive use of the piccolo, Hector Berlioz, in his *Treatise on Orchestration* (1844), picked out two composers in particular — Beethoven and Gluck. Beethoven included a piccolo part in his Symphony No. 6 (the Pastoral, 1808), in which the small woodwind instrument plays high notes above a tremolo in the violas and basses, imitating the whistling wind of a tempest not yet in full spate. Gluck also uses it in an evocation of a storm in his opera *Iphigénie en Tauride* (1779), making a discordant sound in combination with the violins. Admiring effects created by composers who ask the piccolo to shriek or whistle, however, Berlioz goes on to make the point that the instrument is also very effective when played softly. Finally, Berlioz notices that the piccolo can play in tandem with the conventional flute. This combination works well when the standard flute plays a rising scale that is continued upward by the piccolo, so that it sounds as if the music is being played by a single instrument of vast compass — a magical flute effect indeed.

THE PICCOLO OUTSIDE THE ORCHESTRA

✦

The piccolo's similarity to the fife meant that it kept a place in military music, and piccolos were heard in many places where troops marched in the 19th century. In addition, the instrument proved popular in dance music, where people appreciated its combination of high notes and loud volume. Some specialist composers wrote dance music, including the waltzes and polkas that were so popular in the 19th century, for the piccolo. French flautist, piccolo virtuoso and composer Eugène Damaré (1840–1919) was one specialist in this type of music.

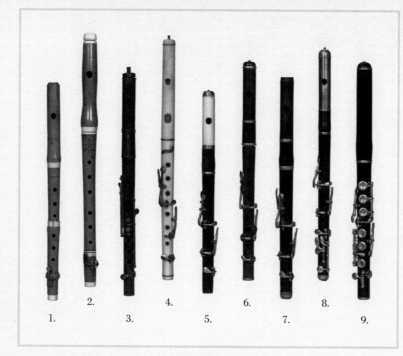

1.   2.   3.   4.   5.   6.   7.   8.   9.

19TH-CENTURY PICCOLOS

A selection of piccolos shows how the instruments were made of a range of different woods, with precious-metal or plated fittings and keys.

1. Piccolo in C, late 18th century, British, boxwood with ivory ferrules, brass key

2. Piccolo in C, 1812, British, boxwood with ivory ferrules, brass key

3. Piccolo in C, 1845–62, British, rosewood with silver keys and ferrules

4. Piccolo in C, 1821, Austrian, ivory, gold fittings, gold-plated keys

5. Piccolo in C, 1880, German, cocus, ivory head joint, with nickel-silver keys and ferrules

6. Piccolo in C, 1875, British, rosewood with nickel-silver keys and ferrules

7. Piccolo in C, 1800, British, grenadilla with nickel-silver keys and ferrules

8. Piccolo in C, 1875, British, grenadilla with nickel-silver keys and ferrules, metal-lined head joint

9. Piccolo in C, late 19th century, origin unknown, lacquered wood with nickel-silver keys and ferrules

IN THE ROMANTIC ORCHESTRA

During the 19th century, makers began to improve the conventional flute by adding keys, making the instrument out of metal rather than wood, and using a conical bore rather than a cylindrical one. They applied these changes in design to the piccolo too, but with the smaller instrument these alterations did not happen very quickly. Possibly the first multi-key piccolo was made in 1824 by Michael Janusch of Prague. But not everybody adopted this design and many different forms of mutli-key piccolo, with different fingerings, were tried. As a result of this non-standardization, many 19th-century players held on to their old single-key wooden instruments.

Among Romantic composers, Verdi sometimes used it to represent storms of lightning, and Tchaikovsky, Richard Strauss and Mahler all wrote parts for the piccolo in their orchestral works, sometimes giving it a solo. As a result of their advocacy, the piccolo became accepted as a regular member of the orchestra and later composers, including Ravel, Stravinsky and Shostakovich, made use of it in their woodwind sections. By exploiting its whole range of effects, from loud, high shrieks to gentle, softer tones, they ensured that this small and often unregarded instrument has kept its place beside the more familiar flutes.

Glass Armonica

Location: London, England

Type: Idiophone

Era: Baroque/Classical

The glass armonica is a musical oddity in which notes are played by rubbing the moistened fingers against glass vessels — either simple drinking glasses (in which case the instrument is sometimes known as the musical glasses) or glass bowls mounted on a spindle. These curious instruments caught the eye and ear of a number of major composers who were fascinated both by the way the instrument produced its sound and the sound itself, which is ethereal and otherworldly.

MUSICAL GLASSES

At least as far back as the Renaissance period, writers noted that rubbing a moistened finger around the edge of a wine glass produces a tone. Galileo was among the scientists who noticed this. A German poet, Georg Philipp Harsdörffer (1607–1658) wrote a series of instructions describing how to make music with wine glasses in 1636. However, his directions about the various pitches possible with half-full and empty glasses are incorrect, so it is unlikely he got very far with turning his idea into a workable instrument.

The first successful glass armonica is usually said to be the one played by the Irish musician Richard Pockrich or Puckridge (c. 1695–1759) in London in 1743. Pockrich's instrument consisted simply of a number of glass goblets set in a frame and filled with varying amounts

FRANKLIN-TYPE GLASS ARMONICA
This instrument, from the late 19th century, is based on Benjamin Franklin's design, with a series of glass bowls on a spindle.

of water to tune them. Pockrich played them by rubbing his fingers around the rims of the glasses. Not much is known about Pockrich, except that he died in a fire in 1759, and his instrument was destroyed in the blaze.

It is not known whether Pockrich invented his instrument or got the idea from somewhere else. The idea was said to be known in Germany at around this time; the composer Christoph Willibald Gluck (1714–1787) performed a concerto for a set of 26 musical glasses in London in 1746.

BENJAMIN FRANKLIN'S GLASS ARMONICA

In 1761 the American inventor and statesman Benjamin Franklin (1706–1790) saw a performance on the musical glasses, was impressed, and thought he could improve the instrument considerably. He devised an instrument consisting of 37 glass bowls mounted on a horizontal metal spindle. A foot treadle linked to the spindle turned all the bowls steadily, and the player moistened the fingers and held them to one or more of the spinning bowls. Franklin introduced another clever feature — painting the rims of the bowls with different colors according to their note, so that all the dark-blue rimmed bowls played the note A, the purple-rimmed bowls the note B, and so on.

FRANKLIN'S INVENTION
Publications such as this Italian engraving helped to bring publicity to Franklin's instrument and to explain how it worked.

Of all my inventions, the glass armonica has given me greatest satisfaction.

Benjamin Franklin

MUSIC FOR THE INSTRUMENT

Handel, Mozart and Beethoven were all taken enough with the unusual sound of the glass armonica to write music for it. Mozart's Adagio in C major and Adagio and Rondo in C minor are still occasionally played, as is a fragment Beethoven wrote as part of some incidental music for the play *Leonore Prohaska* (1815). The composer Gaetano Donizetti seized on the instrument's ethereal tones when writing the mad scenes in his opera *Lucia di Lammermoor* (1839), but rewrote the music for the more accessible flute. Richard Strauss also called for its unique tones in *Die Frau ohne Schatten* (1917) and numerous more recent composers have written for the glass armonica. Although a musical curiosity, the glass armonica is still arresting and, occasionally, entertaining.

THE CRYSTAL ORGAN

♦

An instrument similar to the glass armonica is the crystal organ, which contains 54 metal rods, each attached to a glass rod. The musician plays the glass rods with moistened fingers, but the metal parts provide the resonance. This instrument was invented in France in 1952 by Bernard and François Bachet, who also created musical sculptures. It produces a sound similar to that of the glass armonica, but at impressive volume over its broad compass.

Snare Drum

A lthough it is a small member of the drum family, the snare drum has a clear, brilliant sound that can dominate an orchestra. Whether beating out a steady rhythm or unleashing a torrent of rolls, it can be a forceful presence, its authoritative rhythms recalling its origins in military music. The snare drum has been used by classical composers since the 18th century, not only to imitate military music, but also to reproduce exotic rhythms, or to create a fearsome barrage of sound.

PIPE AND DRUM
Renaissance artist Andrea Mantegna included this player of the pipe (right) and drum in his painting *Triumph of Scipio*, c. 1500.

SMALL BUT LOUD
The snare drum can produce a lot of sound; it punches above its weight in the orchestra.

FROM TABOR TO SNARE DRUM

The snare drum is probably a descendant of the tabor, a type of drum that was popular in the Middle Ages. Tabors had a cylindrical body and often came with two skins, the lower one with a snare consisting of lengths of gut suspended across the diameter of the skin, which pro-

duced a rattling sound when the player struck the drum. Tabors were used in military music and were often played in conjunction with a fife.

Medieval tabors seem to have been quite shallow drums and the instrument-makers of the 15th and 16th centuries began to make drums larger and deeper so that they could produce more volume. Such drums were widely used by the military for signaling and were carried around Europe by troops in the 15th and 16th centuries. By the mid-18th century they began to enter the orchestra and musicians were soon exploiting the snare drum's special character — more brilliant and with a less obvious pitch than a similar drum without snares.

BEATING THE DRUM

The alternative name for the snare drum, the side drum, comes from its position in military use, slung on a strap at the marching player's side. To mimic this position, orchestral snare drums are played mounted on a stand, with the drum held at a slight angle. The usual beaters are tapering, hard wooden sticks with a rounded tip. Players select differently shaped sticks depending on the effect they want to achieve; for example, a stick with a shorter taper or a larger tip is used when the score requires more volume.

The snare drum has its own specific techniques. To play a roll, for example, drummers strike the head twice with the stick in one hand, then twice with the stick in the other hand, and so on; this kind of roll is known as a "mammy-daddy." For embellishment, additional fast strokes may be played before the main stroke — a single embellishment is a "flam," a double a "drag," and a triple decoration a "ruff."

THE INSTRUMENT IN THE ORCHESTRA

Among the first well-known composers to use this type of drum was Handel, who included several in his *Music for the Royal Fireworks*, written in 1749 to accompany a firework display held in London to celebrate the end of the War of the Austrian Succession. Several snare drums (together with timpani) helped to create the military atmosphere required. Other composers, such as Haydn in his Symphony No. 100, the "Military" (1793–1794), and Beethoven in his *Wellington's Victory* (1813), also used snare drums in this way — Beethoven even gave the opposing armies specific snare drum signals in his work.

Although the snare drum is not the most prominent orchestral instrument, its sound is powerful enough to dominate the orchestra when the composer demands it. A famous example is the way the drum defines the constant rhythm in Ravel's *Boléro* (1928). Still more striking is the instrument's appearance in Nielsen's 5th Symphony (1922), in which the snare drummer is instructed to improvise "as if at all costs he wants to stop the progress of the orchestra." The effect is astonishing and a testimony to the power that this small instrument can unleash.

Fashions in side drums have changed almost as often as those of the Paris couturier.

James Blades, Percussion Instruments and their History

THE DRUMMER BOY
A large snare drum, beaten with wooden sticks, features in this painting by William Morris Hunt of Boston, Massachusetts.

VARIETIES OF SNARE DRUM

✦

Snare drums vary a great deal in their size. Most have a diameter of around 14 inches (35 cm). Early military and marching drums, tensioned with cords, are often quite large, and much deeper than their diameter. Snare drums for orchestral use are often around 8 inches (20 cm) deep, modern marching drums slightly smaller still, and snare drums used as part of a drum kit may be less than 4 inches (10 cm) in depth. The snares may be made of gut or of a range of other materials including wire, wire-covered silk or artificial fiber.

1760s French Horn

Location: Paris, France

Type: Aerophone

Era: Baroque

L ike the trumpet, the horn can trace its origins back to the simple signaling instruments of the ancient and medieval worlds. Unlike the trumpet, however, which is made from tubing with a cylindrical bore, the horn has a bore that is generally conical (although modern horns contain quite a lot of straight tubing too). The horn also has a long, narrow, tapering mouthpiece, and the instrument's tube is very narrow where it connects to the mouthpiece. These features, together with its conical bore, give the horn its characteristic sound.

THE NATURAL HORN

In about 1680, a Bohemian nobleman called Count Franz Anton Sporck (1662– 1738) heard a horn played in Paris. The instrument was a *cor de chasse*, a hunting horn with a long tube curled in a large circular loop. It impressed Sporck and he ordered two of his servants, Wenzel Sweda and Peter Rölling, to learn how to play it. He took Sweda, Rölling and their "French" horns back to his Bohemian homeland and in a few decades Bohemia and the neighboring German-speaking areas were a center for horn playing.

Sporck's horns lacked the valves that are found on modern horns. Like all such early brass instruments, they sounded when the player's vibrating lips make the column of air inside the tube vibrate in turn. Altering the way the lips vibrate (by moving the muscles of the cheeks, jaw and so on) changes the frequency of the vibrations inside the instrument, varying the note. But this will only produce a limited range of notes, known as the horn's natural harmonic series, so the early, valveless horn is known as the natural horn. In order to play a complete chromatic scale, the horn player has to find other ways of playing the notes that are missing from the horn's natural harmonic series.

Even with this limitation, the horn found interesting work to do in the music of the early 18th century, in which composers often used the instrument, which closely resembled the hunting horn, to give some of the atmosphere of the chase to their music. Composers liked the horn's combination of a mellow tone and big range

THE MODERN HORN
The horn has a generally conical bore, but the provision of valves means that it also contains a lot of additional straight-bore tubing.

from top to bottom, and wrote melodies for its high notes and simpler passages — recalling hunting calls — for the lower notes. Around 1700 someone, probably the Viennese instrument-makers Michael and Johann Leichamschneider, devised a system of crooks — extra lengths of tubing that could be added to the instrument — so that it could be played in different keys. Makers also devised tuning slides, which similarly altered the length of tubing in use, again enabling the instrument to play in different keys.

NATURAL HORN
The early horn was essentially a long length of conical-bore tubing bent into a convenient shape and ending in a flaring bell.

HAND-HORN TECHNIQUE

Composers and players were still hamstrung by the horn's limited natural harmonic series, however. One solution to this problem was the hand-horn technique, which was developed in around the 1760s in Bohemia and Germany. By inserting the right hand into the bell of the horn and manipulating the hand, the player could lower the instruments "natural" notes. With the hand partway into the bell, the notes would drop a semitone; with the hand a little farther in, they would drop a whole tone.

Hand-horn technique revolutionized horn playing — a skilled exponent could produce whole chromatic scales. However, the key was in the word "skilled." Although the traditional design of the horn, with the bell pointing roughly at right angles to the mouthpiece, made it easy to insert the hand, it required quite a lot of practice to get the hand position right, and to keep the instrument's tone consistent in both the open notes and the ones played with hand-stopping.

No one knows for certain who first came up with the idea of hand-stopping. It may well have been Anton Hampel (1710–1771), a Bohemian musician who played the horn in the court orchestra at Dresden. Hampel was a teacher as

HUNTING HORN AND POST HORN

◆

The most important ancestor of the modern French horn was the hunting horn, used in the Middle Ages to convey signals between hunters. This instrument could be mistaken for the trumpetlike instruments used for military signaling, but as time went on the hunting horn became longer, and was coiled into a circle or more closely wound in a spiral. The greater length gave the horn more deep notes and a less piercing sound than the trumpet. The French form of the instrument made the transition from the hunt to the stage when it was used in hunting scenes in 17th-century operas.

well as a virtuoso and he helped to spread hand-horn technique in Central Europe, stimulating composers in such places as Bohemia, Austria and the German states to write more exciting music for the horn.

Baroque composers who wrote a lot for the horn included Georg Philipp Telemann (1681–1767), whose inventive concertos are still sometimes played. J.S. Bach's Brandenburg Concerto No. 1 (c. 1721) also has parts for two solo horns. The instrument's popularity increased further with the rise of horn virtuosos in the second half of the 18th century. Foremost among these players was Jan Václav Stich (1746–1803), who was born in Bohemia but traveled to Italy, where he changed his name to Giovanni Punto. Under his new Italian identity he toured Europe, giving concerts demonstrating his impressive hand-horn technique, and meeting Mozart and the young Beethoven.

Another notable player, Joseph Leutgeb (1732–1811), inspired Mozart to write his four Horn Concertos between 1783 and 1791. Leutgeb, who was able, according to a contemporary critic, "to sing an adagio as perfectly as the most mellow, interesting, and accurate voice," was an outstanding player. Mozart had a joky, teasing relationship with him, adding humorous comments in his horn parts and at one part instructing the orchestra to play allegro while marking the horn part adagio, probably a joke at the expense of horn players who sounded their notes late.

If composers such as Mozart enjoyed a joke at the horn's expense, they also took the instrument seriously — Mozart's concertos contain passages of great lyrical beauty. The horn could also be a virtuoso instrument. Weber's short but extraordinary Concertino for Horn and Orchestra (1815) includes passages at the extremes of the instrument's register; at one point the player is required to produce a four-note chord by vocalizing one note while playing another, so that the horn produces two further notes as well. Such pieces show that in the hands of players like Leutgeb and his successors, the instrument had come a long way from its hunting-horn ancestors.

THE EARLY CLASSICAL ORCHESTRA

♦

By the time composers were starting to exploit the expressive qualities of the horn, the orchestra was evolving into the ensemble for which the great Classical composers, such as Haydn and Mozart, wrote their symphonies and concertos. By the 1770s and 1780s this early Classical orchestra often contained pairs of horns, oboes and bassoons, as well as the usual complement of strings, including violins divided into two sections. Trumpets and timpani were still optional, and composers could also call upon additional winds to create a particular mood — trombones had somber associations (especially with the underworld), clarinets evoked pastoral scenes, and flutes could imitate birdsong.

THE VALVE HORN

From the late 1780s brass instruments including the horn and the trumpet began to be transformed by the invention of the valve. Valves work by bringing short additional lengths of tubing into play, lowering the instrument's pitch. Among the first attempts at making valves for brass instruments was in 1788 by an Irishman called Charles Claggett. However, the first valves that were taken up in a big way were designed by Heinrich Stölzel (a horn player) and Friedrich Blühmel from Silesia in 1814. The following year the *Allgemeine musikalische Zeitung* of Breslau announced the new mechanism, attributing it to Stölzel.

> ... a chromatic scale of nearly three octaves, with all non-natural notes clear and strong, and similar in sound to the natural notes, is obtained ...
>
> Allgemeine musikalische Zeitung,
> *on Stölzel's horn with valves*

In the late 19th century a further refinement was produced: the double horn. This has a fourth valve that sends the air through a different length of tubing entirely, changing the pitch of the instrument from F to B-flat. Each of the other three valves works in the same way as on a single horn, but has two sets of passages, to control each "side" of the horn. Double horns, introduced at the end of the 1890s, were soon being manufactured by the skilled instrument-maker Alexander of Mainz. Alexander's horns were widely admired and soon players all over the world were seeking out double horns, preferably made by Alexander. The horn used most widely in today's orchestras is based on these instruments.

PLAYING THE HORN
Pressing one of the valves opens up an extra length of tubing, in effect making the horn longer and lowering the note.

HORN AND ORCHESTRA

As valved instruments became more common, the horn was increasingly seen in the orchestra, and by the Romantic era it regularly took its place in the brass section alongside the trumpets and trombones. Of the great Romantic composers, Schumann wrote a Konzertstück for Four Horns and Orchestra (1849) and Richard Strauss, whose father was a renowned horn player, wrote two concertos for the instrument at opposite ends of his career, in the 1880s and 1940s.

However, the horn was most often heard as an orchestral instrument, in the symphonies of composers from Schumann and Brahms to Mahler and Bruckner. Johannes Brahms (1833–1897), who learned to play the horn as a child, although the piano was his main instrument, was a special fan. He preferred the tone of the valveless horn to the modern variety, and he included numerous beautiful horn solos in his four symphonies. He actually begins his Piano Concerto No. 2 (1881) with a horn solo. Brahms also wrote a trio for horn, violin and piano (1865), a beautiful work that he composed after the death of his mother — the sometimes dark tones of the natural horn seem appropriate to the occasion. The orchestra for Romantic music commonly has four horns, with two generally playing high and two playing low. A few works require extra horns — Rachmaninov's *Isle of the Dead* (1908) and Holst's *Planets* suite (1914–1916) ask for six horns, while Richard Strauss's *Alpine Symphony* (1915) requires a vast orchestra that includes 16 horns and four Wagner tubas (see p. 192), an instrument that is a close cousin of the horn.

In the 20th century the solo horn repertoire expanded greatly. This was due in part to the British horn player Dennis Brain (1921–1957), a musician of extraordinary technical facility. Brain's skill not only inspired composers but also attracted other players — there was something of a renaissance of horn playing in the mid-20th century, especially in Britain. The horn part in

JOHANNES BRAHMS
The composer Brahms, seen here at the piano, loved the horn and wrote beautiful passages for it in his orchestral works.

The horn is a noble and melancholy instrument.

Hector Berlioz, Treatise on Orchestration

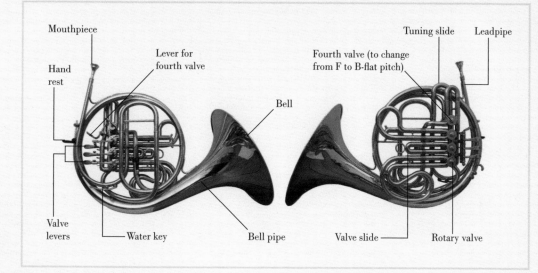

Mouthpiece

Lever for fourth valve

Hand rest

Tuning slide   Leadpipe

Fourth valve (to change from F to B-flat pitch)

Bell

Valve levers

Water key

Bell pipe

Valve slide

Rotary valve

PARTS OF THE HORN
Most modern horns have rotary valves controlled, as here, by levers, although some instruments have piston valves.

Benjamin Britten's beautiful *Serenade for Tenor, Horn, and Strings* (1943) was written for Brain, as were concertos by such composers as Malcolm Arnold and Paul Hindemith; many other composers wrote chamber works for Brain and when he died aged 36, Francis Poulenc composed an *Élégie* for horn and piano (1957) in his memory. Other virtuosos of Brain's and the following generation kept the standard of horn playing high, and encouraged composers to return to the instrument, sometimes stretching its capabilities and creating new sounds. In the meantime, the period-instrument movement stimulated a revival of interest in the natural horn, bringing fresh, historically informed performances of the early horn repertoire. Today listeners can hear period-instrument performances of concertos by Telemann, Bach and Mozart, and even Brahms symphonies are sometimes played with the natural horns that the composer loved.

PISTONS AND ROTARY VALVES

✦

Instrument-makers tried different types of valve mechanism. In some of these the main moving part is a piston, which moves up and down; the enduring type of piston valve is the Périnet valve, patented in 1839.

Another type is the rotary valve, invented by Joseph Riedl in Vienna in 1832, in which there is a rotor that turns to open up the extra length of tubing. Today, many horns have rotary valves, although in Vienna there is a following for horns featuring valves with double pistons.

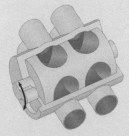

Viola

Location: Austria

Type: Cordophone (bowed)

Era: Classical

- ✦ WOODWIND
- ✦ PERCUSSION
- ✦ BRASS
- ✦ **STRINGS**
- ✦ OTHER

THE ALTO OF THE STRINGS
The viola is the alto member of the string family, slightly larger than but very similar to the violin, which can be regarded as the soprano.

The viola is the alto member of the string section in the modern orchestra, second highest in pitch after the violin, and it forms part of the violin family of instruments that evolved in the 15th century. Its soft tone has meant that it is less common as a solo instrument than the violin or cello, but since the Classical period it has found a strong following, due partly to its pivotal role in chamber music, especially in the string quartet.

A VARIETY OF VIOLAS

During the 15th century, bowed stringed instruments divided into two main kinds (see p. 39), the softer-toned violas da gamba (which were held between the knees) and the more powerful-sounding violas da braccia or violins (held at the shoulder). These violas da braccia included not only the violin itself, the soprano member of the family, but no fewer than three different instruments in the middle (alto–tenor) range. These three instruments were the forebears of the modern viola.

These three types of viola were all included in the five-part string orchestra at the court of French king Louis XIII (ruled 1610–1643) known as Les Vingt-quatre Violons du Roi, founded in 1626, which is sometimes seen as the ancestor of the modern orchestra, so the viola has been at the heart of the orchestra since its very beginnings. The three types were the small *haute-contre*, the medium-sized *taille* and the large *quinte*, which resembled a miniature cello but was played, like the others, at the musician's shoulder. All three instruments were tuned to the same pitches, but their different sizes meant that they had distinct timbres and resonances.

> The viola is commonly (with rare exceptions indeed) played by infirm violinists, or by decrepit players of wind instruments who happen to have been acquainted with a stringed instrument once upon a time.
>
> *Richard Wagner*

Les Vingt-quatre Violons du Roi continued in the same form during the reign of Louis XIV (ruled 1643–1715), but by the time of Louis XV (ruled 1715–1774) a change had taken place: the *quinte* or tenor viola, less agile than its siblings, had fallen out of use. It must always have been a problematic instrument. Holding a viola longer than about 18 inches (45 cm) in length is difficult for most people. As the century went on it became increasingly common for orchestras to feature a single group of violas, all roughly the same size, playing the alto role between violins and cellos.

A LOW PROFILE

The first great center of stringed-instrument production in the 17th and 18th centuries was Italy (see p. 42). Here, great makers such as Stradivari and Guarneri not only perfected the art of violin-making, but also produced beautiful violas and cellos. Stradivari in particular, although he made relatively few violas, put a lot of effort into working out the proportions of the three instruments.

Although the viola found a permanent place in the Baroque orchestra, it did not have a high profile in other kinds of music in this period. One reason for this was the fashion in the late 17th and 18th centuries for the trio sonata. In a trio sonata, two melody instruments (often violins) are accompanied by a continuo (itself often played by two instruments such as a harpsichord and cello, meaning that a trio sonata is often, confusingly, performed by four players). The lack of a part for viola in this most popular of musical forms tended to push the viola out of chamber music in the Baroque period.

There was a similar situation with orchestral music. The prevailing concerto form, the concerto grosso, typically had a concertino group made up of two violins and a cello. There were also few solo concertos for viola. The prolific German composer Georg Philipp Telemann (1681–1767) wrote one, as did a few minor composers such as the Bohemian Johann Stamitz (1717–1757). There are also viola solos in a few

MASTER OF STRINGS
Although he made relatively few of them, Antonio Stradivari's violas are just as highly regarded as his violins.

concertos that feature more than one concertante instrument — Bach's Brandenburg Concertos Nos. 3 and 6 (c. 1721) are the best-known examples. Later viola players have extended the Baroque end of the repertoire by making arrangements of concertos originally written for other instruments, but in the Baroque period itself viola players had few opportunities to shine in a solo role, and they seemed destined to keep a low profile, in the middle of the orchestral string section.

FOUR-PART STRING WRITING

In the Classical period the instrument fared rather better. This was in part due to a change in the world of chamber music. The 18th century saw the creation of one of music's most enduring forms, the string quartet featuring two violins, viola and cello. The quartet came about when composers began to drop the keyboard instrument from the trio sonata, replacing it with another stringed instrument. An example of this was a group of pieces published by Italian composer Alessandro Scarlatti (1660–1725) in the early 18th century; these pieces were called *Sonatas for Four Instruments: two violins, viola, and cello, without harpsichord.*

QUARTET AT HOME
This painting shows Haydn taking part in a string quartet. The performance is in a domestic setting, a typical environment for this type of small-scale music-making.

By adding the words "without harpsichord," Scarlatti was making clear to musicians what they were getting and revealing that a strings-only ensemble was still unusual at this date.

About 50 years after Scarlatti, in 1762, Joseph Haydn (1732–1809) began to write his first string quartets, the group of six that make up his op. 1. He wrote them at the request of an Austrian aristocrat, Baron von Fürnberg, who wanted music for four specific musicians. The pieces were so successful that Haydn wrote more, in the end composing nearly 70 quartets, many of them masterpieces. These entrancing works confirmed the viola's place at the heart of string writing.

At the same time, composers began to discover the viola's potential as a true concerto instrument. Although with its warmer, softer tone it seemed unlikely to be the crowd-pulling concerto star that the violin became, there were enough accomplished players in the Classical period to create a market for viola concertos. Many were written by composers who are little known today but one piece, Mozart's Sinfonia Concertante for violin, viola and orchestra (1779), has a sublime slow movement and is one of the great works of the period; it is still frequently played.

It lies at the heart of the string quartet.
Alec Hyatt King, Mozart Chamber Music *(1968)*

EXTENDING THE REPERTOIRE
In the 19th century the viola underwent changes similar to those applied to the violin (see p. 44) — the use of strings at a higher tension and the adoption of a redesigned bow that made long legato lines easier to play. Several composers of the Romantic era highlighted the instrument — one of the most glorious works for viola is *Harold in Italy* (1834) by Berlioz, a symphony with a solo part for viola, which Berlioz wrote at the encouragement of the violin virtuoso Paganini. Paganini wanted something to play on his

QUARTETS AND QUINTETS
◆

Haydn was the first great composer of string quartets. Although his first quartets do not give the viola a very interesting part to play, by the time of his op. 33 quartets (1781), he was writing more adventurous music for the viola, which was an equal partner with the other three instruments in the group. Haydn's quartets established the viola as a major chamber-music instrument, and instigated a long line of string quartets (and also quintets, sextets and other ensembles) with prominent viola parts. Haydn, Mozart and Beethoven were the greatest quartet composers of the Classical era. Mozart in particular had a liking for the viola and he also wrote a number of string quintets that include two violas, one of which is often asked to play striking and individual music, almost like the soloist in a concerto.

Stradivarius viola, and Berlioz obliged with one of the great works of the period, a description in music of the adventures of the great Romantic hero, the Harold described in Lord Byron's long poem *Childe Harold's Pilgrimage*.

Other Romantic composers concentrated on chamber music for viola. Brahms specified that his clarinet sonatas (1894) could also be played on the viola and included prominent parts for the instrument in works such as his string sextets. Dvořák played the viola and wrote sensitively for it in his chamber music. Mendelssohn and Schumann wrote pieces for viola and piano. Tchaikovsky put the viola section in the spotlight in his Symphony No. 6 (1893), when they play the main theme of the first movement.

In the late-Romantic period, however, many thought that the viola's sound could be strengthened. As a result, there were occasional attempts to redesign the instrument. Wagner, for example, was interested in creating a more powerful viola sound. Hermann Ritter (1849–1926), a German viola player, agreed. Ritter was keen to increase the prestige of his instrument and strengthen its sound. He was especially concerned that in many German orchestras there were viola players, many of whom played small-size violas, who produced a weak and unimpressive sound. He therefore worked with orchestras and students to increase the standard of viola-playing, as well as writing many works for viola, and also transcribed non-viola works by other composers for his instrument.

Ritter is also famous for designing an outsize viola, the 19-inch (48 cm) viola alta, to give the instrument a bigger sound. Some models of the viola alta had the further advantage of an extra string, extending its upper range. When Ritter played his outsize viola to Wagner, the composer was impressed and adopted it in his Bayreuth orchestra. Eventually five of Ritter's pupils were employed in Wagner's orchestra playing the instrument. Richard Strauss was also impressed with Ritter's invention. But the viola alta did not

THE VIOLA D'AMORE

✦

The viola d'amore was a variant of the viola developed in the 18th century in an attempt to produce a viola-based solo instrument. Similar in size to a standard viola, the viola d'amore usually had six or seven strings and the common practice was to tune it to a common chord, to allow chord-playing in a specific key. Although the instrument is rarely played today, several Baroque composers wrote concertos for the viola d'amore, Meyerbeer used it in his opera *Les Huguenots* (1836), and one or two more recent composers, such as Hindemith, wrote pieces for it.

catch on widely — perhaps because of its large size, which did not suit players with average-sized arms, and the physical effort needed to play it. Other attempts to adapt the viola and make it louder or stronger in tone did not last and the instrument, though less standardized than many, has settled down at an average length of 16 inches (41 cm).

VIOLA VIRTUOSOS

The viola owes its success in the 20th century to a number of outstanding players, particularly British-born Lionel Tertis (1876–1975) and William Primrose (1904–1982), and the German composer and violist Paul Hindemith (1895–1963). Hindemith was a prolific composer for a huge range of instruments, including works for viola and orchestra, solo sonatas, and sonatas for viola and piano. His most celebrated viola work is the moving *Trauermusik* for viola and orchestra, written in memory of British King George V in an extraordinary six hours on January 21st, 1936, the day after the king died, for performance by the BBC Symphony Orchestra the same day.

The playing of Lionel Tertis inspired many musicians to take up the instrument. Although Holst, Bax, Bridge and others wrote music for him, Tertis did not always connect easily with the music of his own time and turned down the concerto written for him by William Walton — Hindemith played the work's premiere instead. William Primrose spent much of his life in the U.S., teaching, recording, giving concerts and commissioning the viola concerto that Bartók left unfinished when he died. All three of these great players set an example of excellence and commitment to their instrument that encouraged the next generation of players. They left the profile of the viola at a high point, and there are still many outstanding performers inspiring composers to write innovative music for it. The fortunes of the viola have never been better.

... this hermaphrodite of the orchestra.

Thomas Beecham

Baryton

Location: Esterháza, Hungary

Type: Chordophone

Era: Classical

The baryton is a little-known instrument that looks rather like a cello or viola da gamba, but with extra strings. Although it has never formed part of the classical orchestra, its rich, soft tone was effective in chamber music. The baryton was prized in the 18th century, especially among members of the aristocracy. It was sometimes dubbed "the instrument of kings," and some examples were elaborately carved to indicate the instrument's unusually high status.

+ WOODWIND
+ PERCUSSION
+ BRASS
+ *STRINGS*
+ OTHER

HOW IT WORKS

Though the baryton is of a similar size to a cello, in fact it has more in common with the bass viol or viola da gamba. Like the viola da gamba it is held between the player's knees and the fingerboard has frets. The baryton has six or seven gut strings at the front of the fingerboard, which the musician plays with a bow held as usual in the right hand. But in addition, the baryton has a number of metal strings (often as many as 10) fitted at the rear of the fingerboard, which the player plucks using the left thumb. When not plucked, these rear strings also vibrate sympathetically with the bowed ones, enriching the instrument's tone.

The player can use the two sets of strings in various ways. The bowed strings can be played alone, so that the instrument sounds rather like a bass viola da gamba. The plucked strings may be plucked alone, typically to provide a bass line when higher instruments are playing a melody. Bowed and plucked strings may also be played alternately or together, to provide the kind of blend of bowed and pizzicato effects that are impossible to produce on a normal stringed instrument.

I have this moment received from Haydn three pieces which please me very much. You are accordingly to pay him in my name twelve ducats from the treasury ...

Prince Nikolaus Esterházy, writing to his administrator

ARISTOCRAT OF INSTRUMENTS
The baryton is a visually impressive instrument, with its two rows of tuning pegs and ornate touches on the fingerboard and tailpiece.

THE BARYTON'S HEYDAY

The baryton evolved in the early 17th century, possibly in England, although this is not known for certain. One report recalls that King James I of England, who died in 1625, was an admirer of the instrument. However, the heyday of the baryton was the 18th century, when it became popular in court and aristocratic circles. It was a particular favorite of Prince Nikolaus Esterházy (1714–1790), the Hungarian ruler who employed Joseph Haydn (1732–1809) as his court composer. Haydn wrote more than 120 trios for baryton, viola and cello for the prince to play using an instrument on which the rear strings were tuned higher than usual, so that his instrument could stand out against the cello and viola. Haydn also wrote a number of other baryton pieces for his patron, completing all of them in around 12 years, after which Esterházy laid down his instrument and devoted his energies to staging opera in his court theater.

Once Haydn's patron gave up the baryton, the instrument's golden age was over, and few other works were written for it. However, interest in Haydn and in this unusual instrument stimulated a revival toward the end of the 20th century, and the composer's trios and other works are played and have been recorded. Although quite simply written — Prince Nikolaus was probably no virtuoso — they include many pleasant and entertaining passages and show a composer of genius responding creatively to his patron's needs.

SCHLOSS ESTERHÁZY
Haydn worked at Esterházy Castle at Eisenstadt, Austria, for around 40 years, and many of his greatest works were premiered in the concert hall there.

COMPOSERS AND PATRONS

◆

For hundreds of years composers worked for rich or aristocratic patrons, writing music to order, and this relationship has produced great music. Some composers took full-time jobs in their patron's household — Haydn worked for the Esterházy family for decades, though not always full time. Other composers who, at various times in their lives, took on full-time positions for courtly patrons were J.S. Bach and Handel. Many composers preferred to work as freelancers, taking on commissions on a piece-by-piece basis, just as most composers do today. A huge number of composers worked in this way, and some of the greatest pieces by Mozart and Beethoven began as commissions. An alternative way of working, also pursued by Mozart and Beethoven, and by many Romantic composers, was to write pieces that the composers played or conducted themselves, with the concert revenues providing income.

Tambourine

Location: Paris, France

Type: Membranophone/
Idiophone

Era: Classical

PLAYING THE DAF
This 17th-century Persian
woman is playing the daf
(see right), the large form
of tambourine native to
Central Asia and India.

TAMBOURINE
The Western tambourine
is smaller than the daf,
with small jingles all the
way around the rim.

An ingenious combination of drum and rattle, the tambourine is one of the most familiar percussion instruments, played by dancers, singers and specialist percussionists, and used in everything from religious music to military bands in many different cultures around the world. In orchestral music it can play a variety of roles, from providing crisp, percussive punctuation to adding a sense of the exotic.

A LONG HERITAGE

Tambourines and similar instruments have existed for thousands of years, and are widely used in traditional or religious music all over the world. They are often mentioned in the Bible, where they are usually called timbrels, and they were the main percussion instrument played by the ancient Israelites. They remained popular in the ancient world up to the Roman period and beyond, by which time they had spread widely around the world, taking slightly different forms in a range of cultures. In Portugal and Brazil, for example, the pandeiro has a tunable head and cupped jingles that have a crisp sound. The equivalent instrument in the Arab world is the riq; its pairs of jingles are set in pairs of slits. India and the countries of central Asia have the daf, a large-sized tambourine used to provide the beat in many types of music. All these instruments, and many others, have a similar combination of frame, head and jingles.

Tambourines were used widely in the medieval period, when traveling musicians played them to accompany song and dance; sometimes these instruments had small bells or other jingling objects fitted to the frame in place of the usual flat jingles, but the way they were played was just the same. The instrument remained common in popular and court music — for example, Henry VIII of England had several timbrel players among his large complement of court musicians.

POSITIONS FOR PLAYING

When the player strikes or shakes the tambourine in a horizontal position, the sound is short, punchy and crisp, stopping quickly because the jingles, which lie flat, damp themselves. If the instrument is held vertically, the sound is sustained for longer because the jingles are free to keep moving, but is likely to be weaker. Holding the tambourine diagonally produces a compromise between these two extremes.

INTO THE ORCHESTRA

Like the triangle, the tambourine entered the Western classical orchestra during the 18th century, when composers such as Mozart wanted to imitate music that was seen as "exotic," especially that of Turkey. In its usual form, the modern tambourine as used in classical music consists of a narrow circular wooden frame into which pairs of metal discs are inserted. The frame has a hole for the player's finger and is generally covered with a drumhead, although not all tambourines have a head. The instrument can be played in a variety of ways — by shaking, so that the jingles sound; by beating the head with the knuckle or palm; by hitting with a beater while the tambourine rests on a cushion; or by running the thumb around the head to produce a "roll."

A famous early use is in the opera *Echo et Narcisse* (1779) by Gluck. Weber used it to evoke the culture of the Gypsies in the incidental music he wrote for the play *Preziosa* (1821) and in Bizet's opera *Carmen* (1875) it is one of the percussion instruments used to give the score a Spanish flavor. Tchaikovsky was another composer who used the tambourine to summon up the atmosphere of a different culture, when he included one in the Arabian Dance in his ballet *The Nutcracker* (1892). Since then, the tambourine has been a regular member of the percussion section.

CARMEN
Bizet's opera is set in Spain and has a gypsy heroine. The composer uses the tambourine to evoke both the Spanish setting and the background of Carmen herself.

Tenor Drum

Location: Paris, France

Type: Membranophone

Era: Baroque/Classical

The tenor drum has a military background and has been much used in marching and parade bands for centuries. In the orchestra it has a shorter history, but its distinctive, dull sound (compared by Berlioz to a muffled drum) has been used since the 18th century by composers looking for an atmospheric percussive effect.

THE DRUM'S CHARACTERISTICS

The orchestral tenor drum usually has a depth larger or similar to its diameter — a typical drum measures 20 inches (50 cm) deep, but instruments vary — and sits between the side drum and the bass drum in size and tone. It is beaten with either soft-headed beaters or hard sticks and with either type of beater has a serious and sonorous tone. It is very similar in form to the snare or side drum (see p. 114), except that it lacks snares (lengths of gut, wire, silk or other material stretched across the lower head of the drum). It also has a similar origin to the snare drum — both instruments are descended from the field drums and tabors used from the Middle Ages on by minstrels and in military bands.

In its simple design, the tenor drum is in some ways the most basic of drums, consisting of shell, heads and, originally, ropes to keep the heads in tension. In 1837, Cornelius Ward patented a rod-tensioning system for the side drum; this type of tensioning was soon applied to the tenor and other drums. Such a tensioning system was illustrated on a tenor drum in a French manual of military music of 1848.

The tenor drum was for a long time more common in military bands than in the classical orchestra. It was much used — either in rope-tensioned or rod-tensioned form — in German and French regiments from the early 19th century. In Britain it was present slightly later. Army bandsmen beat it with soft-headed sticks, and players liked to show their speed and dexterity, flourishing

TENOR TONE
Various sizes of tenor drum are produced, all giving the orchestral composer a drum sound that is higher than the bass drum and more sonorous than the snare drum.

> **The quality of the Tenor-drum ... is curiously impressive; its flavor somber and antique.**
>
> *Cecil Forsyth*, Orchestration *(1955)*

their sticks in a showy manner during parades. While the bass drummer could show off in the loud passages, the player of the tenor drum had the chance to shine when the band was playing more quietly.

ORCHESTRAL ROLES

The traditional date for the appearance of the tenor drum in the classical orchestra is 1779, when it was included in the score of *Iphigénie en Tauride* by Christoph Willibald Gluck (1714–1787), a resourceful orchestrator who pioneered several orchestral instruments. Gluck uses the tenor drum to beat out the distinctive rhythm of a chorus of Scythians in this opera. There is actually some dispute about whether Gluck intended this form of drum to be used, because tenor drum and side drum terminology can be confusing. But Berlioz, who was both an expert orchestrator and a great admirer of Gluck, believed the tenor drum to be the composer's chosen instrument.

Among the other composers who have made use of the tenor drum are Wagner, who uses it in several of his operas, including *Lohengrin* (1850), *The Valkyrie* (1870) and *Parsifal* (1882). However, the familiar concert arrangement of the "Ride of the Valkyries" uses a snare drum rather than a tenor.

The tenor drum found favor in the 20th century with composers who were especially interested in colorful percussion effects. Bartók (in the *Sonata for Two Pianos and Percussion*, 1937, and the *Concerto for Orchestra*, 1943), Britten (in the operas *The Rape of Lucretia*, 1946, and *Albert Herring*, 1947) and Darius Milhaud (in *La Création du monde*, 1923) all fall into this category, their use of the tenor drum enriching diverse and multicolored percussion writing.

DRUMMERS
French light infantry drummers of the Napoleonic period set down their instruments and take a break.

DRUM TERMINOLOGY

✦

It can sometimes be difficult to know exactly which drum a composer requires. Names for the tenor drum include the French *caisse roulante*, the German *Rührtrommel*, and the Italian *tamburo rullante*. Sometimes composers ask for a side drum to play without snares, to give an effect similar to a tenor drum.

1791 Glockenspiel

Location: Vienna, Austria

Type: Idiophone

Era: Classical

With its tuned metal bars giving a clear, bell-like sound, the glockenspiel is a percussion instrument familiar to many from its use in schools. It seems to have appeared in the 17th century, but became common in the orchestra and in other kinds of music during the 19th century, when people began to appreciate it for itself, not just as a convenient way of imitating the sound of small bells.

+ WOODWIND
+ **PERCUSSION**
+ BRASS
+ STRINGS
+ OTHER

CARILLON
The monastery of Heiligenkreuz in Austria has a carillon of 43 bells (see right) played using a keyboard.

FROM BELLS TO BARS

For centuries, people have made music using sets of bells, and these sets are sometimes called glockenspiels. Large versions of the instrument were set up in church towers, sometimes with elaborate mechanisms to play tunes on the bells. Smaller sets of bells were played at home, with one or more musicians working together.

The standard orchestral glockenspiel is a development of this idea. Instead of bells, it consists of a series of tuned steel bars, mounted in two rows, either supported on rails insulated with felt or suspended on cords. It has no resonators. The instrument is most commonly played with beaters, like a xylophone or vibraphone, and these beaters are used to strike the bars in the center. The usual beaters have round ends made of a material such as horn, wood or brass, which produce the bright sound usually required. Beaters with rubber heads are

> **... during Papageno's aria with the glockenspiel I went backstage as I felt a sort of impulse to play it myself.**
>
> *Wolfgang Amadeus Mozart*

BARS
The orchestral bar glockenspiel was in part inspired by church bells and carillons.

also sometimes used to give a slightly different tone, like a celesta, and occasionally composers mark a part for either glockenspiel or celesta. There is also a less common version of the instrument fitted with a keyboard, but this is not widely used because players prefer the tone of the instrument played with mallets, and like the way they can alter the glockenspiel's tone by using different beaters.

ON THE STAGE

The first high-profile appearance of the glockenspiel was in Mozart's opera *The Magic Flute* (1791). Here, the bird-catcher Papageno plays a set of magic bells, and Mozart mysteriously labels the part for these "*instrumento di acciaio*" (instrument of steel). Most authorities believe that this music was originally played on some kind of keyed glockenspiel, although today it is also often played on the celesta (see p. 196), an instrument not invented when Mozart wrote his opera — the celesta is in effect a keyed glockenspiel with resonators.

IN THE ORCHESTRA

The glockenspiel turns up in a variety of music from the Romantic era, where composers want a dash of brilliant color in the orchestral texture. Composers sometimes exploit the glockenspiel's ability to imitate small bells and similar instruments. For example, it produces the tinkling tones of a mechanical musical box in Liadov's short piece *The Musical Snuff-box* (1893). Further memorable appearances include Liszt's second Hungarian Rhapsody (1847), the Dance of the Hours in Ponchielli's *La Gioconda* (1876), and Richard Strauss's tone poem *Don Juan* (1888). Mahler, in his Symphony No. 7 (1904–1905), and Messiaen, in *Oiseaux Exotiques* (1956), were other, later composers who added the glockenspiel to make an already rich and colorful musical palette still more vibrant.

THE LYRA GLOCKENSPIEL

✦

To bring some bright tuned percussion to the sound of the marching band, instrument-makers in Germany devised the lyra glockenspiel (or bell lyre) in the 1870s. This consists of an upright metal frame with a series of metal bars arranged in two rows mounted on it. The frame is made in the shape of a lyre, with a pole at the bottom that the player can secure in a harness. The player holds the instrument in one hand and operates the beater with the other. The lyra glockenspiel remains popular in marching bands, especially in North America.

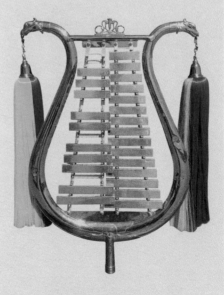

Tam-tam

... its vibrations have an awe-inspiring quality.
Hector Berlioz

Location: Paris, France

Type: Idiophone

Era: Classical

✦ Woodwind
✦ **PERCUSSION**
✦ Brass
✦ Strings
✦ Other

SERIOUS SIGNALS
The crash of the tam-tam is used by composers to signal moments of seriousness or high drama.

The crash of the tam-tam is a powerful sound in Western music, signaling moments of surprise, terror, triumph or sadness — or simply crowning a musical climax with a shattering metallic reverberation. Although it is a familiar part of classical music, the tam-tam, a large flat suspended gong, was introduced into the orchestra only in the 1790s and became common when percussion sections began to expand in the Romantic era.

EASTERN ROOTS

Gongs have their roots in the Far East, and there are two broad types: tuned gongs, which produce a definite pitch, and untuned gongs, such as the tam-tam, which have no distinct pitch. Tuned gongs get their pitch from their shape, which usually has a large boss or nipple at the center. Untuned gongs like the tam-tam are flat discs of bronze. Like cymbals, they give out many different overtones when struck, producing a crash which the human ear hears as lacking a clear single note. The tam-tam is suspended from a stand and the percussionist generally beats it using a stick with a soft, wool-covered head. In China and Japan tam-tams were used in many settings, from religious rituals to martial music.

THE SOLEMN GONG

In 1791 the Belgian-born composer François-Joseph Gossec (1734–1829), by that time living in France, wrote music for the funeral of the French moderate revolutionary politician Honoré Gabriel Riqueti, comte de Mirabeau. In his music Gossec used the tam-tam to produce an atmosphere of great solemnity. The effect of the gong was admired by several composers and the instrument reappeared in the opera house in such works as Lesueur's *Les Bardes* (1804) and Spontini's *La Vestale* (1807). As the 19th century went on, more composers took it up, and the tam-tam gradually came to be used in a range of contexts, though usually with serious or threatening overtones. To master the tam-tam, players learned to exploit the instrument's long-sustaining sound, to cut it off by touching it with the soft head of the beater when required, and to produce resounding rolls and tremolos.

THAI GONG
Large gongs like this are often found in Buddhist temples in Southeast Asia. Unlike the tam-tam, Thai gongs are tuned to a definite pitch.

Since these beginnings, composers of the Romantic era used gongs to symbolize sadness, as in Tchaikovsky's Symphony No. 6 (1893), or to bring extra force to a musical climax, as in the long tremolo followed by a deafening stroke in "Mars," the first movement of Holst's suite *The Planets* (1914–1916). Rimsky-Korsakov made the gong sound like a bell in his *Easter Overture* (1888), Meyerbeer used it to signal the resurrection of three deceased nuns in his opera *Robert le Diable* (1831), and in Elgar's oratorio *The Dream of Gerontius* (1900) a strike of the gong heralds nothing less than the death of the hero.

In the 20th century, composers explored the sounds possible on the tam-tam by calling for a variety of different beaters — from timpani beaters to snare-drum sticks. Richard Strauss included the tam-tam in many of his works, and in several operas (notably *Salome*, 1905, and *Elektra*, 1909) asks for it to be hit with a triangle beater.

MALLETS
The tam-tam is usually struck with mallets like these, which have a wooden head covered with soft material.

Still more unusual sounds can be obtained by using the special effects thought up by more recent composers and percussionists. Some works call for the gong to be vibrated with a violin bow, while composers such as John Cage and Poul Ruders have written parts for the water gong, a tam-tam that is struck and immediately submerged in a trough of water to muffle and modify the sound. Used in this way gongs can display their quieter side, as they can in works scored for smaller ensembles, like *Oiseaux Exotiques* (1956), for a small orchestra, by Messiaen, in which both tuned gongs and tam-tam sound, loud and soft, together.

TUNED GONGS

✦

Gongs that play a specific note have a long history in Asia, the most celebrated being those making up entire orchestras of gongs: the famous gamelans of Java. Not surprisingly, therefore, Western composers have sometimes used tuned gongs to create an atmosphere of "orientalism." A notable example is Puccini, who used them in his operas *Madame Butterfly* (1903) and *Turandot* (1924) — in the latter, combined with xylophones.

Harp

Let them praise his name with dancing and make music to him with tambourine and harp.

Psalm 149.3

Location: Paris, France/ London, England

Type: Chordophone (plucked)

Era: Classical

✦ WOODWIND
✦ PERCUSSION
✦ BRASS
✦ *STRINGS*
✦ OTHER

The distinctive tone of the harp, its plucked strings sounding clearly through the orchestral texture, and often ringing out in upward and downward scales, is one of the most striking sounds in Western music. The Romantic composers of the 19th century especially admired the harp's ability to add color to orchestral pieces, and composers of ballet music liked the way a glissando from the harp can act as a call to attention or a suggestion of mystery and enchantment. The harp found its enduring place in the orchestra during the 19th century, but although it is a relatively recent arrival, it has a long and fascinating history.

THE FIRST HARPS

The harp is one of the most ancient musical instruments of all. In the Bible, harps accompany the rituals and ceremonies of the Israelites throughout the Old Testament — David, the musician-king who, according to tradition, composed the psalms and sang them to the accompaniment of his harp, was the Bible's most celebrated harpist. When David "took an harp, and played with his hand," Saul was refreshed. When the Israelites, exiled in Babylon, sat down by the water and wept, they hung their harps on the trees by the side of the river.

The ancient Egyptians played harps too, and their paintings show us the earliest surviving images of these instruments. These paintings, from the third to the second centuries BCE, show triangular harps in which some 10 to 20 strings are stretched between a vertical wooden neck and a horizontal soundboard. The ancient Mesopotamians and Greeks played similar instruments. Plato mentions the harp, but seems to have preferred the other major Greek stringed instrument, the lyre, which was used for more intimate music-making.

A LATE HEYDAY
Although the harp is an ancient instrument, its heyday in the orchestra came in the 19th century.

EGYPTIAN HARP
In this Egyptian papyrus, a musician plays a triangular harp to the god Re-Horakhty.

THE FRAME HARP

The harp in its ancient form spread across Europe so that by the Roman period harps were well known even in the northern part of the continent. In addition, at some point during the post-Roman "Dark Ages" a new kind of harp appeared, in which the neck and soundboard were attached to a third wooden element, the fore pillar, to make a complete, three-sided wooden frame. No one knows for sure when these frame harps were first produced, but the earliest illustrations of them date to the ninth century CE. They are recognizably the ancestors of modern orchestral harps, although they are much smaller.

ROYAL HARPIST
King David plays a frame harp in this 14th-century illustration from the Chronicle of Rudolf von Ems.

Medieval frame harps also had fewer strings than their modern counterparts — the first illustrations show instruments with around 12 strings; by the 14th century the composer Guillaume de Machaut (1300–1377) wrote about a 25-string harp. The instrument was tuned diatonically (without sharps or flats) so if players wanted a note such as B-flat or C-sharp, they had to tune an additional string specially to produce the note.

One way of offering the missing notes on the medieval harp was to give it extra strings. By the 16th century, instrument-makers were producing double harps, in which a second row of strings provided the chromatic notes missing from the first row. A further elaboration was the triple harp, with three rows of strings, the two outer ones identical and the inner one containing the chromatic notes. These double and triple harps were used in much Renaissance and early Baroque music. Monteverdi specifies a double harp in his opera *Orfeo* (1607), where, according to a list of 1609, it supplemented two harpsichords and two archlutes to create a rich texture of plucked-string sound.

LYRE AND KITHARA

✦

The ancient Greeks played several plucked-string instruments and one of their favorites was the lyre. In Greek mythology, the first lyre, made by Hermes, was played by Apollo, the god of music. Its strings lay parallel to the soundboard, giving the lyre a radically different shape from the harp, in which the strings are roughly at right angles to the soundboard. In Apollo's original lyre, the soundboard was made from the shell of a tortoise, the extending arms from antelope horns, and the strings from the guts of cattle. Other ancient Greek lyres followed a similar design, but the Greeks also produced a large instrument called the kithara, which worked on the same principle but was made of wood. The kithara was used in temple rituals and public ceremonies, while lyres were usually played in smaller gatherings at home.

Some other 17th- and 18th-century composers included the harp in their orchestral or operatic music, but mainly to provide special or striking effects, especially when this was required by the drama, as in operas about the ancient Greek lyre-playing hero Orpheus — both Monterverdi's *Orfeo* and Gluck's *Orfeo ed Euridice* (1762) fall into this category. A few pieces were also written for specific harpists — a good example is Mozart's Concerto for Flute and Harp (1788), which the composer wrote for a flute-playing duke and his harpist daughter.

THE FIRST PEDAL HARPS

Double and triple harps were a big improvement on the simple models of the Middle Ages, but to make the harp really flexible, it was preferable to be able to alter the pitch of all the strings by a semitone, instantaneously, while playing. By the 18th century, harp manufacturers in Central Europe were finding ways of doing this. The first person to create this kind of harp mechanism was probably the German instrument-maker Jakob Hochbrucker (1673–1783), who developed a harp with foot pedals that changed the pitches of the strings in the early 18th century (probably in around 1720). Hochbrucker's harps proved popular, especially when then were taken up in c. 1770 by Marie Antoinette, the French dauphine, who was a keen musician.

French instrument-makers developed similar systems during the following decades. The most successful was the mechanism created by French piano- and harp-maker Sébastien Érard (1752–1831) in 1792. Érard, who was based in Paris but moved to London during the 1790s, developed a system in which a series of pedals at the foot of the harp activates rods and levers in the fore pillar that turn small wheels near the tuning pegs; small metal forks are mounted on these wheels. When the player operates a pedal, the wheels turn and the metal forks grip the strings, shortening their effective length and sharpening each note by a semitone.

IMPROVED PEDAL HARPS

Érard further improved his system by creating the double-action harp, in which the pedal could raise the pitch of the strings by either a semitone or a whole tone. Modern harps use a system very similar to Érard's, with seven pedals, one controlling all the strings tuned to the note A, another connected to all the B strings, and so on. With connections in both England and France, Érard was in a good position to market his invention widely, and his business was a success. By 1810, his double-action harp was selling in large numbers, both to professional musicians and to moneyed amateurs who liked both the sound and the appearance of Érard's richly carved instruments in their music rooms and drawing rooms.

On a modern harp the strings are attached to a hardwood bar that is fixed to the soundboard; they rise to the neck, where each has a tuning key. There are normally some 47 strings, giving the harp a compass of six and a half octaves, the biggest compass of any of the regular orchestral instruments. The harp is also loud enough to be heard in an orchestra, an advantage it has above other plucked-string instruments such as the lute, which, although it was used in some early Baroque bands, is generally too quiet to hold its own in a full-size modern orchestra. As well as plucking the strings, harpists have a range of other techniques at their disposal to produce different sounds — for example, making damped sounds by plucking with the thumb and then quickly damping the string with the fingers, or operating the pedals while the strings are sounding.

HARMONY before MATRIMONY.

ROMANTIC HARP
A satirical print of 1805 by the English artist Thomas Gillray uses the harp as a symbol of "harmony before matrimony."

STRINGING A HARP
An engraving from an 1824 book of trades shows a musical instrument-maker beginning the labor-intensive task of stringing a harp.

THE HARP TAKES CENTER STAGE

The harp really came into its own in the Romantic period, with composers keen to take advantage of its individual sound and newly improved mechanism. Early Romantic composers such as Louis Spohr (1784–1859) and Jan Ladislav Dussek (1760–1812) wrote chamber music that exploited the harp's clear tone — Dussek wrote melodic solo works, while Spohr combined it inventively with violin and cello, so that the harp plays a part similar to that of a piano in a piano trio. The French composer Hector Berlioz (1803–1869) was the first to include harps in a symphony — he called for no fewer than six harps in his *Symphonie Fantastique* (1830). The instrument proved especially popular among ballet-music composers, from Tchaikovsky to Ludwig Minkus, who used delicate harp solos and cadenzas to accompany dances that feature the ballerina.

Harps ever tuned, that glittering by their side Like quivers hung ...

John Milton, Paradise Lost, *Book III*

This use of the harp helped to promote the image of the harp as a "feminine" instrument — since the time of Marie-Antoinette, harp-playing, like singing, had been regarded as a valuable "accomplishment" for well-to-do young women. As a result, it was often played by women in the 19th and early 20th centuries. By the end of the 19th century it had found a permanent place in the orchestra, and some composers, such as Glière and Reinecke, even wrote full-scale concertos for the instrument. Well established as an orchestral instrument, the harp also proved popular in chamber music and kept its strong following among amateur musicians who played at home.

Improvements continued to be made, with harps with extra strings and other upgrades appearing, and in 1905 the Érard company, still a major harp manufacturer, commissioned Ravel to write a demonstration piece to show off the virtues of its latest pedal harp. Ravel's Introduction and Allegro (1905), scored for harp, flute, clarinet and string quartet, was the result. Perhaps surprisingly, given its origin in a piece of product-promotion, it is among the composer's masterpieces, and one of the best pieces in the harp's repertoire. Érard's success, and the example of works like Ravel's, encouraged other composers from the French-speaking countries — Ibert, Françaix, Jolivet and others produced enduring pieces for the instrument. Although the harp still does not have a vast repertoire, and performers often play arrangements of keyboard pieces as well as music written specially for their instrument, the harp has shaken off its "drawing-room" image, and has attracted some of the most innovative composers, such as Luciano Berio, whose *Sequenza II* (1963) is for solo harp.

LADY WITH A HARP
This portrait of 1818 by Thomas Scully (see opposite) shows American heiress Eliza Ridgely. The harp acts as a symbol of her sophistication and accomplishments.

Timpani

Location: Vienna, Austria

Type: Membranophone

Era: Classical

Since the Baroque period the most widely used drums in classical music have been the tuned, cauldron-shaped drums called timpani. In today's orchestras timpani, sometimes known as kettledrums, are usually played in groups of three or more and provide a variety of effects, from ferocious rolls to passages that exploit the drums' different notes or the ability of modern timpani to be retuned while being played.

✦ WOODWIND

✦ **PERCUSSION**

✦ BRASS

✦ STRINGS

✦ OTHER

EASTERN ORIGINS

Drums made in the shape of cauldrons existed in the Middle East in the medieval period; it is thought that European soldiers returning from the crusades brought them back to Europe in the 12th or 13th century. The drums carried by the crusaders were quite small, with wooden shells and goatskin heads, and were known as nakers, from the Arabic verb *naqr*, to beat. A number of illustrations of these drums, played in pairs, survive from medieval Europe, suggesting that they were popular, especially in dance music.

KETTLEDRUM
Played singly or in groups to provide different pitches, timpani or kettledrums are a mainstay of orchestral percussion.

In the Ottoman empire, instrument-makers produced larger versions of the naker, with metal shells. These drums were much louder than nakers and were ideal for military music and battlefield signaling. They were played by musicians on horseback

IN HARNESS
Military musicians from the Middle East sometimes played pairs of timpani mounted on camels.

and made a fearsome sound as the Ottoman troops marched into battle. Again, the drums were played in pairs, one tuned higher than the other, and they were held on either side of the horse using a leather harness. The difference in size could sometimes be quite slight, suggesting that the variation in pitch between the two drums was achieved with a considerable difference in the tension of the heads. The power of these Ottoman kettledrums impressed European musicians and by the 16th century they were being imitated in western Europe, again for military use, in which they combined well with martial trumpets. Military drums did not have to be tuned precisely. Provided that one drum was pitched higher than the other, signals would be effective, and that was all that mattered during a battle.

Used on horseback, kettledrums naturally found a place among the cavalry, and, because of the status enjoyed by these troops, were seen as more prestigious than the side drums used for signaling among the ranks of foot soldiers. Their status was reflected in the fact that kettledrumers belonged to a guild in the Holy Roman Empire and by the fact that monarchs such as Henry VIII of England took pride in their drums — Henry ordered a set of Viennese timpani for court use.

THE TUNABLE KETTLEDRUM

Such drums had royal prestige, were very loud, and looked impressive with their big, curvaceous shells. By the 16th century, orchestral composers were beginning to take an interest in these powerful instruments, but, for them, tuning was a much bigger issue. On early kettledrums, the head was kept in tension by laces running up and down the shell; altering the tuning was impossible without tightening or loosening the laces, which was a slow process. In the 16th century, manufacturers had devised a way of discarding the laces and tensioning the head with a screw mechanism, allowing rapid and precise tuning. By turning a key, the player could tighten or slacken the tension of the head, changing the drum's pitch. Tuned an interval of a fourth or a fifth apart, pairs of timpani soon attracted composers, transforming orchestral music.

The drum heads in this period were made of skin, and musicians and instrument-makers aimed for heads that gave a clear, bright sound. One writer of the 1730s, Joseph Majer, had an

Trompettes ... twelve in nombre besyde two kettle dromes on horsebacke.

Edward Hall, Chronicle *(1548)*

ON HORSEBACK
A pair of timpani produce a loud volume, making them good not only for military signaling but also for striking fear into the enemy.

HAND TUNING

✦

The head of a kettledrum is held in a circular frame called the flesh hoop, which is slightly larger in diameter than the rim of the shell. The head sits on top of the shell and the drum's counter hoop (a metal rim) fits snugly over the top of the flesh hoop. Around the edge of the drum are six or eight screws that pass through fittings on the counter hoop down to brackets on the shell. When the player turns these screws they pull the edge of the head and the flesh hoop downward, increasing the tension and the pitch; turning in the opposite direction decreases the tension.

interesting formula for preparing drumheads: "The covering skin should be only half cured; however, in order that they give a bright sound, the skins should be spread, when dry, with brandy wine and garlic, then dried in the sun or not too close to a low fire." No doubt instrument-makers had their own individual methods of making heads

DRUM WITH SCREWS
This 17th-century kettledrum in the church of St. Peter and St. Paul, Vilnius, Lithuania, has the screw-tensioning facility that came in during the 16th century.

that sounded right. Perhaps tricks such as Majer's went some way toward improving the tone of early timpani, which, having thick skins and being hit with hard sticks, were sometimes accused of having a dull or thudding sound.

Timpani probably began to be used in orchestras in the second half of the 16th century — there is a record of their use in a musical interlude performed in France in 1565. It is likely that early uses paired timpani with trumpets to evoke the style and mood of military music —

the two instruments were very closely associated in the military and the link seems to have persisted in the opera house and concert hall for many years. The drums were usually struck with heavy wooden sticks. One prominent 17th-century composer who employed them was Henry Purcell, who included an early solo passage in his opera *The Fairy Queen* (1692) and used them in conjunction with a pair of trumpets to accompany the alto solo "The fife and all the harmony of war" in his ode for St. Cecilia's Day 1692, *Hail! Bright Cecelia*.

BAROQUE TIMPANI

The next generation of composers, such as the Baroque masters J.S. Bach and Handel, built on the dramatic link between kettledrums and warfare. In his Cantata No. 130 (1724), for example, Bach used the convention to represent the celestial battle between the angelic host and Satan, who is portrayed as a dragon constantly devising new pains for God's followers, while the struggle against him continues to the accompaniment of timpani and drums. Bach used timpani many times — in some 39 religious works alone — usually scoring them with trumpets. Bach's contemporary Handel used kettledrums in a similar way, often bringing them in at dramatic or climactic points in his choral works, famously at the beginning of the "Hallelujah Chorus" in *Messiah* (1741). Both composers use the drums rhythmically, the drums' tuning mechanism allowing no easy change of pitch during the piece.

TUNING IMPROVEMENTS

Screw-tuned timpani found favor with composers, but they raised certain
problems. One was that tuning by turning six or more screws required a
very good ear; another was that it took a lot of time — the player could
not, realistically, retune the drum during a performance, so the instrument was restricted to its tuned pitch. As key changes in music became
increasingly frequent, this became a bigger issue. During the 19th century,
a number of people came up with solutions.

The first solution appeared in Munich in around 1812. Timpanist
Gerardus Mercator (1512–1594; born Gerard de Cremer, or Kremer)
made a mechanism that connected all the screws together so that the
player could adjust them with a single main screw. This sped up
the tuning process and made it more straightforward because each
screw moved the same amount when you turned the master screw.
Other inventors devised a rotary mechanism that
changed the tuning when you turned the shell of
the drum.

TURNING POINTS FOR THE TIMPANI

While these improvements in drum tuning were
being developed, but before they were in widespread use in the orchestra, composers were starting to use the timpani more adventurously, giving
the timpanist more to do than reinforce the
rhythm, emphasize the tonic and dominant with
his two notes, and provide the occasional dramatic
drum roll. The first composer to do this was
Ludwig van Beethoven (1770–1827), who in several works used pairs of timpani tuned at intervals

THE LATER CLASSICAL ORCHESTRA

✦

By the time Beethoven was making
creative use of the timpani, he and
other Classical-era composers were
regularly working with an orchestra
that contained pairs of flutes,
oboes, clarinets, bassoons,
trumpets and horns. All these wind
instruments usually played their own
parts, taking as important a part in
the music as the strings.

ORCHESTRAL SETUP
This arrangement of four
timpani shows a typical
orchestral setup, with a
stool for the musician in
the middle.

BEATERS

✦

Timpanists use a range of different
beaters, which vary in hardness and in
sound. Among the most widely used
beaters are those with a head of cork
covered in varying thicknesses of felt.
There are also beaters covered in
chamois leather or flannel. Beaters
with plain wooden heads are used
especially in music of the Baroque era.
Composers may also require instrumentalists to use unorthodox beaters.
In his *Enigma Variations* (1899), Elgar
uses the timpani in Variation XIII to
imitate the throbbing engines of an
ocean liner; he thought that side-drum
sticks would be the best beaters for
this effect, but, consulting the
timpanist at the first performance,
decided that a pair of coins used to
beat the drum near the edge of the
head would produce a better effect.
Another composer especially aware of
the effects of different beaters was
Gustav Holst. In a dance in his ballet
The Perfect Fool (1922) he asks the
timpanist and bass drummer to use a
felt-covered stick in one hand and
a wooden stick in the other.

different from the traditional fourths and fifths.
Still more striking was his use of the kettledrums at key points in his Violin Concerto
(1806) and Piano Concerto No. 5 (1811). In the
violin concerto, the opening notes of the entire
work are played on the timpani, an astonishing
and daring piece of scoring for the period,
demanding perfect timing and tuning on the
part of the player; it could be said to be a key
turning point in the history of the instrument.
In the piano concerto the timpanist has to play
together with the piano soloist at a key moment
in the final movement.

A vital area that seems to have been
neglected in the Baroque and Classical eras is
the choice of beaters for the timpani. Hector
Berlioz (1803–1869) was the first to specify in
his scores which kinds of beaters he preferred,
and was sensitive to the different sounds they
each produced. Sticks with wooden ends gave a
harsh sound; covering the wooden end with
leather produced a stick that was still dry if less
harsh — this seems to have been the prevalent
beater in the early 19th century. To either of
these types, Berlioz preferred beaters with
sponge heads, which gave a more velvety tone
and enabled his timpanists to play very quietly.

PEDAL CONTROL

Berlioz died in 1869, by which time experiments were underway to control timpani tuning with a pedal, so keeping the player's hands free. These experiments began in around 1840, but the first design that caught on with players was developed, from 1872 onward, by Carl Pittrich of Dresden. Pedal timpani are the most common type in use today. In this type of drum a foot pedal is connected to a disc or frame beneath the drum shell, and this frame is in turn linked to a series of tension rods that rise up to the counter hoop. Moving the foot pedal up and down moves the tension rods, which in turn tighten or loosen the head of the drum.

A conductor is always thankful for the presence of a really reliable timpanist.
Gordon Jacob, The Elements of Orchestration *(1965)*

The pedal drum gave composers a much more flexible instrument, the main aim being not to play tunes using the pedal but to adapt the drum to different keys. Modern orchestras therefore contain not just a single pedal kettledrum, but a number of different sizes tuned to different notes — often two for music from the Classical era, or four for much Romantic and later music.

By the 20th century, composers were taking the timpani in more adventurous directions, using the pedal to produce effects such as glissandi, asking the player to perform at very fast tempi, and including elaborate solo passages. There are even timpani concertos and pieces for timpani solo such as Elliott Carter's *Eight Pieces for Four Timpani* (1950–1966).

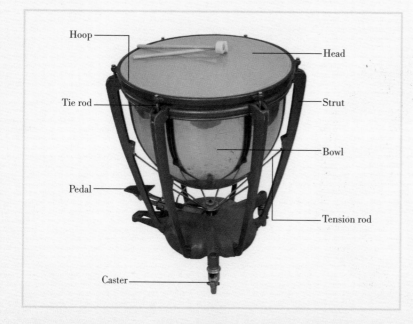

Hoop

Head

Tie rod

Strut

Bowl

Pedal

Tension rod

Caster

PARTS OF THE DRUM
Timpani have a rounded bowl, of copper, fiberglass or aluminum, with strong metal struts that support the bowl as well as providing a framework to hold the tension rods and other parts of the tuning mechanism.

Bass Drum

Location: Paris, France

Type: Membranophone

Era: Romantic

The largest and loudest drum, the bass drum beats the time in orchestral funeral marches and signifies the threat of an approaching army in music that describes warfare. It lends its loud voice to many an orchestral climax, but can also be struck softly to give an impression of distance or loneliness. This variety of uses makes it one of the most powerful of the percussion instruments, and not just because of its loud volume.

A DRUM FROM THE EAST

Most of the common types of drums developed in Europe during the Middle Ages, but the bass drum was an exception. It emerged in the Middle East, where it was played by military musicians. Associated especially with Turkey and the musicians of the Ottoman army, it became known as the Turkish drum, and was not seen widely in western Europe until the 18th century, when Turkish musicians traveled west and brought their large drums with them.

The size and sound of the Turkish drum impressed Western musicians. European bandsmen realized that it was possible to march with the big drum by supporting it on a strap at the player's chest. It was gradually absorbed into Western military music, in which it is still used today.

Composers were struck by the large drum too. They saw it as standing for the two kinds of music from which it came — military and "exotic" Turkish music — so the first orchestral uses of the bass drum appear in these contexts. A famous early example is Haydn's Symphony No. 100 (the "Military," 1793–1794). A contemporary description of an 1803 Paris performance of this symphony refers to the bass drum being played by "a strapping bear of a man," its sound resounding through the hall. It is not certain from the score, however, exactly which type of

THE LARGEST DRUM
The bass drum has two heads, normally of calfskin, stretched over metal hoops attached to a shallow wooden cylinder.

TURKISH DRUM
The ancestor of the modern bass drum used leather thongs for tensioning.

> **... the carrying power of the bass drum is greater than that of any other instrument.**
>
> *Walter Piston*, Orchestration

drum appeared in Haydn's orchestra. Some authorities think it was likely to have been a "long drum," with a head diameter smaller than its depth. In addition, it was probably beaten with short, hard sticks, to give a crisp but deep sound, unlike the soft-headed beaters more commonly used today. Even so, the effect would have been both martial and impressive. Modern period-instrument players of the work have tried various beaters, from small, hard sticks to give a clear sound, to the surprising choice of a birch broom.

Among Classical-era composers, Mozart and Beethoven also called for the bass drum in music with a military or "exotic" theme, in works from Mozart's Turkish opera *Die Entführung aus dem Serail* (1781) to Beethoven's symphony *Wellington's Victory* (1813). When the composer especially wanted to evoke a Turkish atmosphere, the player probably played the drum in the Ottoman manner with two different beaters — a hard stick playing accented notes on one drumhead and a metal rod playing the unaccented notes on the other.

A NEW SOUND

At the beginning of the 19th century, a change occurred in the way the bass drum was used. Composers began to ask players to beat the drum with soft-headed sticks, changing its sound radically in a move away from the "Turkish" sound. Probably the first person to do this was the Italian opera composer Spontini, whose opera *La Vestale* (1807) features a bass drum struck in this way. In this opera it lends solemnity to a triumphal march, and Hector Berlioz (1803–1869) noticed its importance — it could disrupt the march if the player played out of

THE MILITARY BASS DRUM

✦

One of the most prominent members of the military band, the bass drummer traditionally leads the band and sets its tempo (and that of the marching troops) with a roll that takes up a set number of steps. The drummer then marks the time with the stick in his right hand, setting the pace of the march. In the left hand the drummer traditionally holds a smaller stick, which is used to play strokes between the main beats. Instructions to the rest of the band to stop playing, or to switch to another tune, are also given by a simple code such as a double beat by the bass drummer.

MONSTER DRUM
British instrument-maker
Henry Distin produced
this huge drum for the
London Handel Festival in
1857. It was one of the
biggest drums ever used
in classical music.

DISTIN'S MONSTER DRUM AT THE HANDEL FESTIVAL.

time (as he apparently sometimes
did) or if the drum was placed too
far away from the orchestra to be
properly heard.

It was Berlioz who brought the
bass drum crashing into the public
consciousness a few years later,
when he added a bass drum part to
his overture *Les Francs-juges* (1826)
and included it in the vast array of
percussion in his *Grand Messe des
Morts* or Requiem (1837). Berlioz was critical of the way the instrument was often used, with players relentlessly playing each accented
beat, or playing the bass drum and the cymbals at once, a practice he
deplored. In both his words and his music, Berlioz put the bass drum
on the map.

Other great Romantic composers who embraced the bass drum were
Liszt and Verdi. Liszt was the first classical composer to specify a roll on
the bass drum, in his symphonic poem *Ce qu'on entend sur la montagne*
(1849). Verdi sometimes specified exactly the sound he wanted. In his
Requiem (1874), for example, he asks for a very large bass drum and
instructs the player to tighten the ropes of the instrument carefully so
that the offbeat in the "Dies Irae" is dry and loud.

FANFARE
In this painting by
19th–20th-century Polish
artist Stanisław Lentz,
bass drum, cymbals and
brass combine to swell
the volume of an
instrumental fanfare.

THE INSTRUMENT TAKES FORM

Even in Berlioz's time, many percussionists played the old-fashioned long drum, but, increasingly, as time went on, the modern bass drum was becoming more common. Today's orchestral bass drum is a large, two-headed instrument about 40 inches (1 m) in diameter and 20 inches (0.5 m) deep. It is used in a frame that allows the player to set the drum at any convenient angle and is played with a variety of sticks, hitting the drum at a point about halfway between the center and the rim. The sticks vary from hard wooden ones to soft-headed beaters covered with wool. Bass drummers may also use a double-headed stick to play tremolo by shaking the wrist so that the two heads of the stick hit the drum skin alternately.

The bass drum's two heads are tensioned differently, so that when the playing head is struck and sets the other head vibrating, the drum produces a sound that lacks a clear pitch. This is in contrast to a large, single-headed drum (sometimes called a gong-drum), which produces a clear tone. To quell the drum's vibrations and stop it sounding, the player places a hand on each of the heads simultaneously.

The 20th-century bass drum has been used widely by composers from Mahler to Britten. Among those with a particular interest in its percussive power, Stravinsky asked it to be played together with the cymbal in *Petrouchka* (1911) and exploited different beaters in *The Soldier's Tale* (1918). Carl Orff occasionally asked for different sized bass drums to play together and Edgard Varèse included three bass drums of different sizes in his percussion piece *Ionisation* (1929–1931). Meanwhile, the development of pedal-controlled bass drums in the first decade of the 20th century eventually brought the instrument into the jazz and rock-drummer's drum kit. The bass drum has come a long way from imitating the sound of a Turkish band and the predictability of marching music.

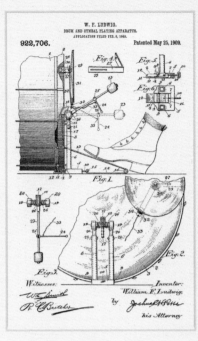

PEDAL ACTION
Instrument manufacturer William F. Ludwig patented his pedal apparatus for playing drums and cymbals in 1909.

JAZZ DRUM KIT
A pedal-operated bass drum, together with snare, toms and other drums, plus a selection of cymbals, is at the heart of the drum kit.

Baton

Location: Vienna, Austria

Type: Not applicable

Era: Classical/Romantic

- ✦ WOODWIND
- ✦ PERCUSSION
- ✦ BRASS
- ✦ STRINGS
- ✦ **OTHER**

There is no more obvious expression of power
than the performance of a conductor.

Elias Canetti, Crowds and Power

Today the baton is the symbol and almost universal tool of the conductor. It stands for a role that is absolutely central in symphonic music, choral music and opera, in which the conductor not only rehearses and leads the musicians, but also presents his or her specific interpretation and way of playing each piece. There have been leaders and conductors for centuries, giving the beat and keeping everyone together, but the high-profile, interpretative role of the conductor is a more recent phenomenon, first coming to prominence at around the same time as the adoption of the baton in the 19th century.

MEDIEVAL LEADERS

Conducting evolved long before the baton became the conductor's accepted tool. In the early Middle Ages, before musical notation had developed — or when it was still rudimentary and not standardized — one singer used his or her hands to lead the others, describing in up-and-down hand movements the rise and fall of pitch, or the rhythm of the music. Illuminated manuscripts from the 14th century and earlier show singers leading their colleagues in this way.

At some point, probably in the late Middle Ages, the leader began to carry a long wooden staff. This was like the staffs of office carried by all kinds of officials, and one purpose of it was simply to identify the bearer as a leader. Some sources show the musician holding the staff in the left hand, while conducting with the right; others show him holding the staff in the right hand and using it as a way of emphasizing his conducting gestures.

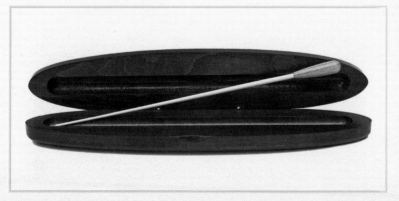

STICK
Although they vary in length and superficial design, batons are usually plain and light-colored, so that the conductor's gestures can be picked up clearly.

As choral music became more complex, especially in the 15th century with the rise of elaborate polyphony, conducting must have become more necessary and more common. With hand or staff, the leader gave a downstroke to indicate an accented beat, an upstroke for unaccented beats. From the 15th to the 17th century, there was no standard baton or staff with which to do this. Some musicians conducted with a rolled-up sheet of manuscript paper, some used a staff, and some probably used their hands and arms alone, as the earliest conductors had done.

BAROQUE ENSEMBLES

There were some major changes in music during the 17th century that made the role of the conductor more important. One was the increasing popularity of complex choral music written for multiple groups of singers and musicians, often arranged separately around a church. Coordinating this complex, spatial music meant that the leader or conductor had a vital role. One thing that unified this complex music and stood at its heart was the continuo part — the bass line that provided the foundation of the harmony and either a rhythmical pulse or important rhythmical punctuation. The leader of the musicians often played the harpsichord as part of the continuo group, and led the proceedings from his seat, cueing in and coordinating the various other groups of players or singers.

LEADER
This 15th-century woodcut is an early image of a musician using a wooden staff while leading what may be a group of singers.

Continuo also had a key part to play in another major development of the 17th century — the rise of opera. This was another complex form of music in which a musical director was needed to keep the orchestra together and to make sure the singers and musicians were synchronized. Again, the continuo keyboard player was a natural choice for such a leader, although the first violinist also took on some of the duties of leading the orchestra.

TEACHER
The staff or baton was a schoolteacher's tool, as this 17th-century German painting shows.

Finally, the other major development in the 17th century was the fashion for instrumental string bands such as the famous French court group Les Vingt-quatre Violons du Roi (see p. 41). In this royal band, the conductor was the composer Jean-Baptiste Lully (1632–1687), who, like his medieval ancestors, carried a wooden staff — but unlike them he banged the staff on the floor to give a precise beat. This French fashion for banging a staff on the floor did not last. The main reason for its demise was probably the obtrusive noise it made. But the staff could also be dangerous. On one occasion, at a performance of a Te Deum in thanks for the king's recovery from an illness, Lully, banging away enthusiastically, hit his foot instead of the floor and sustained a severe injury. The wound turned gangrenous and Lully, refusing the dangerous and painful option of an amputation, died soon afterward.

Other string-based bands, especially those in Italy, found that the natural leader was the first violin, who moved his instrument to indicate time, or gestured with his bow when not actually playing. Because Italian composers such as Vivaldi were great writers of violin concertos, the figure and the leader-soloist became common here.

CLASSICAL LEADERSHIP

In the Classical era, it was still common for composers such as Joseph Haydn (1732–1809) to lead the orchestra from the keyboard. Haydn spent a lot of his life as a court composer and musical director, most famously at Esterháza, Hungary. Here, he supervised and trained the musicians as well as writing and directing the music, so his work combined the modern roles of composer, teacher, conductor and orchestral manager. Similarly, Mozart, who performed his own piano concertos, led the orchestra from the piano.

By the end of the 18th century, however, both music and the way performances were organized

THE SYMPHONY

✦

Classical-era composers such as Haydn and Mozart defined the symphony — both wrote a string of these four-movement works, typically with an opening movement in sonata form (see The piano sonata, p. 84), followed by a slow movement, a more light-hearted third movement, often in the form of a minuet, and a finale. Beethoven extended the scope of the genre, writing longer symphonies than previous composers, pouring inspired musical ideas into his symphonies, and even including parts for singers in his final symphony. After this the symphony became the genre in which Romantic-era composers developed some of the deepest and most adventurous musical thoughts. Berlioz, Liszt, Bruckner and Mahler, in their different ways, pushed the boundaries of the genre, extending its length, enlarging its orchestra, reordering and restructuring its movements, opening up new worlds of sound, and generally placing the symphony at the musical cutting edge. The symphonies of all these composers have enthralled listeners ever since.

were changing. Orchestral music was becoming more complex. The orchestras themselves were larger and the woodwind, brass and percussion sections were expanding with the addition of ever more instruments. These forces all needed marshaling and the job was tough if the leader was also playing an instrument. The answer was to rely more and more on specialist conductors.

At the same time the dedicated court orchestra, like Haydn's at Esterháza, which played music familiar to all the players, was becoming less common. Orchestras were more often formed to play public concerts in halls, often learning and rehearsing the music for a specific event. Again, a dedicated conductor was the best person to help the players handle this challenge.

STANDING UP

The baton, symbol of the importance and leadership of the conductor, appeared in the second decade of the 19th century. Among the first recorded uses of the baton was in Vienna in 1812, and the person wielding it was composer, writer and conductor Ignaz Franz von Mosel (1772–1844). Haydn may have used the baton a few years earlier, and there is also a slightly earlier account of the conducting of one Daniel Türk, whose baton gestures were so broad that he sometimes hit the chandelier above his head, covering himself in bits of glass. Soon others followed suit and by the 1820s and 1830s, specialist conductors, who stood up in front of the orchestra, started to become common. Many of these were composers who were performing their own music. Weber and Mendelssohn were celebrated examples.

IGNAZ FRANZ VON MOSEL
Mosel was a Viennese composer and conductor who played a major part in the musical life of his home city and was director of the Viennese court theaters.

Carl Maria von Weber (1786–1826) was a famed conductor-composer who was well aware of the need for clear direction in orchestral music and, especially, opera. Weber was one of the musicians who worked hard to put German opera on an equal footing with Italian in the early 19th century. To begin with he used a roll of paper to conduct, and critics praised his noiseless beat, but he shocked the cultural coteries of Dresden when he introduced the conductor's baton there. He traveled widely, conducting his and others' works, and in 1824 was invited to London to compose and conduct his opera *Oberon*. He saw the role of the conductor as striking a happy medium between giving a firm beat and allowing the singers the scope to be expressive.

FELIX MENDELSSOHN
Mendelssohn, a prominent
conductor as well as
composer, helped to
promote the use of
the baton.

Felix Mendelssohn (1809–1847) used a baton at his conducting debut in London in 1829, when the baton was still unusual. It caused some surprise among London critics, one of whom wrote: "Mr Mendelssohn conducted his Sinfonia with a baton, as is customary in Germany, France, etc., where the discipline of bands is considered of more importance than in England." When Mendelssohn went back to London three years later, the musicians objected to his conducting with a baton. Mendelssohn was willing to let the matter lie, but colleagues such as Meyerbeer encouraged him to insist on the baton, and in a few years he was vindicated — the baton became standard in England as it was in France and Germany.

In 1835 Mendelssohn became a celebrated conductor of the Gewandhaus Orchestra in Leipzig, where he was famous for conducting not only new music but also music of the past, from Bach to Beethoven, another area in which the interpretative input of a conductor was useful, if not essential. He was praised for his care in orchestral conducting, and for his kindness to his musicians — he seems to have got his way by persuasion rather than by acting the part of musical dictator, as some conductors found it necessary to do. Mendelssohn's conducting was admired by many, including Berlioz (1803–1869), who, in a gesture of friendliness, exchanged batons with him.

The music of Berlioz was both complex and demanding and he, like other conductors of the new Romantic music, demanded long rehearsals. Berlioz also used "sectional" rehearsals, coaching the strings, woodwinds and brass separately before coaching the whole band together.

LISZT, WAGNER AND AFTER

By the second half of the 19th century, conducting with the baton was the norm, and musicians were beginning to think deeply about the conductor's work and role. Franz Liszt (1811–1886), the greatest pianist of his time, was also a transformative conductor. He was keen to convey the emotion in the music he conducted, and insisted on the conductor's importance in interpreting the composer's notes. "We are pilots, not oarsmen," he said. To this end he developed a host of powerful and communicative gestures, moving his baton in precise movements to articulate strong or staccato rhythms, and making gentler, broader hand gestures to indicate a more flowing phrase or melody. For Liszt, the idea of a conductor's "stick technique" became crucial.

Richard Wagner (1813–1883) wrote a book on conducting. Like Weber before him, he stressed the need to combine a clear beat with the flexibility to convey emotions. He also emphasized the importance of balancing the ever-increasing number of instruments and parts in the orchestra so that everything, especially the melody, is heard to its best advantage.

For Wagner, the conductor's importance was great and his role imperious. In complete contrast to Mendelssohn, who wanted to be transparent, for Wagner the conductor's main role was the interpretation of the score — working hard over numerous rehearsals to convey to the orchestra his ideas about each piece and how it should be played, and translating this into often minute instructions concerning tempo, dynamics, timbre and so on.

STICKS, FINGERS OR BOWS

◆

From the 1820s onward, the conductor's most familiar pose was standing on a podium, in front of the orchestra, wielding a baton. Some stuck to the old habit of conducting at the keyboard, but when the composer and pianist Clementi did this in the late 1820s he was probably already seen as old-fashioned. Today, not all conductors use a baton. Some use only their hands — or generally do so, adopting the baton only when conducting large forces that find the stick easier to see. Occasionally, violinists conduct using their bow, a technique used by the Strauss family, composers of Viennese waltzes, and revived by the Viennese conductor Willi Boskovsky when conducting Strauss waltzes and polkas.

FRANZ LISZT
Liszt was a powerful presence on the podium, and insisted on the importance of the conductor's role in bringing out the emotional content of the music.

PERIOD-PERFORMANCE CONDUCTORS

✦

A development that has produced very different sounds from the late-Romantic orchestral norm is the original-instrument or historically informed performance movement. By getting as close as possible to the instruments and performance practices of earlier centuries, specialist conductors have produced widely different sounds, helping us to hear familiar music in new (or old) ways. Often these early-music conductors began as specialist instrumentalists — among the many, Nikolaus Harnoncourt was a cellist, Roy Goodman a violinist, Jordi Savall a player of the viol, Gustav Leonhardt, like many others, a keyboard player. This perspective, combining instrumental playing, historical scholarship and a perceptive ear, has brought a new focus to conducting, and one from which even conductors of conventional symphony orchestras have learned.

Conductors at the end of the 19th and into the 20th century followed the Wagnerian path. The most successful built up long relationships with their orchestras and became known for their interpretations and for the character of the orchestral sound they encouraged among their players. Increasingly high-profile, such conductors became the stars of their profession. Famous examples included Wagner's associate Hans Richter (conductor of Manchester's Hallé Orchestra from 1899 to 1911), Arturo Toscanini (whose career took him from La Scala, Milan, via various American orchestras to the NBC Symphony Orchestra, which he conducted from 1937 to 1954) and Wilhelm Furtwängler (principal conductor both of the Berlin Philharmonic and the Leipzig Gewandhaus orchestras at various periods between the 1920s and 1950s).

There were huge differences in approach between these star conductors. Where Toscanini fostered precision and minute attention to detail, Furtwängler was much more flexible and encouraged a warm, bass-heavy sound. Such differences brought them large followings and if anything increased their prestige.

THE QUEST FOR PERFECTION

In the 20th and 21st centuries, the leading role of conductors in orchestral music has continued, but with one or two significant differences. In spite of the multiplicity of talented conductors, many critics and listeners find that orchestral sound has become more homogenous and orchestras more like one another than before. This is partly the result of the rise of the recording industry, with its power to edit recordings until they are note-perfect. The wish that every recording should

RICHARD WAGNER
Wagner stressed the role of the conductor as interpreter and made full use of rehearsals to explain his ideas to the orchestra.

be "perfect" and worthy of the repeated re-listenings that purchasers will give it has encouraged very high standards of playing, but also great similarity between orchestras and between the approaches that conductors often take. Modern economic conditions, with minimal rehearsal time, have also tended to encourage this development, as has the ability of the recording industry to market recordings internationally.

In spite of this movement toward similarity, there has still been room in the concert hall for the charismatic individual — the conductor who is committed to working hard with an orchestra to get a performance that is both effective and very different from the norm. From the emotionally charged performances conducted by Leonard Bernstein in the post–World War Two period to the meticulously prepared concerts of the great Romanian maestro Sergiu Celibidache, notable individual conductors have still made a huge difference — to orchestral playing, to sound and to the audience's appreciation of the music.

Other developments, from the success of a number of small orchestras who play without a conductor at all to the rise of the original-instrument movement, have also helped to make conductors reassess their role. And when a conductor responds sincerely to the music, and strives to get the best out of the musicians, the players follow and a memorable performance is likely to follow.

A LEADING ROLE
By the 1880s, the conductor was a well-established, integral part of the orchestra.

HANDS AND BATON
The baton helps to magnify and clarify the gestures of the conductor.

1829

Cornet

Location: Paris, France

Type: Aerophone

Era: Classical

Similar to the trumpet but with a conical bore and a mellower tone, the cornet appeared first in France in the second quarter of the 19th century soon after the invention of valves for the brass. It was taken up by players as a flexible, pleasant-sounding high wind instrument, and is still heard today in classical pieces specially written for it, although listeners are more likely to come across it in performances of jazz, where it was the favorite instrument of the famed Bix Beiderbecke.

THE VALVED POST HORN

The post horn was a familiar instrument in the 18th century from its use to signal the arrival or departure of mail coaches, the postilions of which also sounded their horns when the coach was in motion as a warning for other road users to get out of its way. The post horn was a long brass tube (with either a cylindrical or a conical bore and a flared bell); it could be either long and straight or, more often, coiled in a round or elongated "trumpet" shape to make carrying and holding it more convenient.

The post horn makes occasional appearances in classical music. Mozart wrote a Post Horn Serenade (1779) that features the instrument, and, as late as the beginning of the 20th century, Mahler wrote a part for the post horn in his Symphony No 3. In the Mahler symphony, the post horn is played offstage, and its haunting sound is sometimes played today by the flugelhorn (see p. 166).

TRUMPET'S RELATIVE
Apart from its conical bore, the cornet is very similar to the modern trumpet and is played in the same way, so players can swap instruments easily.

At some point around 1820, someone had the idea of adding valves, newly invented during the second decade of the 19th century, to the post horn, to produce the instrument known as the cornet. It is not known exactly who came up with the idea of the cornet, but one of the early makers may have been the instrument-maker and professor of music Jean Hilaire Asté, also known as Halary. Another likely candidate is Périnet. By 1829 the design was refined enough for Périnet to patent the instrument, and Périnet's patent mentions that the valved cornet has been known for about four years. In the late 1820s, therefore, the instrument was still new and unusual, and this accords with a comment by Berlioz in his *Memoirs*, where he relates the performance of the cantata he wrote as his prizewinning entry for the Prix de Rome in 1830. The composer notes, with a tone of pleased surprise, that the orchestra for his prize piece included "even cornets — modern instruments!"

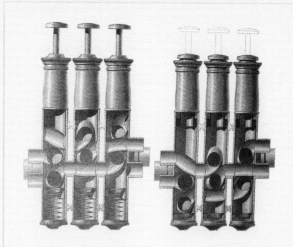

VALVES
Pressing the valves reroutes the air, so that the pitch changes.

BECOMING ESTABLISHED

Because makers of trumpets were for some reason relatively slow to apply valve technology to their instruments, the cornet caught on as a high brass instrument, and many players also admired its tone, which is mellower than the trumpet, as a result of its usually conical bore. Its popularity increased and it was produced in a variety of different pitches, in various metals and with numerous valve systems.

The cornet was popular first in its French homeland, especially after Dufrène, cornet player at the Champs-Elysées Promenade Concerts, wrote a book on playing the instrument in 1834. As a result it was often known by its French name, the *cornet à pistons*. In France, as in England, it often replaced the keyed bugle, and in Germany and Austria it was also popular, although here the

CORNET VS TRUMPET
♦
Although trumpets were well established in the orchestra by the time the cornet came along, they were "natural" instruments, lacking valves, and so the valved cornet, with its simple way of playing full, chromatic scales, was preferred by many composers and players. In addition, the trumpet had strong links with martial music; the cornet had no such associations, and so composers felt they could write for it more lyrically. Therefore, especially in France but also in other countries, the cornet found a welcome place in many orchestras, often alongside trumpets, until the valved trumpet became more popular in the 20th century.

flugelhorn was also much played, so the cornet's use was not quite so widespread. Nevertheless, the cornet became an increasingly familiar sight in brass bands as the 19th century went on, and it was also quite common in concert orchestras and theater bands.

One key to the cornet's sound and playability is the mouthpiece. On modern cornets, this has a deeper cup than the trumpet mouthpiece, which makes it easy to play in long stretches. However, the mouthpiece began, appropriately for an instrument that evolved from the post horn, as rather similar to that of a horn (more tapering than cuplike inside); this was said to give early cornets a round, rich sound. The more cup-shaped mouthpiece that evolved later produced a rather more piercing sound that was popular with French players at the end of the 19th century.

CORNET WITH PISTONS
A late 19th-century cornet with piston valves is shown in this Spanish engraving.

JEAN-BAPTISTE ARBAN
The French virtuoso Arban did as much as anyone in the 19th century to popularize the cornet and to raise standards among players.

THE FIRST CORNET VIRTUOSO

The most renowned cornet player of the 19th century was Jean-Baptiste Arban (1825–1889), who wanted to do for his instrument what Paganini had done for the violin. Arban, who favored the cup-shaped cornet mouthpiece, certainly achieved a very high degree of virtuosity, and wrote a number of pieces designed to show off his talent, including a set of variations on *Carnival de Venise* (1864) and a *Fantaisie Brillante* (1864). He wrote a book on playing the cornet and saxhorn and in 1869 he was appointed Professor of Cornet at the Paris Conservatoire, where he attracted numerous talented pupils.

A lot of the music played by Arban and his pupils was for the cornet as part of a brass band. Nowadays, this music might be classified as "light music" or put in the "easy listening" category, but it still stretched the players and found a ready audience. But by Arban's time various classical composers had been inspired to write parts for the cornet too. Berlioz scored for cornets, adding two to the trumpet section in his

Symphonie Fantastique (1830), Bizet included them in his popular opera *Carmen* (1875), Franck wrote them into his Symphony in D minor (1888–1889), and many other composers included them in the orchestra.

The cornet's use was on the whole more widespread in France than in Central Europe, where good valved trumpets established themselves more rapidly. French composers often included a pair of them in the orchestra alongside the trumpets, and the cornet players were often given the faster parts.

Not all the cornet's appearances in the orchestra gave the instrument prominence, but occasionally a composer wrote a solo that showed audiences the qualities of the cornet. Tchaikovsky used it in his ballet music, and the cornet has a memorable solo, with an especially impressive fast section, in the Neapolitan Dance in *Swan Lake* (1875–1877).

The trumpet became more widespread again in the orchestra in the 20th century, but the cornet has a high profile in a few 20th-century classical pieces (although sometimes these parts are played on the trumpet). It plays a key role in the small ensemble of Stravinsky's ballet *The Soldier's Tale* (1918), in which it is the only brass instrument except for the trombone. In Prokofiev's suite *Lieutenant Kijé* (1934), a cornet opens the final movement, "The Burial of Kijé," and a muted cornet portrays the last journey of the hero's soul.

... solos ... in Tchaikovsky's *Swan Lake* **show up only too well the instrument's fundamentally plebeian nature.**

R. Morley Pegge, in Anthony Baines, ed., Musical Instruments Through the Ages

THE CORNET IN JAZZ

✦

The role of the cornet in jazz goes right back to Buddy Bolden (1877–1931), one of the pioneers of ragtime, who played the instrument in New Orleans in the early years of the 20th century. Bolden was a famous improviser and a pivotal figure in the early history of jazz, adding the element of blues to the ragtime then fashionable in New Orleans. Among the other great early jazz cornettists were hot-jazz exponent Muggsy Spanier (1901–1967) and Bix Beiderbecke (1903–1931), who was known for his purity of tone and his role in developing the jazz ballad. After these pioneers, the best-known jazz players to adopt the instrument were Joe "King" Oliver (1881–1938) and Louis Armstrong (1901–1971), who learned much from Oliver and played cornet with him before switching to the trumpet. From the 1930s onward, jazz players tended to prefer the more piercing tone of the trumpet to the cornet, but sometimes trumpeters switch to the other instrument when they want a different sound.

Flugelhorn

Location: Germany

Type: Aerophone

Era: Romantic

+ WOODWIND
+ PERCUSSION
+ **BRASS**
+ STRINGS
+ OTHER

FLUGELHORN
With its wider bore, the tubing of this instrument is wound more broadly than that of the trumpet.

Although it looks superficially like a trumpet, the flugelhorn has a much mellower tone that has won it admirers in fields from classical music to jazz. Its early ancestors were the signaling horns of the ancient Romans and the hunting horns of Central Europe. These were semicircular metal horns played by the *Flügelmeister*, who used the instrument to signal to the rest of the hunters.

FROM BATTLEFIELD TO BAND

During the Seven Years War (1756–1763), some of the forces on the Hanoverian side took up the semicircular hunting horn for signaling on the battlefield, and its use soon spread to other states (including England, which was ruled by the House of Hanover in this period). In Germany it was known as the Halbmond (half-moon), from its distinctive shape. During the 19th century, various modified forms of bugle were produced, including ones made in single or double loops, which were presumably more convenient to carry than the large Halbmond horns.

In 1810 the Dublin-based bandmaster Joseph Halliday had the idea of making the bugle more musically flexible by fitting it with keys — something that had been tried with the trumpet in Central Europe a decade and a half previously. The resulting keyed bugle was still primarily a military instrument and was named for the Duke of Kent, Commander of British forces in Ireland, as the Royal Kent bugle. But the instrument soon caught on beyond the battlefield and parade ground, finding a place in wind bands both in Britain and mainland Europe. Players were soon showing off their agile fingerwork in solos and the keyed bugle started to acquire a following.

ENTER THE VALVE

By the end of the 1830s, brass instruments with valves were becoming popular and at some point around this time an instrument-maker, probably in Germany, had the idea of producing a bugle with valves instead of keys. One of the instrument-makers to whom this development is attributed is Michael Saurle of Munich, who produced an instrument referred to as a "chromatic flugelhorn" in 1832. But the precise history of how the instrument developed is not clear and, as is common with the evolution of musical instruments, several makers were probably refining similar bugles at around the same time.

Whoever first produced it, it was the bugle with valves that became generally known as the flugelhorn. The resulting instrument is similar to a cornet, in that it is pitched in B-flat and has the same compass. But because the flugelhorn retains the shape of the bugle's tube, which expands quite widely toward the bell, it has a broader tone than the cornet. Soprano versions of the instrument, pitched in E-flat, are also produced.

A UNIQUE SOUND

The flugelhorn's unique sound is most widely heard in brass and military bands, where it can have quite a prominent role, especially in European ensembles. Its brass band role was beautifully evoked in the 1996 film *Brassed Off*, in which the heroine Gloria plays the solo part of Joaquín Rodrigo's *Concierto de Aranjuez* (originally written for guitar in 1939) on her flugelhorn, to showstopping effect. The flugelhorn has also been used a lot by jazz musicians — mostly trumpeters, including Miles Davis and Chet Baker.

Although the flugelhorn has not often been taken up by classical composers, there are a few works in which the instrument makes its mark. Vaughan Williams's Symphony No. 9 (1958) has a solo part for flugelhorn, Stravinsky's *Threni* (1958, settings of texts from the Biblical Book of Lamentations) also has a solo, and in Respighi's *Pines of Rome* (1924) the instrument is used to evoke the sound of the ancient Roman horns that are the distant ancestors of the flugelhorn. Michael Tippett liked the flugelhorn too, featuring it in his Symphony No. 3 (1972) and his *Festal Brass with Blues* (1984). Elsewhere the instrument is sometimes used to imitate or stand in for the post horn, as sometimes happens in performances of Mahler's Symphony No. 3 (1893–1896).

This beautiful and neglected instrument is not usually allowed in the select circles of the orchestra and has been banished to the brass band, where it is allowed to indulge in the art of vibrato.

Ralph Vaughan Williams

ADOLPHE SAX AND THE FLUGELHORN

◆

When in 1845 he created and patented his family of saxhorns, the Belgian instrument-maker and inventor Adolphe Sax included in the range an instrument that is very similar to the flugelhorn. He originally designed his saxhorn in B-flat with the bell pointing upward, as it does on the tenor and baritone horns used in brass bands. When modified as a trumpet-shaped instrument, Sax's horn resembled the flugelhorn closely. But Sax did not invent the flugelhorn, which already existed by this time.

CHET BAKER
The multitalented Chet Baker was known for both his singing and trumpet-playing, but often switched to flugelhorn during the 1970s and 1980s.

1835

Location: Berlin, Germany

Type: Aerophone

Era: Classical/Romantic

Tuba

... the most intestinal of instruments, the very lower bowel of music.

Peter de Vries, The Glory of the Hummingbird

The largest of the brass instruments, the tuba was developed in the 19th century to provide the lowest voice in brass bands and in the orchestra's brass section. It replaced a number of other instruments such as the ophicleide, all of which had a large following but eventually gave way to the low, smooth tone of the tuba.

ANCIENT TUBAS

The ancient Romans used the term "tuba" (which clearly relates to the Latin *tubus*, a tube) to describe a long, straight brass instrument that probably sounded quite high — Pliny compares its sound to the cry of an elephant. Similarly, medieval instruments given the name tuba were also high, trumpetlike horns, and in the "Dies irae" section of the requiem set by many composers the Latin words *"tuba mirum spargens sonum"* are usually translated as "the trumpet's astonishing sound."

SERPENT VARIATIONS

During the period when the modern orchestra began to evolve, therefore, a very different instrument, the serpent (see p. 30), provided the bass voice in many bands and instrumental ensembles. From the 17th century onward, the serpent was also used to accompany choirs and appeared occasionally in the symphony orchestra and more often in the opera house.

The serpent was far from perfect. Many players yearned for a brighter, more focused sound. Instrument-makers responded with a number of variations on the serpent, most of which were upright, bassoon-shaped instruments and often had a hybrid name such as the French *serpent-basson*. However, these diverse bass instruments had all kinds of names, from Russian bassoon to bass horn. Some of them were extraordinary-

LONG TUBE
Depending on the pitch of the instrument, a tuba can contain between 12 and 18 feet (3.5–5.5 m) of tubing.

looking objects, often made in metal or a mixture of wood and metal and sometimes with a metal dragon-head instead of a rounded bell, in imitation of ancient Roman instruments.

THE OPHICLEIDE

The serpent was difficult to play well and none of the other bass horns had a strong following, so by the second decade of the 19th century, instrument-makers sought an alternative bass wind instrument. They found inspiration in the keyed bugle, a high brass instrument that first appeared in 1810. The keyed bugle was agile and had a strong sound. Within a few years of its appearance, instrument-makers were experimenting with a lower-pitched instrument built along similar lines. These experiments produce the ophicleide, a tenor-bass brass instrument with a widely conical tube shaped rather like a bassoon and with a series of keys. It was the creation of the instrument-maker Halary of Paris, who patented it in 1817.

The ophicleide had an impressive sound, rich in its upper register and less smooth lower down. With a good player with plenty of breath it could play loudly and combined an ability to blend with the other brass with the facility to play stentorian, coarse-sounding low notes that stood out magnificently.

The ophicleide proved popular with composers who liked its clear sound. Berlioz, Mendelssohn, Schumann and Verdi all wrote parts for it, appreciating its rich bass and strong tone, and capitalizing on both its ability to stand out and its potential to add a bass voice to its neighbors in the brass section, the trombones. Hector Berlioz (1803–1869)was a particular enthusiast, asking for four to play at once in his Requiem (1837) and including no fewer than six in his *Symphonie Funèbre et Triomphale* (1840). By using two ophicleides and a serpent in the *Symphonie Fantastique* (1830), he produces a particularly rich and varied bass sound. The instrument was also popular in wind bands, and some of its orchestral appearances — for example, in the Berlioz Requiem and in Spontini's opera *Olimpie* (1819) — it was

SERPENT
The serpent, seen here (left) in an Italian print of 1723, was sometimes used to provide low wind sounds in the orchestra before the invention of the tuba.

ROMANTIC BASS
The ophicleide, which resembles a very low-pitched keyed bugle, had a vogue during the Romantic period.

SOUSAPHONE AND HELICON

✦

Manufacturers devised various ways of arranging the long tubes that make up the lower brass instruments. One solution, first produced in Austria around the 1840s, was the "circular bass," often known as the helicon. With its circle of tubing, the helicon was designed to be lifted over the player's head and rested on the left shoulder, an arrangement suited to players in marching bands. As a result, it became popular with military musicians. A variation on this theme was the sousaphone, created in the 1890s by the manufacturer Conn and named after the celebrated American bandleader and composer John Philip Sousa. The sousaphone (pictured) has a very large bell, which originally pointed upward. Later models were made with forward-facing bells, and these proved especially useful in the early years of recording, where their bells could be turned toward the microphone and their sound could reinforce the soft orchestral double basses.

part of a wind-band in a classical setting. It was not always easy to get good players for these parts, however — Berlioz complained in his *Memoirs* that the instrument was not taught at the Paris Conservatoire and "... of the hundred or hundred and fifty persons in Paris at present blowing this exacting instrument, hardly three are fit to be in a good orchestra."

THE COMING OF THE TUBA

The ophicleide was impressive but had its weaknesses. Its keys were delicate and wore out quickly, and it required fingering that was entirely different from the other brass instruments. This was because brass instruments other than the trombone increasingly had valves, mechanisms that alter the working length of the instrument's tubing, enabling the musician to play the full chromatic scale. Valves, invented by the Silesian wind players Stölzel and Blühmel, were patented in Berlin in 1818. By about 1830, instrument-manufacturers were beginning to add valves to the lower brass instruments.

Among the first of these were known as bombardons, developed by the instrument-maker Riedl in Vienna in around 1829. Bombardons were upright instruments resembling ophicleides, but with loops and curves of extra tubing and with three or more piston valves. Others were valved ophicleides, which looked similar and retained the somewhat coarse-sounding lower end, while the bombardons had a generally smoother sound.

However, the most enduring of these valved low brass instruments was the bass tuba, introduced by Prussian court instrument-maker Johann Moritz and trombonist Wilhelm Wieprecht in 1835. Clearly related to the ophicleides, this original bass tuba had a generally upright design, but its tubes were bent less tightly, giving the whole instrument a broader appearance, and its conical bore ended in a bell with a very small flare.

The new tuba was steadily taken up in both bands and orchestras, although when used in bands, players often referred to it as a bombardon. As a result, there is a lot of confusion between the two instruments — and between these two and the ophicleide, which remained in use long after the tuba appeared. In its Prussian homeland, however, the tuba was especially popular. Because of Wieprecht's position as head of the Prussian Royal Military Corps, it was soon adopted in Germany military bands, and orchestral use followed quickly. Berlioz, on his travels through Germany, met it often.

Berlioz complained in his *Memoirs* that, as with the ophicleide, the Paris Conservatoire offered no teaching of the tuba, and went on to define its position in the brass: "We have no class in the bass tuba, a powerful valved instrument differing from the ophicleide in timbre, mechanism, and range, its position in the trumpet family being exactly equivalent to the double bass in the violin family."

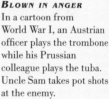

BLOWN IN ANGER
In a cartoon from World War I, an Austrian officer plays the trombone while his Prussian colleague plays the tuba. Uncle Sam takes pot shots at the enemy.

SAX AND THE TUBA

Berlioz especially approved of tubas made by Adolphe Sax (1814–1894), holding that they were steadier in tone, better made, and brighter in sound than the ophicleide, although he praised the agility of the older instrument, advising composers to include parts for both in their orchestral works. Sax enters the story of the tuba via his saxhorn family of instruments, which he demonstrated to good effect at a famous contest between old and new brass instruments on the Champ de Mars, Paris, 1845.

In their final form the saxhorn family were tuba-shaped instruments ranging in pitch

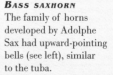

BASS SAXHORN
The family of horns developed by Adolphe Sax had upward-pointing bells (see left), similar to the tuba.

MODERN TUBA
The tuba remains the lowest brass instrument in use in the classical orchestra.

from a high E-flat soprano to a low E-flat bass. A number of these instruments evolved into horns used widely in brass and wind bands — for example, the modern tenor horn, baritone horn and euphonium. The E-flat bass saxhorn formed a template for many modern tubas, including those produced in Britain and elsewhere.

THE TUBA AT WORK

Slowly, composers and orchestras saw the virtues of the tuba and in the second half of the 19th century it became a regular feature of classical orchestras, at last giving the brass section a sweet-toned bass member that stood the test of time. Although other instruments were added to the orchestra for special effects and to provide distinctive voices, the addition of the tuba in effect rounded out the Romantic-era orchestra, which took on the form in the late 19th century that it retains today.

All the Romantic-era composers who wrote large-scale music, including Brahms, Bruckner, Wagner, Mahler and Strauss, made the tuba a regular part of their orchestra. Many composers seized on the way the tuba blends well with the double bass section and also, in its higher register, with the French horn. The tuba also has a close relationship with the trombone section, with the tuba player sometimes

CELEBRATION
Boston Symphony
Orchestra Principal Tuba
Mike Roylance performs at
composer John Williams'
80th Birthday tribute in
2012, at Tanglewood,
Massachusetts.

playing the fourth trombone part. Composers
generally use the tuba's lower notes, which are
hard to play but resonant, quite softly to reinforce the bass, while scoring more audible,
melodic passages for the instrument's middle
and higher registers.

The tuba is not seen by most composers as
a solo instrument, but Vaughan Williams
wrote a memorable and melodious tuba concerto (1954), while Hindemith (who wrote solo
or chamber works for virtually every instrument) composed a sonata for tuba and piano
(1955). Tuba players also make arrangements
of a wide variety of classical works to give
their instrument a solo repertoire, so that as
many listeners as possible can appreciate the
scope of this instrument that, large as it is, is
rarely in the limelight.

TUBAS AND HÉLICONS
Left: Two members of this
group of 19th-century
police musicians play tubas
made in helicon form.

THE ROMANTIC ORCHESTRA

✦

By the second half of the 19th century,
the Romantic symphony orchestra was
growing into a large-scale ensemble,
although it still varied in size. The
Romantic orchestra in its various
forms is still familiar today, playing
the symphonies and concertos of
composers such as Schumann and
Brahms, and swelling still more to take
part in Wagner's operas and Bruckner's
vast symphonies. In the hands of
Romantic composers from Brahms
onward it included a generous complement of strings, trombones
and valved brass instruments such
as trumpets, French horns and tubas,
and a range of woodwind including
piccolo, flutes, oboes, English horns,
clarinets, bassoons and contrabassoon.
A large body of percussion was also
common, and these forces could be
augmented when required with all
kinds of instruments, from the
celesta to the Wagner tuba.

Bass Clarinet

Location: Paris, France

Type: Aerophone (single reed)

Era: Classical/Romantic

The bass clarinet is pitched at least an octave below the standard clarinet and is admired for its depth of voice and rich timbre. It is primarily an orchestral instrument, and its role combines reinforcing the bass of the woodwind section with playing the occasional stunning solo, in which it emerges from the shadows to enchant listeners with its beautiful, liquid tone.

+ **WOODWIND**
+ PERCUSSION
+ BRASS
+ STRINGS
+ OTHER

A CLARINET LIKE A BASSOON

Many admirers of the clarinet liked the rich notes of its lower register, and instrument-makers in the late 18th century began to find ways of producing a bass instrument that capitalized on these notes and took them still lower. Among the pioneers were the French maker Gilles Lot and the German Heinrich Grenser. Grenser's bass clarinets of the 1790s were pitched in B-flat (an octave below the conventional clarinet) and were made rather like bassoons, with a double tube connected by a U-bend at the bottom to make the instrument relatively short and easy to handle. Also like bassoons, these early instruments had thick tubing so that the maker could drill the tone holes at an angle, making it easier for the player's fingers to reach them.

By the early 19th century, several French work-shops were producing similar bassoon-shaped instruments, some called *basse guerrière* (to indicate their use in military bands) and some called *basse orgue* (to show an affinity with low organ notes and perhaps as a nod toward their use in church ensembles). There is evidence that instruments like these were popular in America — the *Oxford Companion to Music* cites an engraving of around 1810 that shows one at the head of an American marching band.

FUNCTIONAL DESIGN
The striking funnel-shaped bell of the bass clarinet (see right) is turned upward and this provides space for a spike so that the player can rest the instrument on the floor.

When well and thoughtfully handled ... an entry of the bass clarinet is really something to look forward to ...

Anthony Baines, Woodwind Instruments and Their History

THE BASS CLARINET TAKES THE SPOTLIGHT

The bass clarinet was soon appreciated by orchestral and opera composers too. In Act V of his 1836 opera *Les Hugue-nots*, Giacomo Meyerbeer wrote an elaborate solo for the instrument. This virtuoso passage showed its stunning ability to plumb great depths, while also ascending and keeping its beautiful, liquid tone.

In the 1830s, the bass clarinet in its modern form appeared — a mainly straight instrument with an upward curve toward the bottom, terminating in a slightly flaring bell. This design was pioneered by manufacturers such as Buffet of Paris and, above all, Adolphe Sax (1814–1894) of Brussels, whose straight-bodied bass clarinet appeared in 1838. Sax's good ear and talent for producing instruments that both sounded good and handled well meant that his form of the bass clarinet stood the test of time.

REACHING THE DEPTHS

Romantic composers such as Liszt, Wagner, Puccini and Delius used the bass clarinet to contribute to deep wind harmonies and established it as a regular member of the orchestra from the second half of the 19th century. However, Wagner particularly liked the instrument's low notes and in many of his operas requires a bass clarinet in A, a lower instrument than the original one in B-flat. The extra range can be accommodated by giving the standard instrument more length and an additional key.

HANDFUL
The tone holes on this extra-large instrument are very far apart and would be impossible for the player to reach unaided — every one is therefore covered by a key.

Russian composers seem to have been particularly drawn to the bass clarinet. Tchaikovsky makes telling use of it in his famous "Dance of the Sugar Plum Fairy" from the *Nutcracker* ballet (1892). Russian makers also produced a bass clarinet even lower than the one that Wagner asked for, and this low bass clarinet inspired Russian composers such as Prokofiev (in *Romeo and Juliet*, 1935) and Shostakovich (in Symphony No. 8, 1943, and the opera *Lady Macbeth of Mtsensk*, 1932). Such solos, and occasional pieces like Luciano Berio's *Chemin IIc* (1972) for bass clarinet and small orchestra, make up for the dearth of concertos for the instrument.

PLAYING SOFTLY

✦

It was not just the low notes and striking timbre of the instrument, but also its ability to play very quietly that was attractive to many composers. In Tchaikovsky's Symphony No. 6 (1893), there is a bassoon solo that the composer marks *pppppp* — a way of saying "as quiet as possible." The bass clarinet being much easier to play very quietly than the bassoon, this passage is now often given to the instrument.

Harmonium

Location: Paris, France

Type: Aerophone (free reed)

Era: Romantic

✦ WOODWIND
✦ PERCUSSION
✦ BRASS
✦ STRINGS
✦ **OTHER**

CHURCH KEYBOARD
The typical church harmonium has an ornamented case and a row of stops above the manual.

A small keyboard instrument with foot-bellows, the harmonium sounds rather like an organ but produces its notes with reeds rather than pipes — because of the way the reeds work it is described as a free-reed instrument. It was invented for use in the home and became popular for accompanying hymn-singing in churches. It also acquired a small repertoire of classical pieces from composers as different as Rossini and César Franck.

HOW IT WORKS

The harmonium contains a series of reeds attached to plates, and these reeds can vibrate freely when air passes over them. When the player pedals, the mechanism pumps the bellows, filling the wind chest beneath the reeds with air. When a key is pressed, air passes from the wind chest to its corresponding reed, which vibrates so that a note is sounded. Reeds of different sizes produce different pitches; variations in the shape and breadth of the reed affect the timbre.

Above the reeds is a board containing channels into which the air flows when it has passed the reed. These channels affect the tone quality, and the harmonium has various stop controls, looking like organ stops, that can adjust the size of these channels, altering the timbre. There are also stops to change the instrument's volume by opening or closing wooden flaps.

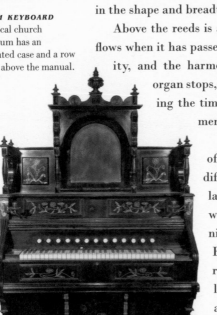

Harmoniums have up to four separate ranks of reeds, which can be selected to provide further differences in timbre and pitch. Their stops are labeled, often with names that recall the woodwind instruments that come closest to the harmonium's sound. A basic or "unison" rank (flute and English horn) plays at quite high pitch; another rank (clarinet and bourdon) sounds an octave lower; a third rank plays an octave higher (fife and clarion); and a fourth rank may have reeds at a similar pitch to those of the "unison" rank but with a different tone (oboe and bassoon).

... the things ... that you blow wi' your foot.
Thomas Hardy, Under the Greenwood Tree

THE EMERGENCE OF THE HARMONIUM

Free-reed instruments, and free-reed stops for conventional organs, appeared in the 18th century and experiments with this kind of instrument probably also led to the invention of the harmonica and accordion. Various reed organs were marketed in the early 19th century, but a particular inventor, Alexandre-François Debain (1809–1877), made the first one that allowed air to be routed from the reeds to different-shaped chambers, each giving a different timbre. Debain called this instrument the harmonium, patenting it in 1842 and selling production rights (but not rights in the name "harmonium") to the Alexandre company, which was a manufacturer of accordions, free-reed instruments that work in a similar way to the harmonium.

The Alexandre instrument, marketed as the "orgue melodium," caught the attention of players and composers. Alexandre's employee Victor Mustel (1815–1890) set up on his own as a harmonium-builder and introduced improvements such as separately controllable wind sources for the treble and bass. Mustel's instruments were especially well made, and became sought after by players.

ACCORDION
The accordion, another free-reed instrument, was probably invented around 1822 and was becoming popular at around the time the harmonium was invented.

REPERTOIRE

The harmonium was principally conceived as a domestic instrument. Harmoniums were also bought by small churches without the funds for an organ, theaters, and other clients. In church and home alike its natural role was accompanying hymns and playing music written for organ, and some specialist organ composers, such as the Frenchman Louis Vierne (1870–1937), wrote pieces with the harmonium in mind. Other composers who admired the instrument included Dvořák (who wrote a set of bagatelles for harmonium and chamber group, 1878) and Saint-Saëns. The Belgian composer César Franck wrote several pieces for the instrument, including some duos for harmonium and piano. Rossini originally scored his *Petite Messe Solonelle* (1863) for the unusual combination of two pianos, harmonium and voices, and in it the harmonium has an almost orchestral part, sometimes imitating a group of strings, sometimes evoking woodwind solos.

HARMONICA

✦

The harmonica, also known as the mouth organ, is a small, hand-held free-reed instrument. Developed in the 1820s, it has established a foothold in virtually every type of music, from folk to rock, and its use by blues musicians has earned it the alternative name of "blues harp." A few classical composers have written for it, including Vaughan Williams, who wrote his *Romance for Harmonica and Orchestra* (1951) for the renowned player Larry Adler.

Castanets

Location: Russia

Type: Idiophone

Era: Romantic

✦ WOODWIND

✦ **PERCUSSION**

✦ BRASS

✦ STRINGS

✦ OTHER

With a sound that instantly recalls Spain, the castanets are both beautifully simple and highly evocative. Familiar to everyone who has watched traditional Spanish dance, they often appear in concert music with a Spanish theme, or sometimes when composers require a light pointing-up of a piece's rhythm. The instrument's origins are in the ancient world, but castanets only became familiar in classical music after the Russian composer Glinka began to write for them in 1845.

FOLK ROOTS

The ancient Egyptians played clappers, flat pieces of wood or ivory, one held in each hand, that they hit together. Sometimes the pieces were shaped like human hands, suggesting that their sound was seen as a kind of amplified hand-clapping. The Greeks and Romans held a pair of clappers in each hand, snapping them together, and these are probably the ancestors of the flat castanets that are used in folk music in many different places across Europe.

The castanets used in the orchestra, however, derive from the traditional castanets of Spain, which evolved in a slightly different way. Instead of being flat, they are shell-like in form. The shells are made of a hard wood such as ebony or rosewood. They are held together by cord so that the two hollow sides of the shells face one another. The player puts the loops of the cord through one thumb so that the two shells are held over the palm, leaving the fingers free to click one shell against the other. In Spanish folk music, the player holds a pair of castanets in each hand, the so-called "male" pair, played by the left hand, having a lower pitch than the "female," played on the right hand.

SPANISH CASTANETS
These examples take the traditional form, with a cord joining the pair of wooden shells.

ADAPTATION FOR THE ORCHESTRA

In traditional Spanish music, the castanets are played continuously, but in classical music, the orchestral percussionist often has to change instruments rapidly. The Spanish castanets, held tightly by the thumb, take too long to remove from the thumbs before switching, so orchestral players generally use castanets mounted on a central wooden handle, so that the shells beat against the handle when they are shaken.

The player can produce different rhythms by continuous shaking, by beating the instrument against the thigh, or by clicking one of the shells using the fingers. Orchestral players also use so-called machine castanets, in which two pairs of shells are mounted on a base, with the upper shells held by elastic. Percussionists can play these either using the fingers or with a soft-headed beater.

Mikhail Glinka (1804–57), the father of Russian classical music, was among the first to use castanets in an orchestra. He became interested in Spanish music and dance when he traveled to the country in 1845, and was able to master the dance steps, although he confessed himself unable to play the castanets at the same time. When he returned to Russia he included castanets in some pieces inspired by what he had seen and heard in Spain, in particular his *Jota Aragonese* (1845) and the *Recuerdos de Castilla* (1848).

MIKHAIL GLINKA
Although identified with his own Russian culture, Glinka was fond of Spanish music, and of the castanets in particular.

A VARIETY OF ROLES

Classical composers of the 19th century typically followed Glinka and used castanets to create a vividly Spanish atmosphere — well-known examples are Emmanuel Chabrier's orchestral rhapsody *España* (1882) and Bizet's opera *Carmen* (1875), which is set in Seville. Castanets, with their associations with exotic dancing, were also employed to evoke a mood of sensuality by composers such as Wagner (in his Venusberg Music in the opera *Tannhäuser*, 1845) and Richard Strauss (in *Salome*, 1905). Sometimes, even when there is no specifically Spanish setting or atmosphere, composers use the crisp clicking sound of the castanets to define the rhythm of a piece, as Prokofiev does in his Piano Concerto No. 3 (1921).

Happy, like a pair of castanets.

Spanish saying

NATIONALIST MUSIC

♦

In his "Spanish" pieces, Glinka (following the lead of Berlioz, who wrote a Hungarian March) uses music to evoke national character and culture. Soon Glinka was creating musical portraits of his own culture in orchestral works such as *Kamarinskaya* (1848), which is based on Russian folk themes, opening up the way for composers from many other countries to express their national identities in music. From Smetana in Bohemia to Liszt in Hungary, and from Grieg in Norway to Albéniz in Spain, musical nationalism became a strong vein in the late 19th and early 20th centuries. In many of these places, composers formed part of a wider movement to promote national culture, especially in new nations, or states, like Bohemia, part of the Austro-Hungarian empire until 1918, trying to assert their cultural independence.

1846 Saxophone

Location: Paris, France

Type: Aerophone (single reed)

Era: Romantic

+ **WOODWIND**
+ PERCUSSION
+ BRASS
+ STRINGS
+ OTHER

The jazz instrument par excellence, the saxophone is also used occasionally in classical music. When included in the orchestra it is part of the woodwind section because, like its relative the clarinet, it is a single-reed instrument. Its strong, vocal tone adds something unique to the orchestral palette and has been admired by composers from Berlioz to Debussy.

ADOLPHE SAX

The inventor of the saxophone was Adolphe Sax (1814–1894) the son of Charles-Joseph Sax, a maker of musical instruments from Dinant, Belgium. Charles-Joseph encouraged Adolphe in his interest in instruments and by the time the young man was 15 he had already produced several instruments of his own, including two flutes and a clarinet that he made out of ivory. Adolphe was a player too, and studied flute and clarinet at the Royal Conservatory of Brussels.

THE SAXHORN

Adolphe Sax's first major work was to redesign the bass clarinet (see p. 174), patenting his new version of the instrument in 1838. The Sax bass clarinet was the ancestor of the modern bass clarinet and was an important contribution to instrument design, but while working on it Sax ran up debts in his home country. By 1841 he decided to leave Belgium and moved to Paris with his last 30 francs. Here, he found an old shed in which to work and began an ambitious project to create a whole new family of brass instruments. These became known as the saxhorns.

Sax conceived the saxhorns because he was dissatisfied with the diverse collection of instruments played in the brass and wind bands of the time. The various brass horns, bugles and trumpets — some with valves, some with keys, some with neither — had evolved independently and Sax thought their sounds did not blend very well. Bands with woodwinds were also imperfect in outdoor music, with tales of poorly blending oboes and bassoonists, their faces puffed up with effort, vainly

> It is the most beautiful amalgam of sounds that I know of.
>
> *Gioachino Rossini*

TENOR SAX
Probably the most popular saxophone, the tenor is in the middle of the family, below the alto and above the baritone.

trying to produce enough sound to carry effectively. It would be better, Sax argued, to design an integrated family of instruments that all worked along the same lines. The resulting saxhorns were based on existing, mostly German, valved bugles, tenor horns and tubas, and all had a conical bore, cup-shaped mouthpiece and valves. They made up a family of seven horns, contrabass up to sopranino and pitched alternately in E-flat and B-flat.

SAX AND THE SAXOPHONE

At around the same time Sax also had his eye on the woodwind instruments. He wanted to make the woodwinds more powerful and to improve the clarinet, which he wanted to overblow at the octave (rather than the 12th). His solution was to produce an instrument with a single reed but, instead of the clarinet's cylindrical bore, his new instrument had a conical bore.

Sax was not the first to combine a reed and a conical bore in this way. At least one French maker, Desfontenelles, had made a conical-bore wind instrument along these lines. But Sax, coming later, also had the advantage that he could use the keywork becoming common on wind instruments on his new horns. And Sax, unlike earlier experimenters, went for a comprehensive family of new woodwinds, just as he had with his brass saxhorns. By the early 1840s he was a long way toward perfecting his saxophone family.

The new instrument had its first high-profile outing at the National Exhibition at Brussels in 1841. Sadly for Sax it was damaged by a rival and rendered unplayable. But the instrument-maker had some compensation the following year when Hector Berlioz (1803–1869), not only a great composer but an outspoken writer about music, got hold of a saxophone. Writing in the *Journal des Débats*, Berlioz pronounced himself impressed and predicted that in a few years every orchestra would include saxophones. His article in particular singled out the saxophone's tone and versatility, which the composer praised in typically romantic words: "Its principal merit in my view is the varied beauty of its accent, sometimes serious, sometimes calm, sometimes impassioned, dreamy or melancholic, or vague, like the

SAXHORNS
These horns usually have upward-facing bells, although saxhorns with backward-facing bells were also popular in some 19th-century marching bands.

ADOLPHE SAX
The Belgian inventor Sax produced the saxhorns, the saxotrombas (which had a narrower bore) and, most successful of all, the saxophones.

THE FAMILY OF SAXOPHONES

✦

Voices and many instruments are classified by their pitch range in four categories: in descending order, soprano, alto, tenor and bass. The saxophone family, however, has no fewer than seven members.

Sopranino in E-flat
The type originally called for by Ravel in the *Boléro* (though the rarity of the sopranino means that this part is usually taken by a soprano).

Soprano in B-flat
The highest saxophone that is widely heard; plays the top part in saxophone quartets and became well known in jazz through the superb playing of Sidney Bechet.

Alto in E-flat
Quite widely used in classical music, by Ravel, Berg, Rachmaninov and others.

Tenor in B-flat
The most widely used jazz saxophone.

Baritone in E-flat
Quite commonly used in jazz, less so in classical music, although it does feature in Gershwin's jazz-influenced scores, such as *Rhapsody in Blue* (1924).

Bass in B-flat
Rare except in saxophone groups and occasionally in concert bands; classical composers who have written for it include Richard Strauss.

Contrabass in E-flat
A very rare instrument indeed.

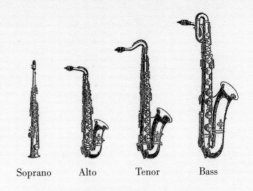

Soprano   Alto   Tenor   Bass

weakened echo of an echo, like the indistinct plaintiff moans of the breeze in the woods and, even better, like the mysterious vibrations of a bell, long after it has been struck ..." Berlioz was also the first well-known composer to write music for the new instrument, making an arrangement of his song "Chant Sacré" in 1844. He went on to include the saxophone in the orchestra for his *Te Deum* (1849) and his opera *Les Troyens* (1858).

By the mid-1840s Sax had produced a whole family of saxophones. Each had a conical metal tube, pierced with some 20 tone holes covered by keys. The higher instruments have a straight tube, but the longer tubes of the lower instruments have a U-shaped bend with the bell turned out slightly toward the front, a shape that has become instantly recognizable. The mouthpiece is similar to that of a clarinet, but the embouchure is different, with the mouthpiece entering the mouth at a flatter angle, and the reed is proportioned slightly differently from the clarinet reed.

CONTRABASS SAX
This is one of the largest of all woodwind instruments. Its range goes down an octave below the baritone sax.

Success and Disaster

There had been a decline in French military music by the mid-1840s, and Sax suggested to the military that they adopt his instruments to improve the performance of the military music corps. The minister for war, General de Rumigny, considered Sax's proposal, and decided to organize a competition in which a band equipped with Sax's instruments would be pitted against a band with traditional instruments.

The competition took place on the Champs de Mars in April 1845 and around 20,000 people turned up to listen to the contest alongside members of the military and war ministry. The traditional band was made up of 45 players; Sax's group was slightly smaller, because some of the participants did not turn up and Sax himself, as well as leading the band, had to take a turn at two different instruments. In spite of this problem, the rich tone and well-blended sound of the saxhorns and saxophones impressed both the public and the military bigwigs present. The military men also liked the way the saxhorns were easy to carry.

By August the same year the army had adopted Sax's idea for a reorganized music corps, equipped with his instruments. His prestige was at a high point and it looked as if he would become rich from a large military order.

SAX FACTORY
The factory of Adolphe Sax had a variety of equipment for bending, machining and polishing the tubing from which he made his instruments.

STOREFRONT
Sax's premises on the rue
Saint-Georges in Paris had
an elegant baroque frontage
to catch the eye of potential
customers.

But rival manufacturers alleged that Sax's horns were not original inventions at all and accused him of plagiarizing ideas from other manufacturers. Rivals took out numerous writs against Sax, and there were also dark stories of a mysterious fire at his workshop. Sax responded by defending himself vigorously and by taking out counter-writs against those who had sued him. He soon found himself tangled up in lengthy and costly litigation, which drained away the money he made from selling his saxhorns and saxophones. Political developments were against him too. When the French monarchy fell in 1848, the new Republican government banned Sax's instruments, which were associated with the old regime. By 1852, the inventor was declared bankrupt.

However, by the time of Sax's bankruptcy the French republic had ended, Napoleon III was emperor, and in 1854 Sax found himself appointed instrument-maker to the imperial army. His patents were upheld in 1856 and Sax was awarded substantial damages. Yet his troubles were not over — there were more lawsuits that led to a further bankruptcy in 1873. By the time Sax died in 1894, he had made tens of thousands of instruments, made and lost fortunes, and left a lasting legacy to the musical world.

ORCHESTRAL ROLES

Although the saxophone never became a permanent member of the classical orchestra, its unique sound and powerful voice were admired by many classical composers. The saxophone therefore appears in quite a large number of orchestral pieces, and when it does so it adds something special to the effect. Having been praised by Berlioz and invented in Paris, it is not surprising that the saxophone was taken up most widely by French composers, but it was the 20th century before they exploited it widely and gave it a major solo role. One of the first was Claude Debussy (1862–1918), whose Rhapsody for Saxophone and Orchestra appeared in 1901; in this piece it is a solo instrument and the rhapsody is like a miniature concerto. The best known saxophone concerto is by Alexander Glazunov (1865–1936), written for alto saxophone.

More often the saxophone is used in the orchestral woodwind section, where it can add body to the sound when the winds are playing together. In addition, composers value it for its power — it can project

SOPRANO SAX
The highest commonly
played saxophone has a
short, straight tube.

a solo melody even when many other instruments are playing — and for its mournful quality when it plays softly. The saxophone plays a key role in Ravel's famous *Boléro* (1928), which has parts for both sopranino (or soprano) and tenor saxophone. When, in 1922, Ravel orchestrated Mussorgsky's *Pictures at an Exhibition* (originally written for piano) he included an alto saxophone part that evokes the song of a troubadour.

Russian composers also took to the instrument — Prokofiev used it in several works and Rachmaninov included an alto in his late, great work the *Symphonic Dances* (1940). Vaughan Williams included three saxophones (two altos and a tenor) in his Symphony No. 9 (1957), and said that on the whole he allowed these instruments to "be their own romantic selves." Richard Strauss, who liked large orchestras, put a whole quartet of saxophones (soprano, alto, baritone and bass) into his *Symphonia Domestica* (1903).

In recent decades the jazz and classical worlds have come closer together via the saxophone. Saxophonists from the jazz world, including John Harle, have collaborated with classical musicians, playing new work by classical composers, such as Harrison Birtwistle. Another approach is the one adopted by saxophonist Jan Garbarek and the vocal group the Hilliard Ensemble, who have joined together to combine ancient musical material, such as Gregorian chant, with Garbarek's soaring soprano saxophone. The ability of the saxophone to cross musical boundaries continues.

JAZZ SAXOPHONISTS

✦

The saxophone has been very closely associated with jazz and popular music since John Philip Sousa added it to his wind band in the 1890s. As jazz developed in New Orleans at the beginning of the 20th century, one of the first players to take to the saxophone was the great clarinetist Sidney Bechet (1897–1959), who liked the soprano sax because it was louder than his clarinet and could hold its own against instruments like the cornet. Since Bechet (pictured) began his long career, many musicians have played jazz saxophone. The tenor sax has been a particular favorite, eloquent in the hands of players such as Coleman Hawkins, Ben Webster and Lester Young. The alto has also been a great jazz instrument — Charlie Parker and Cannonball Adderley were two of its greatest exponents.

Triangle

Location: Weimar, Germany

Type: Idiophone

Era: Romantic

+ WOODWIND
+ **PERCUSSION**
+ BRASS
+ STRINGS
+ OTHER

The triangle is the simplest of musical instruments and has a long history. Dating back at least to the Middle Ages, it was incorporated into the orchestra in the 18th century by composers who wanted to recreate the "exotic" effect of Turkish music, for which there was a fashion at the time. In 1855, however, the premier of Liszt's Piano Concerto showed in an astonishing way that this small, apparently simple percussion instrument could take a solo role in a large-scale orchestral work.

PLAYING THE TRIANGLE

The triangle consists of a metal rod, bent to form a three-sided shape, which is left open at one corner. Triangles are generally made of steel, although some are made of beryllium copper, and struck with a metal beater, though occasionally a wooden beater is used if the composer or player prefers a less ringing tone. Playing it is simply a matter of striking the triangular rod with the beater, but this is not always as straightforward as it sounds, since some pieces involve quite complex rhythms and the volume is not always easy to control. Players produce rapid runs of notes by moving the beater quickly back and forth inside one corner of the triangle. The sound produced is normally a clear ringing tone, but the way the triangle is constructed means that this has no definite pitch, so the effect is very different from other struck metallic instruments such as bells.

Triangles come in various sizes, and those used in orchestral music are usually between 6 and 9 inches (15.25–23 cm) across. There is no single standard size, and percussionists choose a size suitable for the music they are playing, tending to go for larger triangles in the lusher, more richly textured music of the Romantic period and later. The player either holds the instrument using a loop of gut or synthetic fiber, or plays it suspended from a stand. When using the instrument suspended, players are usually careful to hang it from a thin line (some use fishing line), so that it is completely free to vibrate.

ROD OF STEEL
Triangles for orchestral use are generally between 6 and 9 inches (15.25–23 cm) across and made of steel.

THE DEVELOPMENT OF THE TRIANGLE

The medieval triangle could be three-sided, trapezoid or stirrup-shaped, and had a series of metal rings along the bottom bar. When a player struck the instrument, these moved around, producing a sound very different from the pure tone of the modern instrument. Some writers have described the early triangle's sound as a "zing," whereas today's triangle produces a clear "ting." The triangle with rings survived into the 19th century, while the ringless instrument, which has existed since the 14th century, has gained in popularity over the centuries and is now the norm.

The triangle found an occasional place in the orchestra in the 18th century and it appears in works by the three major Classical-era composers, Haydn, Mozart and Beethoven. These composers use it mainly for special effects, to provide bright and exotic color, especially when imitating the music of the Janissary soldiers of Ottoman Turkey. Mozart, for example, uses it (along with cymbals and bass drum) in imitations of Turkish music in his opera *Die Entführung aus dem Serail* (*The Abduction from the Seraglio*, 1782), which is set in part in a Turkish harem.

By the 19th century, the triangle was used in more mainstream orchestral music and was accepted as a regular member of the percussion section, where it often provided a regular, rhythm-defining beat. Its great breakthrough came in Piano Concerto No. 1 by Liszt (first performed in 1855). In the third movement of this piece, the triangle has a prominent role alongside the solo piano. Never again could the triangle be dismissed as a minor instrument with a purely supporting role. Since then many composers have taken advantage of the bright, ringing sound of the instrument. Memorable examples include Wagner, who enhanced the color of his bridal chorus in *Lohengrin* (1850) with the instrument, and Elgar, who used it in his *Enigma Variations* (1899) to portray a bulldog's tinkling metal collar, a job only the triangle could do.

THE SISTRUM

✦

In ancient Egypt, priests and priestesses played the sistrum, a percussion instrument in the form of a rattle. The sistrum has a metal frame shaped like an upturned "U" crossed by horizontal rods that bear loose discs or plates. The instrument was used in religious ceremonies in Egypt and in the first century BCE its use spread with the worship of the goddess Isis to the Roman empire. The sistrum is sometimes seen as an ancestor of the triangle, although the latter is played with a beater and the sistrum is shaken. The sistrum has also been used in percussion pieces by 20th-century composers such as John Cage and Lou Harrison.

Xylophone

Location: Paris, France

Type: Idiophone

Era: Romantic

Familiar first as a folk instrument with local forms played all over the world, the xylophone arrived in the classical orchestra in the 1870s. Composers soon learned to like its crisp, clear sound, and it heralded an interest in tuned percussion, with the development of other instruments such as the marimba.

XYLOPHONES AROUND THE WORLD

The xylophone is a common instrument among the indigenous peoples of both Africa and Asia. In Africa it takes various forms but typically consists of a series of wooden bars of different sizes, each one set above a gourd that acts as a resonator. The gourds, like the bars, are graduated in size. Different methods of supporting or suspending the bars, and spacing them evenly, evolved. The traditional Indonesian xylophone is similar, but instead of many gourds has a single wooden trough-like resonator, running the length of the instrument.

OUT OF AFRICA
Musicians in Cameroon play traditional portable xylophones, using large wooden beaters.

TUNED BARS
Xylophones without resonators, like the one pictured right, have a harder sound than the more usual modern instrument with resonators beneath the bars.

Xylophones like these came to the notice of European explorers when they traveled to Africa in the 16th century. One traveler of the 1580s, João dos Santos, described xylophones in Ethiopia in which the wooden bars were "suspended by cords so that each key is held in the air above the hollow of its gourd." He also observed how the musicians played the xylophone using carefully constructed beaters that had ends bearing a ball of sinews. He and other explorers stressed both the sweetness of the sound produced by these traditional xylophones and the skill of the players. Modern historians have also noted the careful construction of the instruments, from the selection of hardwoods that retain their density, and therefore pitch, to the careful trimming of the bars to ensure that they are perfectly in tune. European writers from the 16th century onward describe xylophones, and there is an interesting illustration of one in Holbein's print *The Dance of Death*, in which the instrument is played by a skeleton. The German composer Michael Praetorius included the xylophone among the many musical instruments he described in his book *Syntagma Musicum* (1614–1620), illustrating it in one of the woodcuts. This was a basic instrument — no resonators are visible in the picture — and similar to the medieval xylophone described

by James Blades in his study of percussion instruments: "the wooden slabs loosely strung together, or resting on ropes of straw, giving rise to the name 'straw fiddle'." It was the kind of instrument played by itinerant musicians, and would remain so for hundreds of years.

RENAISSANCE EXAMPLE
A xylophone is found among the instruments illustrated in the *Syntagma Musicum*, by Michael Praetorius (above left).

FROM FOLK INSTRUMENT TO CONCERT HALL

The medieval instrument of wood and straw was still being played by traveling entertainers in the 19th century. One of these was a brilliant Jewish player, Joseph Gusikov (1806–1837), who was born in what is now Belarus, but traveled widely in Europe, introducing klezmer music to new audiences. When he toured major cities such as Prague, Frankfurt, Vienna and Paris, a number of composers heard him play and most admired his musicianship. He made a deep impression on Mendelssohn, who wrote that Gusikov was "inferior to no virtuoso in the world, both in execution and feeling; he therefore delights me more with his instrument of wood and straw than many with their pianofortes."

Gusikov undoubtedly did a lot to raise the profile of the xylophone and bring it to the notice of composers, from Meyerbeer to Mendelssohn. He may also have stimulated instrument-makers such as the Parisian Charles de Try, who produced a new xylophone design, the tryophone, around 1870. Some think that seeing a demonstration of Try's instrument encouraged Camille Saint-Saëns (1835–1921) to write his *Danse Macabre* (1874), the piece in which the xylophone enters the classical orchestra for the first time.

WOOD AND STRAW
This 19th-century German illustration of a xylophone is labeled: "Wood and straw instrument."

Unusually, in *Danse Macabre* the instrument is played with its resonating tubes removed, to produce a sound that imitates the rattling of bones. Saint-Saëns followed this up with a further, more conventional, use of the xylophone in the "Fossiles" movement of his *Carnival of the Animals* (1886), where the tune is the same, but the meter different.

THE MARIMBA

✦

A very close relative of the xylophone, the marimba used in classical music derives from Latin American instruments with wooden bars and wooden resonators. When American manufacturers began to adapt these instruments for Western classical use, they replaced the wood resonators with aluminum tubes, but kept the wooden bars, which are shallower than those on the standard xylophone. The result is a larger, lower-pitched version of the xylophone. The bars are made of softer wood than those of the xylophone and this helps to give the marimba its distinctive soft, mellow tone. Since the 1950s it has caught on with orchestral composers, who use it to reinforce the low and middle notes of the tuned percussion. Darius Milhaud wrote a concerto for marimba and vibraphone (1947), and Pierre Boulez included one in his piece *Le marteau sans maître* (1955).

Both of these pieces have become popular classics, although the *Carnival of the Animals* was only performed privately during its creator's lifetime because Saint-Saëns thought it would detract from his image as a "serious" composer.

Although the xylophone originally used by Saint-Saëns may have been similar to Gusikov's wood and straw instrument, later orchestral xylophones became more sophisticated. A xylophone has bars made of a carefully selected timber such as rosewood, precisely tuned and arranged in two rows, the back row corresponding to the black notes of the piano. Each bar is paired with a tube resonator that matches the pitch of the bar. There is a compass of three and a half or four octaves. Players use hard glockenspiel-type beaters, changing to ones with softer heads when the music requires it.

NEW SOUNDS FOR THE XYLOPHONE

By the early 20th century, the orchestral xylophone had evolved and caught the notice of numerous composers. Prominent among these were the Russians, who made especially strong use of percussion. Shostakovich used the xylophone in several of his symphonies, including the popular 5th (1937) and 10th (1953), in his Cello Concerto No. 2 (1966) and in the ballet *The Golden Age* (1930). Prokofiev used it to add color to works such as the Scythian Suite (1915), and Khachaturian gives the instrument a lot of work to do in his famous Sabre Dance from the ballet *Gayaneh* (1941–1942). Stravinsky was another Russian composer who was aware of the power of the xylophone, combining its high, brittle sound with the upper notes of pianos in *Les Noces* (1923).

Many composers wrote only simple passages for the xylophone, using it to play patterns of repeated notes to provide bright rhythmic highlights. But in the late 20th century, a great deal of music appeared that explored the less well-known reaches of the orchestra as composers explored fascinating new sound worlds. The xylophone has played its part in this movement, and there are important parts for it in the concertos for orchestra by Tippett and Lutoslawski. Two French composers, Olivier Messiaen and Pierre Boulez, used the xylorimba, a xylophone with an increased compass, to produce a range of stunning orchestral colors. Messiaen gave it a solo part (along with solos for piano, horn and glockenspiel) in his orchestral work *Des canyons aux étoiles* (*From the canyons to the stars*, 1971–1974), and in *Le marteau sans maître* (*The hammer without master*, 1954–1955) by Pierre Boulez it is teamed up with voice, alto flute, vibraphone, guitar, viola and other percussion. Pieces like these stretch the player, and musicians are now expected to display speed and agility, often playing with four mallets at once. With more and more percussionists able to play such works, the composers increasingly write for percussion alone, and the xylophone and other tuned percussion instruments often play a key role in their pieces. In less than a century and a half since it took to the concert stage, the xylophone has achieved a secure place among the orchestral percussion.

... a very agile instrument.

Gordon Jacob, Orchestral Technique

MALLET MUSIC
A street musician playing a xylophone uses a two-mallet grip in the right hand.

Wagner Tuba

Location: Munich, Germany

Type: Aerophone

Era: Romantic

+ WOODWIND
+ PERCUSSION
+ **BRASS**
+ STRINGS
+ OTHER

A kind of cross between a French horn and a tuba, the Wagner tuba was created at the request of the German composer Richard Wagner, who wanted it to fill a specific role in his operas. It has always been a niche instrument in classical orchestras, but some composers have prized it for the way in which it can blend with both the higher brass and its lower-pitched counterparts, the trombones and tubas.

A 20-YEAR SEARCH

In 1853 Richard Wagner (1813–1883) was composing *Das Rheingold*, the first opera of his four-part Ring Cycle. He had written a Valhalla theme, originally scoring it for a quartet of trombones, but decided he wanted to change the sound to something between the timbre of the French horn and the trombone. He changed the marking on his manuscript from Trombones to "Tuben" ("tubes") and discussed with instrument-makers the creation of a new type of tuba that would produce the sound he wanted — as well as creating a more homogenous, blended sound in the brass section as a whole.

> Harsh, awkward Wagner tubas with their demoniac sound.
>
> *Richard Strauss*

LONG GESTATION
The Wagner tuba took about 20 years to develop before the composer was happy with the result.

However, the development of the new instrument did not go as quickly as the composer would have liked. Wagner met the Belgian-born inventor and instrument-maker Adolphe Sax (1814–1894) in 1853. Sax had vast experience in developing wind instruments — as well as inventing the saxophone (see p. 180), he had developed the saxhorn family. Sax may have helped Wagner decide what kind of tuba he needed for *Das Rheingold*, but the German composer seems not to have been impressed with the quality of Sax's instruments. By the time *Das Rheingold* was ready for its first performance, no Wagner tuba had been made and it is likely that the parts were played on other instruments. Subsequently, Wagner turned instead to German manufacturers such as Georg Ottensteiner of Munich, who produced a quartet of Wagner tubas that were first used in a performance in 1875. The Wagner tuba had taken more than 20 years from initial idea to the production of a playable instrument.

TUBA AND HORN

Wagner tubas are produced in two different pitches, the tenor in B-flat and the bass in F. Both have four valves and a wider bore than the French horn, but the bore tapers so that the tuba can take a horn mouthpiece. The Wagner tuba has a characteristic oval shape and the bell is turned upward, so the player cannot hand-stop the instrument. The similarities to the horn are such that in Wagner's operas, and other pieces using the instrument, the Wagner tubas are played (and often doubled) by hornists. This means that the Wagner tuba and horn players generally sit together in the orchestra. However, sometimes composers write for four Wagner tubas and the bass tuba as an ensemble within the orchestra, so Wagner tuba players occasionally have to sit next to the bass tuba.

The Wagner tuba has never been a mainstream orchestral instrument. It was initially adopted by some followers of Wagner, especially those who worked on a large scale. Anton Bruckner (1824–1896), perhaps Wagner's most devoted disciple, took up the Wagner tuba in the slow movement of his Symphony No. 7 (1881–1885), also using it in three of the four movements of his vast Symphony No. 8 (1887–1890). Bruckner's final symphony, his ninth, was left unfinished at his death, but the tubas play a key part in the slow movement and in the finale that the composer did not complete. Richard Strauss also employed the instrument (for example, in *Don Quixote*, 1897, and *Ein Heldenleben*, 1898) although his view of it as harshsounding is curious. In addition to its use in the orchestra, the Wagner tuba has found a lasting place in brass bands, especially in Central Europe.

RICHARD WAGNER

✦

The German composer Richard Wagner transformed music through his innovative operas, in which music, drama and scenery were integrated to create a total work of art that could be overwhelming in its impact. To this end, Wagner wrote for a very large orchestra, with a large body of strings, multiple winds and a battery of percussion instruments. This enabled him to produce a variety of effects. The multiple woodwinds, for example, meant he could write different parts and give each part the strength it needed — in turn allowing him to exploit to the full the color of the instruments and to produce a smooth, rich overall woodwind sound. With the brass he took full advantage of the latest instruments with valves, which gave them the ability to play in different keys in a way unknown to earlier composers, who had to be content with valveless instruments. To extend the scope of his brass section still further, Wagner also commissioned new instruments — not only the Wagner tuba but also a bass trumpet and a contrabass trombone. In its large size and vast scope, Wagner's orchestra is the star of his operas.

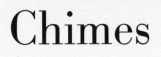

Chimes

Location: Warwick, England

Type: Idiophone

Era: Romantic

+ WOODWIND
+ **PERCUSSION**
+ BRASS
+ STRINGS
+ OTHER

C himes first became popular as a way of providing a convenient bell sound in the orchestra. They enable opera composers to conjure up the atmosphere of a church or to imitate a striking clock, and their timbre is also used in all kinds of other musical contexts, where they can do everything from livening up the palette of orchestral colors to evoking the solemn tolling of a funeral bell.

THE NEED FOR BELLS

At various points in history — especially in Romantic-era opera — composers have wanted to include the sound of bells in the orchestra. Church bells are designed for permanent installation in towers and are too heavy to move around easily; percussion instruments such as the triangle do not produce a clear pitch like a bell, because they produce many diverse "inharmonic" overtones. To imitate a bell, on the other hand, an instrument has to produce overtones that harmonize with the main or fundamental note, creating a combination of a rich bell-like sound with a distinct pitch. Opera houses tried various ways of doing this — one that was quite successful involved tuned metal bars or discs struck with a beater.

The solution that gave the best combination of rich sound, distinct pitch and portability was the chimes or tubular bells, steel or brass tubes of various lengths, suspended from a stand. Chimes were probably first made during the 1860s, but their first appearance in classical music seems to have been during the 1880s. British inventor and clockmaker John Harrington patented a clock chime with tubular bells in 1885. Soon afterward, the composer Arthur Sullivan tried them in his popular cantata *The Golden Legend* (1886), giving musicians

Exhibitors.   145

Messrs. HARRINGTON, LATHAM & CO.,
EARLSDON, COVENTRY.
Harrington's Patent Tubular Bells.

A PEAL of eight Church Bells can be fixed complete, from £120 to £250, ready for
ringing, equal in tone to the finest Cathedral Bells. Prospectus free on application.

EXTRA-LARGE CHIMES
Large tubular church bells
were advertised by British
firm Harrington, Latham
& Co. in the 1890s.

the chance to hear them in an orchestral context. The chimes were also used to imitate church bells in various operas, often where other bell substitutes had been previously used. Verdi's *Il Trovatore* (1853) and *Un Ballo in Maschera* (1859) fall into this category, while the doom-laden tolling bells in Puccini's *Tosca* (1900) appeared after chimes were established as an orchestral instrument.

BELLS TOGETHER

Grouping together a number of chimes so that they can play a full chromatic scale produces an instrument known either simply as the tubular bells or as the chromatic chimes. Modern chimes setups also have a damper pedal arrangement, allowing the player either to cut off the notes, or to let them continue to sound undamped. Grouping the bells together in this way opens up new musical possibilities, and it was not long before composers saw the potential of using tubular bells for their own sake rather than as church-bell substitutes.

Since the 1890s, chimes have rung out in symphonies by Mahler and orchestral works by Debussy and have been included in the orchestra for operas by Leoncavallo and Richard Strauss. More recent composers who have used them to add color to already colorful orchestral sounds include Messiaen (in his vast *Turangalîla Symphony*, 1948) and Benjamin Britten in his opera *The Turn of the Screw* (1954). For some parts, however, such as the bell notes in the *Symphonie Fantastique* (1830) by Berlioz, church bells sound best and this is especially true with very low notes, where it is difficult to make chimes with precise pitch.

Chimes also appear in percussion-only pieces. Here, they not only add color but also an element of tuned percussion to works featuring mainly untuned instruments. A landmark work in the percussion repertoire is Varèse's vibrant piece *Ionisation* (1931).

CHROMATIC CHIMES
A full set of chimes arranged on a stand gives the composer the scope to write melodic passages for the instrument.

GONGS AND WIRES

✦

Because very deep-toned chimes do not work well, musicians have experimented with different solutions to the problems set by composers who ask for deep bell notes. Mushroom-shaped bells and clock gongs have sometimes provided the answer to this problem. One notable example is Wagner, in his opera *Parsifal* (1882). At the opera house at Bayreuth, the bell notes required in *Parsifal* were originally produced by very thick piano wires on a resonator and played together with sounding gongs.

Bells, the music nighest bordering upon heaven.

Charles Lamb, Essays of Elia

Celesta

Location: Paris, France

Type: Idiophone

Era: Romantic

T he clear, bell-like tone of the celesta has an unearthly quality that is immediately recognizable. The instrument's delicate sound is produced when hammers, controlled by a keyboard, hit vibrating metal bars set above wooden resonators. This mechanism produces an enchanting effect that earned the instrument its name, which comes from the French word for "heavenly." The celesta has been much used by composers — especially of opera and ballet music — to conjure up a mood of mystery, otherworldliness or mysticism.

+ WOODWIND

+ *PERCUSSION*

+ BRASS

+ STRINGS

+ OTHER

BEGINNINGS

The celesta was invented in the instrument workshop of Charles Victor Mustel and sons, Parisian builders of organs and harmoniums, in the 1880s, and Mustel patented it in 1886. Mustel's patent was for an instrument in which a piano-like keyboard controls a series of felt hammers that strike metal bars from above. Mustel's invention therefore resembles a glockenspiel, except that the bars are struck with hammers rather than with beaters and the bars, which are usually made of steel, are set above wooden resonators, which give the celesta a more delicate tone than that of the glockenspiel. The celesta also has a wider range than the glockenspiel's two and a half octaves — four- or five-octave celestas are the norm.

MINI KEYBOARD
Since it is a keyboard instrument, the celesta is often played by a pianist, although it is regarded as a member of the orchestral percussion section.

HISTORICAL INSPIRATION

In inventing the celesta, Mustel drew on knowledge of keyboards and instrumental actions gained from his work as an organ-builder. But his crucial idea — the use of metal bars — may have been inspired by earlier instruments such as the mysterious *"strumento d'acciaio"* (instrument of steel) used by Mozart in his opera *The Magic Flute* (1791) to represent the magic bells played by the bird-catcher Papageno; this was probably some kind of keyed glockenspiel. Another possible inspiration is the dulcitone, a keyboard instrument in which hammers strike a series of tuning forks. The dulcitone, invented by Scottish instrument-maker Thomas Machell in 1860, did not catch on widely, but the celesta began to inspire composers almost from the day that Mustel announced his new invention.

An instant hit

Since the celesta was invented in Paris, it is not surprising that the first of the composers to take it up was French. Ernest Chausson used it in some incidental music he wrote for a translation of Shakespeare's *The Tempest* in 1888, no doubt finding its ethereal tones ideal for the enchanted island that forms the setting of the play. However, the first famous piece to feature the celesta was by Tchaikovsky, who was taken with the celesta when he heard one on a visit to Paris. His "Dance of the Sugar-Plum Fairy," from the ballet *The Nutcracker* (1892), highlights the instrument. Although *The Nutcracker* was reviewed badly when it was first performed, in the "Dance of the Sugar Plum Fairy" Tchaikovsky combined the soft tone of the celesta with contrasting instruments such as woodwinds and plucked strings to create a sound that was completely new in orchestral music, and that has been enchanting listeners ever since. Other composers to take advantage of the celesta's otherworldy sound are Mahler (1860–1911), in his 6th and 8th symphonies, and Holst, who used it to contribute to the haunting sound world of "Neptune, The Mystic," in the last movement of his suite *The Planets* (1916). Bartók's *Music for Strings, Percussion and Celesta* (1936) gives the instrument still greater prominence.

The celesta today

The celesta continues to find a place in the modern orchestra. Although technically a percussion instrument, it is normally viewed primarily as a keyboard instrument and played by a pianist. Most modern celestas work in exactly the same way as the one designed by Mustel in the 19th century, although instruments with slightly different actions (for example, with hammers that strike the bars from below rather than from above) are also available and are commonly marketed as celestas. Composers such as Conrad Susa and Philip Glass — as well as jazz musicians and writers of film music — have prized the subtle timbre of the celesta and incorporated the instrument into their scores.

The carillon, an early ancestor

◆

In his oratorio *Saul* (1738), Handel used an instrument he called a carillon to imitate the sound of the shalish, the triangle-like instrument with which the women of Jerusalem welcome back Saul and David to the city. Handel's librettist Charles Jennens described this carillon as having a tone like "a set of Hammers striking upon anvils," adding that it had keys like a harpsichord. Handel's carillon must therefore have been an 18th-century ancestor of the celesta.

EARL HINES
The great American pianist Earl Hines brought the celesta to jazz, playing it on the track "Basin Street Blues" (1928), with Louis Armstrong on cornet.

Heckelphone

Location: Wiesbaden, Germany

Type: Aerophone (double reed)

Era: Romantic

+ **WOODWIND**
+ PERCUSSION
+ BRASS
+ STRINGS
+ OTHER

> ... so manly and baritone-like that one might be listening to the male voice.
>
> *Wilhelm Heckel on the heckelphone*

LOW WIND
The heckelphone (see right), a development of the bass oboe, adds weight to the low end of the woodwind section in some large-scale orchestral works.

I n the early 20th century, the instrument-maker Wilhelm Heckel developed the heckelphone, a low member of the oboe family, to fill out the bass of the woodwind section. The heckelphone, which looks rather like an outsize English horn, is a rare instrument, but its deep tone was admired by some composers, especially those, such as Richard Strauss, who liked to write for a very large orchestra.

BASS AND BARITONE OBOES

In the 1820s some French manufacturers started to produce a low oboe with a U-bend and upward-pointing bell (usually called a baritone oboe) and later in the century a similar instrument was made with a straight tube (when it is generally known as a bass oboe, although its compass is similar to the baritone version). The straight bass oboe found some favor among Romantic composers, but not everyone was satisfied with its rather thin tone.

Wilhelm Heckel redesigned the bass instrument by changing the bore. The bass oboe got its lower compass by having a long tube and a wide bore — the cross-sectional area of the bore was roughly twice that of the standard oboe. Heckel decided to produce a wider bore — one in which the diameter was double that of the oboe, giving a still greater cross-sectional area than on the bass oboe. The result was an instrument with a much richer, fuller sound. Heckel added his own system of key-work, and launched the instrument that bears his name in 1904.

The heckelphone is a large instrument — about 4 feet (122 cm) in length with a large bulbous bell. It is equipped with a peg at the end, so that the player can rest it on the floor. It takes a large reed, rather like a bassoon reed.

In use

Heckel succeeded in making his new instrument sound fuller and richer than the old baritone and bass oboes; he described its sound as "voluptuously sonorous yet sweet." The first composer to discover its virtues was Richard Strauss (1864–1949), who included it in the large woodwind section of the orchestra for *Salomé* (1905), his opera based on the play of Oscar Wilde. Strauss later included the heckelphone in his opera *Elektra* (1909) and his *Alpine Symphony* (1915). A master of the large orchestra and the effects created by different instruments, Strauss produced an updated edition of Berlioz's book on orchestration and instrumentation. In it, he mentions the heckelphone alongside the bass oboe, ensuring that people referring to this widely read reference book would know about both instruments.

Because the heckelphone is a rare instrument, not every composer is familiar with it. Delius, when writing *A Mass of Life* (1905) and the first *Dance Rhapsody* (1908), had not heard a heckelphone, and wrote parts for bass oboe in his scores. Later, when he was able to hear the instrument, he said that he would prefer it instead of the bass oboe in these pieces. Other works with bass oboe parts are sometimes played on the heckelphone — which instrument is used sometimes depends on the preference of the conductor, sometimes simply on which instrument is available. The instrument's chamber-music repertoire is tiny, but the German composer Paul Hindemith, who was always interested in trying new instruments, wrote a trio for heckelphone, viola, and piano (1928). More recent composers who have written for the instrument include the Finnish composer Kalevi Aho, who uses it in various orchestral works.

RICHARD STRAUSS
The German composer Richard Strauss (pictured left) did a lot to promote the heckelphone, using it in some of his works and including it in his book on orchestration.

THE LATE-ROMANTIC ORCHESTRA

✦

At the end of the 19th century and the beginning of the 20th, when the heckelphone began to appear in orchestral works, the late-Romantic symphony orchestra could be a vast band. The orchestra for Mahler's enormous Symphony No. 8 (1906), for example, contains multiple numbers of the usual woodwind and brass instruments, including four oboes, four flutes, eight horns and eight trumpets, plus various unusual orchestral instruments such as organ, harmonium, piano, celesta and, in many performances, several mandolins and harps. Richard Strauss, and Arnold Schoenberg in his cantata, *Gurrelieder* (1900–1911), sometimes used even bigger orchestras. However, there was a corresponding trend toward smaller ensembles, with many composers writing for strings alone, or for groups made up of a few carefully selected winds, strings and percussion.

Vibraphone

Location: Indianapolis, U.S.

Type: Idiophone

Era: Modern

W ith its metal bars and clear, vibrato tone, the vibraphone is one of the most distinctive of the tuned percussion instruments and a favorite with many players. Well established in jazz, it also features in many modern orchestral works and is often at the heart of pieces for percussion alone. In the hands of a skilled player using four sticks at once to play chords in rapid succession it can be visually as well as sonically spectacular.

+ WOODWIND

+ **PERCUSSION**

+ BRASS

+ STRINGS

+ OTHER

FOUR-MALLET GRIP
Vibraphonists have to learn how to use four mallets at once. American player Joe Locke shows his personal version of the four-mallet grip (see above, right).

BARS AND RESONATORS
The aluminum bars of the standard vibraphone (see below), arranged like the white and black keys of a piano, produce a range of three octaves.

HOW IT WORKS

The vibraphone looks rather like a xylophone, except that instead of wooden bars it has two rows of metal ones. The key feature of the vibraphone, however, is what goes on under the bars. Each bar has a tubular resonator beneath it, and this resonator contains a round

vane, connected to an electric motor. When the player turns on the motor and strikes a bar, the vane spins, alternately opening and closing the resonator. This turns on and off the resonance, producing the instrument's characteristic vibrato effect. The player can also change the speed of the vanes to produce longer or slower vibrato pulses as required. The instrument has a damper, in the form of a felt-covered strip controlled by a pedal, which damps a whole row of bars, although the player can also damp notes individually by placing a finger on a bar.

The vibraphone has two rows of bars, one consisting of natural notes, one of sharps. Whereas on many xylophones the rear row is set slightly higher than the front row, overlapping it to bring the striking points of the two rows closer together, on a vibraphone the rows are level.

I like the sparkle of the vibraphone.

Evelyn Glennie

This enables a player holding two sticks in each hand to play chords of up to four notes using both rows of bars — some players have even experimented with three beaters in each hand.

DEVELOPMENT

Probably the first vibraphone-style instrument was the one produced by the instrument-maker Herman Winterhoff (1876–1945) for the American Leedy Drum Company in 1916. It had a motor that raised or lowered the resonators to produce a variable tone. Winterhoff produced the first instrument with spinning disc-shaped vanes in the resonators in 1921 and soon afterward another American firm, Deagan of Chicago, began to market a similar instrument under the name of vibraharp.

By the beginning of the 1930s these instruments were well established in jazz, and were becoming widely known as "vibes." Soon classical composers and writers of film music were taking an interest too. Alban Berg was one of the first to write for it — in his opera *Lulu* (1934–1935) — and other composers to use it included Benjamin Britten, whose scores for the *Spring Symphony* (1949) and *A Midsummer Night's Dream* (1960) benefit from its striking color. In addition, Britten also asked the player to turn off the vanes so that the bars could sound like bells in works such as the *War Requiem* (1961–1962), while other composers sometimes ask for the vibration speed to be varied during performance. Aaron Copland and Michael Tippett made good use of the vibraphone among the large percussion sections sometimes employed in their works and the vibraphone is also one of the instruments in *Le Marteau Sans Maître* (1954–1957), by Pierre Boulez.

THE VIBRAPHONE IN JAZZ

◆

From the beginning, the vibraphone quickly established itself as a jazz instrument. Lionel Hampton, who started out as a drummer, took it up in the late 1920s and when asked in 1930 to play vibes with Louis Armstrong, his career on the instrument took off. His own big band, with which he played countless solos on vibes, was especially successful in the 1940s and 1950s. His styles ranged from swing to rhythm and blues. The other great jazz vibes player was Milt Jackson, most famous for his cool, bluesy solos with the Modern Jazz Quartet from the 1950s to the early 1970s. These two players, with their very different styles, showed the enormous scope of this percussion instrument.

<table>
<tr><td>

c. 1923
</td><td>

Wood Block
</td></tr>
</table>

Location: London, England

Type: Idiophone

Era: Modern

The wood block, consisting essentially of a piece of wood with a slit cut into it, is apparently one of the simplest of musical instruments. However, the size of the block, the dimensions of the slit, and the kind of beater used provide variations in pitch and timbre. The wood block, and its relative the temple block, have been used for a variety of musical effects.

AN ANCIENT ANCESTOR

The ancestor of the wood block is the slit drum, a traditional instrument consisting of a wooden box with one or more slits carved through it. The slit drum, which is found in many parts of the world, from Africa to Oceania, is usually played by hitting it with wooden beaters or mallets. Slit drums have a very long history and were used in all kinds of musical contexts, from religious rituals to military music. In some cultures they were also used to convey messages, when their impressive carrying power, especially when placed in a resonant space such as a long valley, was especially prized. In China, where there is a long tradition of making various kinds of wooden drums, slit drums made in the form of wooden fish were used in Buddhist and Confucian rituals.

TEMPLE BLOCK
A Chinese musician plays a temple block in this 17th-century engraving (see above).

BLOCKS AND BEATERS
A mallet with a hardwood head is a common choice to produce a strong, clear tone with the wood block.

THE CLASSICAL WOOD BLOCK

The wood block that entered Western classical music in the 1920s was smaller than many of its traditional forebears, but works in the same way when struck with a wooden or rubber-tipped beater. It is designed to be used singly, placed on a soft, flat surface to allow it to resonate, and its clear clacking sound can pierce through quite a thick instrumental texture when played loudly. Its first appearance was in the "Popular Song," part of William Walton's eccentric "entertainment" *Façade*, which was first performed in public in 1923. Other composers who added wood blocks to their scores included Prokofiev, two of whose symphonies, No. 5 (1944) and No. 6 (1947), include the instruments.

Though outwardly simple instruments, wood blocks can tackle a variety of tasks, including special or imitative effects. They can recreate the sound of horses' hooves or clog-wearing dancers, they help portray the mallet blows of Noah when he builds the ark in Britten's opera *Noye's Fludde* (1957), and they are sometimes used to conjure up an oriental atmosphere. The wood block's usefulness in special effects, as well as its distinctive clacking sound, is also favored by some rock and jazz percussionists, who add the instrument to their drum kit.

TEMPLE BLOCKS

In addition to single wood blocks, percussionists sometimes play sets of blocks at different pitches, usually called temple blocks (also known as Chinese blocks). These are descendants of the carved wooden fish found in China, and Western temple blocks are sometimes carved in a bulbous form that recalls the Chinese instruments and also gives them their nickname of "dragons' mouths." Rectangular temple blocks are also available. Once again, Walton took to them and used two temple blocks in *Façade*. Other British composers followed, including Constant Lambert, whose Piano Concerto (1931) includes a set of six. More recent composers to take up the temple blocks include, not surprisingly, those who have shown an interest in extending the range of sounds produced by the orchestra, from Messiaen (in his *Turangalîla Symphonie*, 1948) to Harrison Birtwistle (in his opera *The Minotaur*, 2008).

UNUSUAL PERCUSSION

✦

A host of different objects make occasional appearances in the percussion section, to provide specific, unusual sounds. Among these, the whip is quite popular among 20th-century composers. It is usually in fact a wooden instrument consisting of two strips of wood hinged together and brought together to make a whip-like slapping sound, and is heard to striking effect right at the beginning of Ravel's Piano Concerto (1931). The ratchet, with a cog and tongue of wood like a football rattle, appears in several works, as do metal items such as the anvil (its metallic sound featuring in many operas) and the chain (rattled in a metal container in some modern pieces). A wooden plank beaten with a wooden hammer and a sandpaper block rubbed on wood are further examples of the simple items that composers call on to extend and enliven their palette of sounds.

CARVED AND CURVED
Traditional temple blocks are carved to a rounded shape out of a single piece of hardwood. They are generally played with wooden or rubber-headed beaters.

Microphone

Location: U.S.

Type: Sound reproduction

Era: Romantic/Modern

+ WOODWIND
+ PERCUSSION
+ BRASS
+ STRINGS
+ **OTHER**

Should we not fear this domestication of sound, this magic that anyone can bring from a disc at will?

Claude Debussy

SOUND SOURCE
The microphone makes possible all the recorded sound we hear today, from the iPod to surround-sound cinema.

The microphone is a device that turns sound waves into electrical signals that can then be amplified, processed or recorded using other electronic equipment. By making possible good quality recordings, the microphone has transformed music, not just in pop and rock, where records, CDs and downloads have been pivotal, but also by bringing the classics to a larger audience than ever before and delivering the most stunning professional performances into the homes of anyone with a CD player, a computer or an iPod.

PHONOGRAPH AND GRAMOPHONE

The idea of sound recording began in the 19th century, when a number of engineers and inventors developed mechanical ways of capturing the vibrations caused by sound waves and transferring them to a recording medium, from which the sound could then be played back. The first widely used example of this process was the phonograph, which the eminent American inventor Thomas Alva Edison developed in the 1870s. The phonograph used a diaphragm to capture vibrations, which were then transferred to a stylus that cut a groove in a cylinder covered in wax or tinfoil. A similar mechanism could play back the sound by tracing the groove with a stylus and amplifying the resulting vibrations using a horn. Listeners marveled, even though the recorded sound was crackly and indistinct.

EDISON
The prolific inventor Thomas Alva Edison shows off the phonograph, one of his best-known creations.

During the following decade a similar method was developed to record sounds on a rotating disc. The disc-based machine was known generally as the gramophone, and, like the phonograph, it used a mechanical system, called acoustic recording. It had severe limitations — the sound reproduction was still poor and the system was not very sensitive, so players had to huddle close to the recording machine. Some instruments were difficult to reproduce — double basses, for example, were often replaced with tubas; special violins fitted with amplifying horns were often used; and singers had to stand very close to the recording apparatus. In spite of these drawbacks, the idea of recordings of favorite music appealed, and gramophone records gradually became popular.

A NEW PROCESS

The breakthrough that led to a leap in sound quality came in 1925 with the adoption of an electrically powered method of producing recordings to disc and the use of the microphone. The electrical signal from a microphone was amplified using vacuum tubes before an electric recording mechanism cut the disc. Early inventors, such as Edison, Berliner and telephone pioneer Alexander Graham Bell, had begun to develop microphone technology in the 1870s, but the kind of precision microphones needed for recording finally became available in the 1920s. Electrical recording and amplification equipment was developed at around the same time.

Much more sensitive than the acoustic system, electric recording using the microphones of the 1920s and 1930s enabled better sound reproduction — it picked up a wider compass of frequencies and had a much wider dynamic range. In addition, it could handle

MULTITRACK RECORDING

◆

The adoption of stereo recording in the 1950s involved using two microphones, one placed or pointing to the right and one to the left, to record a performance and give a sense of physical space when the recording was played back through the right equipment. This process involved two simultaneous recordings on separate "tracks" of the magnetic tape. It is also possible to use more tracks, placing the corresponding microphones so that they pick up sound from different instruments of an orchestra, for example. The engineer can then mix the tracks together to create the best blend, and this provides the opportunity to increase the volume of particular instruments or sections, for example, emphasizing an instrument when it plays a solo. This technique has been used in classical music, but often creates an artificial effect and many engineers prefer to use a pair of microphones, or a single stereo microphone, positioning the players with care to get a well-balanced, realistic result.

larger groups of players. Musicians and listeners alike began to realize that recordings could provide real entertainment, lasting pleasure and a permanent record of great musical performances.

The sound reproduction possible with these early recordings was far from perfect. But it was a major advance on what had gone before, and listeners spoke of how records reproduced the color of instruments and voices and a lot of the detail of instrumental sound. The recording revolution had begun.

One result of the success of electrical recording was that systems started to be standardized. Manufacturers settled on a standard speed of 78 rpm, for example, so that, in theory at least, discs produced by one manufacturer would play on gramophones made by another. These 78 rpm discs were made until the 1950s, and were mostly made of brittle shellac. Some tougher vinyl 78s were made, but vinyl was a costly material and they were mainly intended for use by radio stations.

Developing technology

Recording technology developed beyond recognition in the second half of the 20th century. From 1948, long-playing vinyl records enabled lengthy symphonic works to be fitted onto a single disc. At around the same time, recording on magnetic tape made editing straightforward. The arrival of stereo, developed in the 1930s but adopted commercially in the late 1950s, enhanced sound reproduction. In the 1980s, digital recording and the compact disc hugely improved the medium's convenience and ease of use. The transition to the internet and downloading in the last 10 years has revolutionized the way people access and purchase recorded music. Recording companies continue to find ways of improving sound reproduction with everything from the SACD (Super Audio CD) to "lossless" download formats.

VINYL
From the late 1940s to the arrival of the CD, vinyl discs dominated the market. Unlike this rare example from Romania, they were usually black in color.

At the same time the sheer amount of recorded music has multiplied. In popular music, recording became king, with the recorded performance rather than the live concert becoming the way that most fans heard their favorite performers and bands. In the classical world, thousands of historical recordings, capturing great performances from the birth of recording onward, have been transferred to digital format. All the best orchestras, chamber groups and other ensembles make recordings. Nearly every player of standing wants to record their repertoire.

More recorded music is therefore available than ever before. The number of different recorded versions of pieces such as the major symphonies, concertos, operas and choral works is almost countless. A huge variety of less well-known pieces from obscure composers has also been put on record, making it easy to explore the byways of music — to discover the work of everyone from South American Baroque composers to contemporary Australian musicians, and to listen to every instrument from the crumhorn to the theremin. Recording has given listeners a greater sense of the richness of classical music, and of the multitude of talented musicians, than ever before.

ACCESS TO MUSIC

Recording has completely changed the world of classical music, in ways unthought of by its inventors. First, it has transformed access to music. Before recording, the only way to listen to a piece of music was to go to a performance or to perform it oneself. Travel restrictions before the age of mass communications meant that most people had a limited opportunity to go to concerts, but countless people made music at home. Millions of 19th-century households owned a piano, and many people's experience of classical music involved playing piano music or piano arrangements of larger-scale pieces, such as Liszt's arrangements of Beethoven's symphonies. Composers and amateurs also made arrangements of orchestral works for chamber ensembles, so that groups of friends could play them at home.

... music of a sort is everywhere and at every time; in the heavens, the lower parts of the earth, the mountains, the forest and every tree therein.

Constant Lambert, Music Ho!

With the coming of recording, all this changed. Once a piece had been recorded, people could listen to it whenever they liked. To begin with, records were not cheap, and the short playing time of a 78 meant that a symphony could occupy several discs. But once the prices came down, and reproduction quality improved, music was everywhere. This made classical music far more accessible than before, though listening to a recording lacks the sense of occasion (and sometimes of close concentration) that listening in a concert hall can bring. Many lament the devaluing of art that has occurred because classical music is now everywhere — not just on the iPods of joggers, but also in shopping malls, in elevators, on station platforms, and even transformed into cell phone ringtones.

RECORDING AND THE ORCHESTRA

✦

The recording process does not always work well with players positioned as they would be in a concert hall. This was one factor that led to a widespread change in orchestral layout in the early 20th century when the first and second violins, instead of being split left and right of the stage, moved together on the left, giving the lower strings a better chance of being clearly heard. Better recording equipment, and more experienced technicians, now make it easier to record instruments clearly, and many conductors have reverted to the kind of positioning used in earlier times.

THE SEARCH FOR "PERFECTION"

For many, the search for "perfection" can lead to performances that are too similar. Knowing that a recording will become a lasting "document," players are less inclined to take risks and more likely to concentrate on refining details. Critics of recording say that the result is performances that are bland and uninteresting, especially compared with live performances or concerts from the early days of recording when editing was impossible and spontaneity was the keynote.

However, in many ways interpretations and performances are as diverse as they have ever been. There is a huge variety of approaches available to, say, playing the symphonies of Beethoven or the concertos of Mozart, approaches that vary with factors such as the instruments played, the size of the orchestra, the edition of the score used, the spatial arrangement of the players, the acoustics of the hall — let alone the decisions of the conductor about tempo, balance and countless points of detail. Thanks to recording, any listener can experience this variety of choices by sampling different recordings of the same piece.

CLOSE MIC
The best placing for a microphone when recording a solo cello will depend on the player, the instrument and, perhaps above all, the acoustics of the room.

LISTENING AND EDITING

Recording has consequences for the performer, too. The ability to listen to oneself playing, after the event, helps musicians understand the impact of a performance and to iron out imperfections in future performances. When the advent of tape recording made editing possible, players could improve a performance by cutting out and replacing unsatisfactory passages, eliminating everything from wrong notes to stretches where the musician or recording producer felt that a slightly different approach would improve the effect.

CONTROL ROOM
The control room of a recording studio contains the mixers, computers and other equipment that the recording engineer uses to control and record the signals from the microphones in the studio itself.

BUSINESS AND MARKETING

Recording rapidly became a big business, and this brought advantages and drawbacks in turn. Once records were established as the way to listen to music, a recording contract could bring a performer or ensemble worldwide fame on a scale undreamed of even by such 19th-century "stars" as Paganini and Liszt. Singers, from Caruso to Domingo, and conductors, from Toscanini to Karajan, were soon among the biggest global names, reaching vast audiences via recordings. While this is good in many ways, it also increases the amount of effort musicians are expected to spend marketing themselves, and can add further pressures to already highly pressurized careers.

Like the whole history of music, however, this aspect of the business is constantly changing and evolving. The recording industry was once largely in the hands of a few major companies with smaller, independent labels operating alongside. Today, technology, internet sales and downloads make it possible for very small companies, or even individual performers, to have their own recording label. Digital recording can also be an astonishingly fast process. It is now possible, for example, for an orchestral concert to be recorded and for discs of the performance to be ready for audience members to buy as they leave the hall. This is just one example of how such technology, which has sometimes seemed to threaten the freedom of the musician, can also be liberating. The microphone is an instrument that can help foster the artistry of composers and performers, ensuring that their rich creativity is both set down for posterity and allowed to progress, develop and flourish.

Ondes Martenot

Location: France

Type: Electronic

Era: Modern

+ Woodwind
+ Percussion
+ Brass
+ Strings
+ **Other**

In 1928, the French musician and electronics expert Maurice Martenot (1898–1980) unveiled the ondes musicales (later named the ondes Martenot), an instrument that produced an eerie, wavering sound in a range of timbres. Martenot developed the instrument several months after meeting Léon Theremin, the Russian inventor of the theremin, a similar electronic instrument, but had been working on the idea independently. Martenot certainly had an ideal background to develop an electronic instrument: he had been a radio engineer during World War I and was also a musician — he played the cello.

THE ELECTRONIC ERA

The first few decades of the 20th century saw key developments in electronics. After Marconi sent the first radio signals in the 1890s, electronic engineers began to develop components such as vacuum tubes that made practical radio transmission possible. Soon engineers discovered that they could perform all kinds of tasks using such components, which would go on to have a huge impact everywhere from the telephone system to sound recording.

It was not long before people noticed that the electrical circuits used in radios and similar devices sometimes made interesting sounds. While the sounds were not usually welcomed, a few pioneers realized that there might be a musical use for them. Maurice Martenot was just one of a number of engineers working in this field in the 1920s and 1930s, people who were attracted by the purity of these sounds, the potential to control them precisely using electronics, and by the fact that pro-

CONTROLS
Playing the ondes Martenot involves the keys, the switches in the drawer and the ribbon control.

THE THEREMIN

✦

The theremin was invented in 1920 by the Russian physicist Lev Sergeyevich Termen (1896–1993), later known as Léon Theremin, who was working on a project researching proximity sensors. On the outside of the instrument are two metal rods known as antennae but technically parts of a capacitor. Inside the theremin are electronic circuits that produce an audio signal and allow it to be varied in volume and pitch. By moving his or her hands closer or farther away from the antennae, the player can vary the volume and pitch of the sound. Classical composers from Grainger to Martinů have written for the theremin, but it is most popular among film composers, who like its atmospheric wailing tone. Miklós Rózsa used it in several film scores including *Spellbound* and *The Lost Weekend*, and Shostakovich wrote a part for it in the music for the film *Odna* (1931). The industry's fascination with the theremin has continued in the music for movies such as *Ed Wood* and *The Machinist* and for the popular British television series *Midsomer Murders*.

ducing music in this way seemed to point toward an exciting technological future. The ondes Martenot, an instrument that combines a traditional keyboard with modern items such as a loudspeaker, was one of the most lasting products of this work.

PLAYING THE INSTRUMENT

The ondes Martenot relies on the way in which circuits called frequency oscillators can be made to produce sounds. The way these work allows continuous changes in both pitch and dynamics, making it easy for the player to slide from one note to another and providing great expressive power. The first ondes Martenot produced sounds that were rather similar to the theremin — cellolike tones at one end of the range and more violin-like sounds at the other. The basic control with which to regulate these sounds is the ribbon, along which the player slides a metal ring, which is worn on a finger of the right hand. Moving the

ring along the ribbon changes the pitch, and on the original instrument, the ribbon was positioned above a painted dummy keyboard, so that the player could see which note would be played at which position of the ring. Later instruments replace this dummy keyboard with a working keyboard, so that the player can choose whether to control the pitch using the ribbon (allowing smooth glissandi from one note to the next) or the keyboard (enabling one note at a time to be played). Unlike a piano or organ keyboard, the keys on the ondes Martenot also move laterally, allowing the player to use vibrato.

While the player's right hand is controlling the pitch, the left hand operates a group of controls in a small drawer below one end of the keyboard. This contains a volume control (the deeper you push it in, the louder the note) and a number of switches that change the timbre, rather like stops on an organ. The sound emerges through one of several loudspeakers, including a lyre-like unit with strings that produce sympathetic vibrations.

MUSIC FOR THE ONDES

The instrument's debut in 1928 featured a work specially written for it by Dimitri Levidis, a Greek composer living in Paris, called *Poème Symphonique*; Martenot himself played the ondes. Martenot continued to play his new instrument, performing with the renowned Philadelphia Orchestra under conductor Leopold Stokowski in 1930 and winning a prize at the Paris World's Fair in 1937. He also taught a number of others — including his sister, Ginette Martenot, and Jeanne Loriod — to play the ondes, ensuring that the instrument's use spread more widely.

Since then, a number of composers, especially from the French-speaking world, have featured the instrument in their works — Honegger, Milhaud, Varèse and Jolivet have all written for it. They exploited its ability both to soar into a high register as well as to

produce very low notes to underpin the bass in an orchestra — Honegger was said to prefer it to the contrabassoon for this purpose.

The composer who has given the ondes most prominence was Olivier Messiaen (1908–1992), who included ondes Martenot parts in his opera *Saint-François d'Assise* (1975–1983) and in his vast *Turangalîla Symphonie* (1946–1948), as well as writing a piece for six ondes, *Fêtes des Belles Eaux* (1937). The whistles and vibrating squeals of the ondes rising above the vast waves of orchestral sound in *Turangalîla* are probably the place where most concertgoers first meet the instrument. Jeanne Loriod, sister of Messiaen's wife, the pianist Yvonne Loriod, often played the ondes part in his works and wrote a three-volume treatise on playing the instrument, which has helped to promote the ondes in France and beyond.

In popular music, the ondes Martenot has been exploited by bands from Radiohead to Muse. It has also attracted film-music composers. Probably the first was Honegger, whose score for the 1930s film *The Idea* uses the ondes. Later film composers such as Richard Rodney Bennett (*Billion Dollar Brain,* 1967) and Elmer Bernstein *(Heavy Metal,* 1981) are among the many who have seized on its evocative sound when writing for the big screen. The popularity of films like these, together with the enduring quality of Messiaen's works, keeps the ondes Martenot in the public eye and stimulates modern composers to add its haunting tones to their music.

Pianists or organists could master it quickly.

Richard Taruskin, Music in the Late Twentieth Century

VOLUME AND PITCH
A player adjusts the volume with the left hand using the control drawer while altering the pitch using the ribbon with the right (see left).

GINETTE MARTENOT
Maurice Martenot's sister Ginette (1902–1996) was a concert pianist. She became one of the first performers of the ondes Martenot.

Synthesizer

+ WOODWIND
+ PERCUSSION
+ BRASS
+ STRINGS
+ **OTHER**

During the second half of the 20th century, electronic music developed at a rapid pace and had a huge impact on a variety of musical fields, from classical to pop. A range of electronic experiments from the 1930s to the 1950s led eventually to the invention of the synthesizer, the instrument that creates all kinds of sounds using electronic circuits. Music has never been the same since.

TWO APPROACHES

The 1930s pioneers of electronic instruments such as Léon Theremin and Maurice Martenot (see pp. 202–203) showed that electronic circuits could be used to make musical sounds. The instruments they created, the theremin and the ondes Martenot, had a distinctive sound but the eerie quality of that sound was suitable for a fairly narrow range of music. But they showed the potential of electronics to produce sound, and others developed this potential after World War II. These postwar pioneers developed electronic instruments using a different approach, creating instruments that could produce a wide variety of instrumental sounds, from the flute to the violin, the piano to the harpsichord.

ELECTRONIC KEYBOARD
Thanks to microelectronics, the circuits of today's synthesizers are tiny — the biggest part of the instrument is the keyboard.

Some of the most advanced work making music using oscillating circuits was done in Germany during the 1950s. At the WDR Studio for Electronic Music in Cologne, physicist Werner Meyer-Eppler, sound engineer and composer Robert Beyer and composer Herbert Eimert developed a form of music initially made only of electronically generated sounds. The trio, with others such as the young composer Karlheinz Stockhausen (1928–2007), created complex combinations of circuits that could be wired together in different ways — in effect a vast synthesizer that could be reconfigured with different electronic modules — to produce a vast range of sounds.

A separate group of musicians and technicians were working in France with magnetic tape. Using the facilities of broadcaster RTF in Paris, they recorded all kinds of sounds — not just musical ones — and spliced them together in interesting ways, or manipulated them by play-

MIXER
The German company Lawo developed this mixing console in the late 1980s. It was used by Stockhausen to produce his work *Octophonie* in 1991.

ing them back at different speeds or backward. They dubbed this kind of music, made from preexisting or "concrete" sounds, *musique concrète*. *Musique concrète* mixed sounds recorded in the natural world with the sounds of human voices and conventional instruments, plus electronic sounds — and all this material could be combined without regard to normal musical ideas about harmony or rhythm. The pioneers of *musique concrète* included Pierre Boulez, Jean Barraqué and Edgard Varèse.

Combining approaches

Although at first seen as opposed, the two early approaches to electronic music did not remain separate for long. Composers were soon combining the techniques, using equipment such as filters, which could remove selected frequencies from sound, reverberation units and mixing desks, with which the composer could combine various signals, capturing the final result on tape. Performances involved playing back the tapes, sometimes in conjunction with live sounds produced on conventional instruments.

Many of the most influential European composers came to the Paris RTF studio to work before setting up their own sound studios — Greek composer Iannis Xenakis (1922–2001), Italian Luciano Berio (1925–2003) and Frenchman Pierre Boulez (b. 1925) were notable examples. Boulez eventually founded IRCAM (Institut de Recherche et Coordination Acoustique/Musique), the large electronic music studio, located underground near the Centre Pompidou, which became a major center for electronic music-making. Berio founded the Studio di Fonologia, a studio for electronic music in Milan. He and cofounder Bruno Maderna invited various important composers to work there and he also produced a journal of electronic music.

Magnetic tape

✦

The first commercially available tape recorder appeared in Germany in 1935. It provided good sound quality and was a huge advance on the previous magnetic recording machine, the wire recorder. This was because the tape was easy to edit — anyone with a sharp knife could cut and join lengths of tape together. Magnetic tape was soon being widely used to record music — and soon composers were using it to create music from scratch.

The synthesizer and modern electronics

The equipment to produce sounds in the early decades of electronic music was bulky, costly, specially built, and relied on components such as vacuum tubes that were large and heated up when running. But with the coming of transistors all this changed and from 1965 onward the American engineer Robert Moog (1934–2005) was producing small, commercially available synthesizers. Moog's synthesizers caught the attention of pop and rock musicians, and in 1967 the Rolling Stones ("2,000 Light Years From Home") and The Doors ("Strange Days") were both early adopters. There were also examples of using the Moog synthesizer to imitate classical instruments and to play arrangements of classical

music — the most famous early recording was Wendy Carlos's *Switched-on Bach* (1968), produced using Moog synthesizers.

For classical musicians who want to break new ground, though, studio-based composition, with or without traditional instruments, has remained the chosen route for many. When computer control and sound-processing were added, especially in and after the 1980s, composers such as Pierre Boulez produced extraordinary, large-scale pieces, such as his *Répons* (1981), in which live electronics were used to manipulate the sounds of classical instruments to striking effect. Works such as this, combining a chamber orchestra, instrumental soloists and computer-controlled electronics, show that, in creative hands, combinations of instruments and the latest technologies can continue to provide sounds that are dramatic, arresting and new.

ANALOG SYNTHESIZER
This Studio-66 Synthesizer uses analog circuitry to produce a huge range of adjustments and manipulations to the sound it produces.

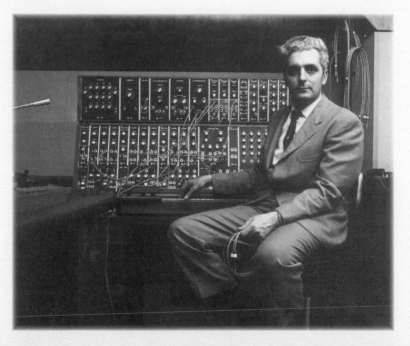

ROBERT MOOG
The American inventor Robert Moog sits in front of one of his state-of-the-art synthesizers from the late 1960s.

Further Reading

Agricola, Martin (1994)
Musica instrumentalis deudsch,
translated by William E.
Hettrick, Cambridge:
Cambridge University Press

Arnold, Denis, ed. (1983)
*The New Oxford Companion
to Music*, Oxford: Oxford
University Press

Bacon, Tony (1991) *The Ultimate
Guitar Book*, London: Dorling
Kindersley

Baines, Anthony (1976)
*Brass Instruments: Their
History and Development*,
London: Faber & Faber

Baines, Anthony, ed. (1961)
*Musical Instruments Through the
Ages*, Harmondsworth: Penguin

Baines, Anthony (1967) *Woodwind
Instruments and Their History*,
London: Faber & Faber

Bate, Philip (1975) *The Oboe*,
London: Benn

Bate, Philip (1978) *The Trumpet
and the Trombone: An Outline of
Their History*, London: Benn

Berlioz, Hector (1991) *Treatise on
Instrumentation*, translated by
Theodore Front, New York:
Dover

Blades, James (1971) *Percussion
Instruments and Their History*,
London: Faber & Faber

Bond, Anne (1997) *A Guide to the
Harpsichord*, Portland, OR:
Amadeus Press

Boyden, David D. et al. (1987)
Strings, London: Macmillan

Brymer, Jack (1976) *Clarinet*,
London: Macdonald & Jane

Campbell, Murray, Clive Greated
and Arnold Myers (2004) *Musical
Instruments*, Oxford: Oxford
University Press

Carse, Adam (1939)
Musical Wind Instruments,
London: Macmillan

Cole, Michael (1998) *The Pianoforte
in the Classical Era*, Oxford:
Clarendon Press

Crombie, David (1984) *The
Synthesizer and Electronic
Keyboard Handbook*, London:
Dorling Kindersley

Dearling, Robert, ed. (1996) *The
Ultimate Encyclopedia of Musical
Instruments*, London: Carlton

Diagram Group (1976) *Musical
Instruments of the World*, New
York: Bantam

Donington, Robert (1982)
Music and Its Instruments,
London: Methuen

Ehrlich, Cyril (1991)
The Piano: A History, Oxford:
Oxford University Press

Herbert, Trevor and John Wallace,
eds. (1997) *The Cambridge
Companion to Brass Instruments*,
Cambridge: Cambridge
University Press

Hotteterre le Romain, Jacques
(1968) *Principles of the Flute,
Recorder and Oboe*, translated by
D. Lasocki, New York: F.A.
Praeger

Jenkins, Lucien (2006) *The
Illustrated Musical Instruments
Handbook*, London: Flame Tree
Publishing

Lawson, Colin, ed. (1995) *The
Cambridge Companion to the
Clarinet*, Cambridge: Cambridge
University Press

Lawson, Colin, ed. (2003) *The
Cambridge Companion to the
Orchestra*, Cambridge: Cambridge
University Press

Marcuse, Sibyl (1975) *Survey of
Musical Instruments*, Newton
Abbot: David & Charles

Meylan, Raymond (1988)
The Flute, London: Batsford

Montagu, Jeremy (1979) *The World
of Baroque and Classical Musical
Instruments*, Newton Abbot:
David & Charles

Montagu, Jeremy (1976)
*The World of Medieval and
Renaissance Musical Instruments*,
Newton Abbot: David & Charles

Montagu, Jeremy (1981)
*The World of Romantic
and Modern Musical
Instruments*, Newton Abbot:
David & Charles

Morley-Pegge, Reginald (1973)
The French Horn, London: Benn

Pollens, Stewart (1994) *The Early
Piano*, Cambridge: Cambridge
University Press

Quantz, J.J. (1966)
On Playing the Flute, London:
Faber & Faber

Remnant, Mary (1990) *Musical
Instruments: An Illustrated
History from Antiquity to the
Present*, London: Batsford

Ripin, Edward M. et al. (1989)
Early Keyboard Instruments,
London: Macmillan

Rowland, David, ed. (1998) *The
Cambridge Companion to the
Piano*, Cambridge: Cambridge
University Press

Sadie, Stanley and J. Tyrrell, eds.
(2001) *The New Grove Dictionary
of Music and Musicians*, London:
Macmillan

Stowell, Robin, ed. (1999)
The Cambridge Guide to the Cello,
Cambridge: Cambridge
University Press

Stowell, Robin, ed. (1992)
*The Cambridge Guide to the
Violin*, Cambridge: Cambridge
University Press

Wills, Arthur (1984) *Organ*,
London: Macdonald

USEFUL WEBSITES:

American Musical Instrument Society:
www.amis.org

Bate Collection of Musical Instruments:
www.bate.ox.ac.uk

Berlioz Treatise on Instrumentation and Orchestration:
www.hberlioz.com/Scores/BerliozTreatise.html

ClassicOL String Family History:
*www.classicol.com/classical.cfm?music=instrumentInfo&section
=StringHistory&title=String+Family+History*

Finchcocks Musical Museum:
www.finchcocks.co.uk

Galpin Society:
www.galpinsociety.org

Horniman Museum:
www.horniman.ac.uk/collections/musical-instruments

Musical Instrument Museum:
www.mim.org/

National Museum of American History:
*http://americanhistory.si.edu/collections/subjects/music-
musical-instruments*

Royal College of Music: Historical Performance:
www.rcm.ac.uk/hp

Syntagma Musicum by Michael Preatorius:
https://archive.org/details/imslp-musicum-praetorius-michael

Vienna Symphonic Library:
www.vsl.co.at/en/70/149/152/48.vsl

Yale University Collection of Musical Instruments:
www.yale.edu/musicalinstruments

Index

A

accordion 177
Aho, Kalevi 199
Albinoni, Tomaso 48, 109
Almenräder, Carl 55, 56
Amati family 40, 42
anaconda 31
Antonii, Giovanni 70
anvil 207
Arban, Jean-Baptiste 164
archlute 13
Armstrong, Louis 93, 165, 201
Arnold, Malcolm 121
arpeggione 69
Asté, Jean Hilaire (Halary) 163
aulos 46

B

Babcock, Alpheus 86
Bach, C.P.E. 72, 83, 100
Bach, J.C. 82, 83
Bach, J.S. 18, 19, 27, 28, 29,
   42, 43, 47, 48, 71, 81–2, 91,
   94, 100, 105, 109, 118, 121,
   124, 129, 146
Bachet, Bernard and
   François 113
Bachmann, Carl Ludwig 60
Baker, Chet 167
Bartók, Béla 67, 87, 127,
   133, 197
baryton 128–9
bass clarinet 174–5
bass cornet see serpent
bass drum 150–3
bass violin see violone
basset clarinet 75
basset horn 75
bassoon 52–7
baton 154–61

Bechet, Sidney 185
Beethoven, Ludwig van 13, 29,
   50, 54, 65, 76, 84, 85, 92, 101,
   110, 113, 115, 125, 129,
   147–8, 151, 187
Beiderbecke, Bix 162, 165
Bellini, Vincenzo 31, 107
Bennett, Richard Rodney
   213
Berg, Alban 201
Berio, Luciano 37, 51,
   103, 143, 216
Berlioz, Hector 31, 32,
   48, 50, 66, 67, 78, 90, 92,
   107, 108, 110, 125–6, 133,
   143, 148, 149, 151–2, 156,
   158, 163, 164–5, 169, 171,
   179, 182, 185, 195
Bermudo, Juan 21
Bernstein, Elmer 213
Bernstein, Leonard 161
Beyer, Robert 215
Biber, Heinrich 42
Birtwistle, Harrison
   51, 93, 185, 203
Bizet, Georges 131, 165
Blühmel, Friedrich 119, 170
Boccherini, Luigi 72
Boehm, Theobald 76, 101–3
Bolden, Buddy 165
bombardon 170, 171
Boskovsky, Willi 159
Bottesini, Giovanni 61
Boulez, Pierre 103, 190, 191,
   201, 215, 216, 217
Brahms, Johannes
   45, 62, 68, 73, 78, 87,
   120, 121, 126, 172
Brain, Dennis 120–1
Britten, Benjamin 73, 121,
   133, 195, 201, 203
Broadwood, John 83–4
Bruckner, Anton
   19, 156, 172, 193

Buffet, Louis-Auguste 76–7, 175
Bull, John 27
Buxtehude, Dieterich 18
Byrd, William 27, 59

C

calvicembalum 24
carillon 197
Carlos, Wendy 217
Carter, Elliott 149
Carulli, Ferdinando 22
Casals, Pablo 71
castanets 178–9
Cavaillé-Coll, Aristide 19
celesta 196–7
Celibidache, Sergiu 161
cello 68–73
Chabrier, Emmanuel 179
chain 203
chalumeau 74
Chausson, Ernest 197
chi 98
Chickering, Jonas 86
chimes 194–5
Chopin, Frédéric 73, 87
Claggett, Charles 119
clarinet 74–9
clavichord 24, 80
Clavitur-contrafaggot 96
Clementi, Muzio 83, 84, 159
concertos 29
contrabassoon 94–7
Copland, Aaron 93, 201
cor anglais see English horn
Corbetta, Francesco 22
Corelli, Arcangelo 36, 43
cornet 162–5
Corrette, Michel 109
Couperin, François 28
Cristofori, Bartolomeo 80–1
crotale 66, 67
crumhorn 54
crystal organ 113
cymbals 64–7

Image Credits

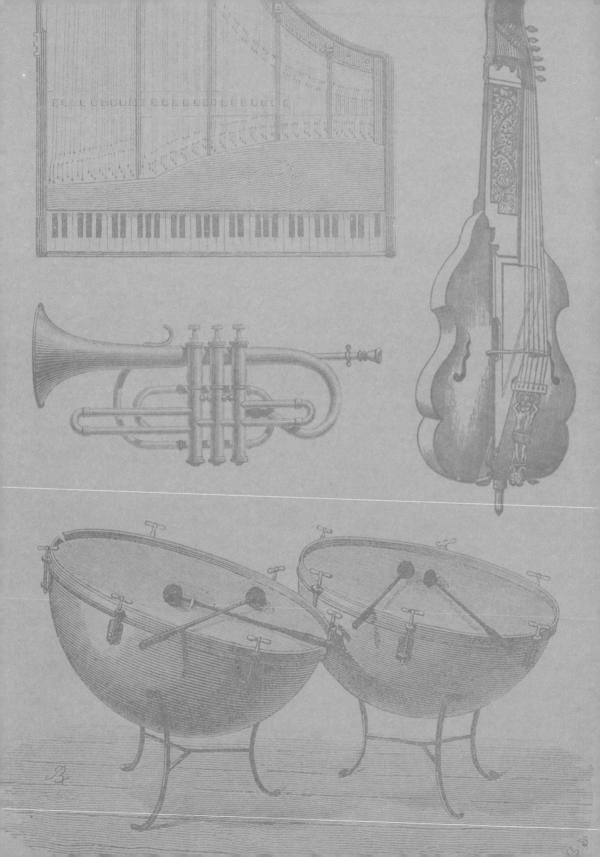